Workshop on Induction of Linguistic Structure 2012

Held at the 2012 Conference of the North American Chapter of the Association for Computational Linguistics: Human Language Technologies (NAACL-HLT 2012)

Montreal, Quebec, Canada
3-8 June 2012

ISBN: 978-1-62276-547-8

Printed from e-media with permission by:

Curran Associates, Inc.
57 Morehouse Lane
Red Hook, NY 12571

CURRAN ASSOCIATES INC.
proceedings
.com

Some format issues inherent in the e-media version may also appear in this print version.

Printed by Curran Associates, Inc. (2013)

Association for Computational Linguistics
209 N. Eighth Street
Stroudsburg, Pennsylvania 18360

Phone: 1-570-476-8006
Fax: 1-570-476-0860

acl@aclweb.org

Additional copies of this publication are available from:

Curran Associates, Inc.
57 Morehouse Lane
Red Hook, NY 12571 USA
Phone: 845-758-0400
Fax: 845-758-2634
Email: curran@proceedings.com
Web: www.proceedings.com

Introduction

Welcome to the proceedings of the NAACL Workshop on the Induction of Linguistic Structure (WILS). This workshop solicited papers addressing the challenges of learning in an unsupervised or minimally supervised context with questions of linguistic structure. Inducing structured linguistic representations from text has long been a fundamental problem in Computational Linguistics and Natural Language Processing, drawing from theoretical Computer Science and Machine Learning. The popularity of the area is driven by two different motivations. Firstly, it can help us to better understand the cognitive process of language acquisition in humans. Secondly, it can help with portability of NLP applications into new domains and new languages. Most NLP algorithms rely on syntactic parse structure created by supervised methods, however in many cases there is no available training data, thus limiting the portability of these algorithms. Consequently work on unsupervised induction of the linguistic structure of language holds considerable promise, although current approaches are a long way from solving the general problems. This workshop aimed to foster continuing research in structure induction, and bring together different communities working on these problems, be it from a cognitive or a text processing perspective.

The workshop also hosted the PASCAL Unsupervised Grammar Induction Challenge, which aimed to foster continuing research in grammar induction and part-of-speech induction, while also opening up the problem to more ambitious settings, including a wider variety of languages, removing the reliance on gold standard parts-of-speech and, critically, providing a thorough evaluation.

Trevor Cohn, Phil Blunsom and João Graça, Workshop Chairs

Organizers:

Trevor Cohn, University of Sheffield
Phil Blunsom, University of Oxford
João Graça, Spoken Language Systems Lab, INESC-ID Lisboa

Program Committee:

Ben Taskar - University of Pennsylvania
Percy Liang - Stanford University
Andreas Vlachos - University of Cambridge
Chris Dyer - CMU
Mark Drezde - John Hopkins
Shai Cohen - Columbia University
Kuzman Ganchev - Google Inc.
André Martins - CMU/IST Portugal
Greg Druck - Yahoo
Ryan McDonald - Google Inc.
Nathan Schneider - CMU
Partha Talukdar - CMU
Dipanjan Das - CMU
Mark Steedman - University of Edinburgh
Luke Zettlemoyer - University of Washington
Roi Reichart - MIT
David Smith - University of Massachusetts
Ivan Titov - Saarland University
Alex Clarke - Royal Holloway University
Khalil Sima'an - University of Amsterdam
Stella Frank - University of Edinburgh

Invited Speakers:

Alex Clark - Royal Holloway University
Regina Barzilay - MIT
Noah Smith - CMU

Table of Contents

Conference Program

Thursday, June 7, 2012

9:00–10:00 Invited talk by Alex Clark

Session 1: Spotlight talks

10:30–11:00 Break

11:00–12:00 Invited talk by Regina Barzilay

Session 2: Spotlight talks

Thursday, June 7, 2012 (continued)

1:00–2:15	Lunch
2:15–3:15	Invited talk by Noah Smith
	Session 3: PASCAL challenge and poster session
3:15–3:30	*The PASCAL Challenge on Grammar Induction* Douwe Gelling, Trevor Cohn, Phil Blunsom and Joao Graca
3:30–4:00	Break and poster session
4:00–5:30	Poster session continues. Posters include the above spotlight papers and the following system descriptions
	Two baselines for unsupervised dependency parsing Anders Søgaard
	Unsupervised Dependency Parsing using Reducibility and Fertility features David Mareček and Zdeněk Žabokrtský
	Induction of Linguistic Structure with Combinatory Categorial Grammars Yonatan Bisk and Julia Hockenmaier
	Turning the pipeline into a loop: Iterated unsupervised dependency parsing and PoS induction Christos Christodoulopoulos, Sharon Goldwater and Mark Steedman
	Hierarchical clustering of word class distributions Grzegorz Chrupała
	Combining the Sparsity and Unambiguity Biases for Grammar Induction Kewei Tu

Transferring Frames: Utilization of Linked Lexical Resources

Lars Borin
Markus Forsberg
Richard Johansson
Kaarlo Voionmaa
University of Gothenburg
first.last@svenska.gu.se

Kristiina Muhonen
Tanja Purtonen
University of Helsinki
first.last@helsinki.fi

Abstract

In our experiment, we evaluate the transferability of frames from Swedish to Finnish in parallel corpora. We evaluate both the theoretical possibility of transferring frames and the possibility of performing it using available lexical resources. We add the frame information to an extract of the Swedish side of the Kotus and JRC-Acquis corpora using an automatic frame labeler and copy it to the Finnish side. We focus on evaluating the results to get an estimation on how often the parallel sentences can be said to express the same frame. This sheds light on the questions: Are the same situations in the two languages expressed using different frames, i.e. are the frames transferable even in theory? How well can the frame information of running text be transferred from one language to another?

1 Introduction

To our knowledge, there is no ongoing effort to create a framenet for Finnish. This experiment gives information on whether it is feasible to build a preliminary framenet for Finnish by transferring the frames with their lexical units from Swedish. The building of semantically annotated language resources from scratch is a costly and time consuming effort. In this experiment, we test the feasibility of utilizing Swedish and Finnish lexical resources for building a Finnish framenet.

Transferring lexical units from Swedish to Finnish is possible because of the wordnet connections of both languages: both the Swedish wordnet and the Finnish wordnet are linked to the Princeton wordnet. This connection is described in more detail in Section 2.

We evaluate the transferability of the frames and their lexical units from Swedish to Finnish. In the evaluation, we use Swedish–Finnish parallel corpora to see whether the same sentence is expressed using the same frames in both languages. Using parallel corpora, we can evaluate not only the theoretically similar content of frames in two different languages, but also their use in actual texts.

The idea of semantic role transfer across parallel corpora is not novel (see Section 2.3), but to our knowledge, the use of linked lexical resources proposed here is. The language pair Swedish–Finnish is also one for which this methodology has not been attempted earlier. With our experiment we can see whether transferring the frame information from Swedish to Finnish could work, given that the languages are not demonstrably related, and structurally quite different. The work presented here consequently provides a data point for the evaluation of the language-independence of this kind of methodology, which can arguably only be convincingly demonstrated by actually attempting to apply it on a range of typologically diverse languages (Bender, 2011).

From a more practical point of view, there may well be as much Finnish–Swedish as Finnish–English parallel data, since Finnish and Swedish are the two official languages of Finland, and all public documents must by law be available in both languages, and for practical reasons also a large amount of other texts. In addition, despite their non-relatedness and large structural differences, the two languages have a long history of contact and bilingualism. Finnish has borrowed words and structures from Swedish on a large scale, and the lexical semantics of the two languages have converged in many domains. This means that we may expect frames to transfer well across the two languages, whereas the structural differences may make us more pessimistic about the transferability of frame elements.

2 Language Resources

2.1 Wordnet Connections

Wordnets are lexical databases that group words of a language into synonym sets – or *synsets* – each synset supposedly expressing one distinct concept in the language. Wordnets further provide general definitions of the synsets, and encode the semantic relations between the synsets. Typically they are monolingual, but efforts have been made to produce multilingual wordnets as well; see e.g. Vossen (1998).

FinnWordNet (Lindén and Carlson, 2010) is a wordnet for Finnish that complies with the format of the Princeton WordNet (PWN) (Fellbaum, 1998). It was built by translating the Princeton WordNet 3.0 synsets into Finnish by human translators. It is open source and contains 117 000 synsets. The Finnish translations were inserted into the PWN structure resulting in a bilingual lexical database.

SweFN++ is an integrated open-source lexical resource for Swedish (Borin et al., 2010; Borin, 2010). It includes the Swedish framenet (SweFN) and Swesaurus, a Swedish wordnet. The wordnet has been semi-automatically assembled from freely available Swedish lexical resources (Borin and Forsberg, 2011), and part of it has been linked to the Core WordNet, a 5000-synset subset of PWN. All resources in SweFN++ are linked together on the word sense level using the persistent sense identifiers of the SweFN++ pivot resource SALDO, a large-scale lexical-semantic resource (Borin et al., 2008; Borin and Forsberg, 2009). Using these links, we can collect a set of 434 frames and 2 694 word senses that have a direct PWN – Swedish wordnet – SweFN – FinnWordNet connection. Using these connections, we can transfer the frame information of the words from Swedish to Finnish. We used the Korp pipeline (Borin et al., 2012) to analyze the Swedish part of the parallel text to get hold of the SALDO sense identifiers. The analysis is not able to distinguish senses that do not differentiate themselves formally (by different word forms or morphosyntactic descriptions).

2.2 Framenet and the Semantic Labeler

Framenets are lexical databases that define semantic relations. The best-known framenet is Berkeley FrameNet which is based on the theory of frame semantics (Fillmore, 1976). SweFN is built using the same principles as the Berkeley Framenet (Ruppenhofer et al., 2006) of English. The frames are mostly the same as in English.

In the experiment, we use an automatic semantic role labeler for Swedish, developed by Johansson et al. (2012). The labeler is based on the Swedish framenet and it uses the same frame and frame element labels.

2.3 Related Work

From a methodological point of view, the first question to ask should be whether the semantic frames are meaningful in both languages: for instance, if the Swedish FrameNet has defined a frame SELF_MOTION and a list of associated frame elements (SELF_MOVER, GOAL, PATH etc.), does it make sense to define an identical frame in a Finnish FrameNet? This question has been studied by Padó (2007) for English–German and English–French, and although most frames were cross-linguistically meaningful, a number of interesting discrepancies were found. Whether the number of discrepancies is higher in a pair of more typologically different languages is an important question.

As far as we are aware, there has been no previous attempt in using multilingual WordNets or similar lexicons when deriving lexical units in frames in new languages. The WordNet–FrameNet combination has seen some use in monolingual applications: for instance, Burchardt et al. (2005) and Johansson and Nugues (2007) attempted to extend the coverage of FrameNet by making use of WordNet. Padó and Lapata (2005a) used word alignment in sentence-aligned parallel corpora to find possible lexical units in new languages.

There have been several studies of the feasibility of automatically producing the role-semantic annotation in new languages, although never for languages as structurally dissimilar as Swedish and Finnish. Padó and Lapata (2005b) projected annotation from English to German, and Johansson and Nugues (2006) implemented a complete pipeline for English–Swedish by (1) automatic annotation on the English side; (2) annotation transfer; and (3) training a Swedish semantic role labeler using the automatically produced annotation.

3 Frames from Swedish to Finnish

3.1 Outline of the Experiment

We start off by locating such Swedish word senses that are both represented in SweFN and linked to PWN in two Finnish–Swedish parallel corpora. The sentences that include such a word make up the evaluation data set. After this, the Swedish half is enriched with frame labels using the framenet-based semantic role labeler for Swedish.

After running the semantic labeler on the evaluation data, we pick the 20 most commonly occurring frames from both corpora. For each of the most common frames, we pick the 6 first occurrences for closer scrutiny. Due to the differing nature of Swedish and Finnish, we make one change before selecting the 20 most frequent frames: We exclude the frame which is evoked (erroneously) only by the Swedish indefinite articles *en/ett* – homonymous with the numeral 'one'– among the 6 first occurrences. We take the 21st most frequent frame instead because there are no articles in Finnish. To sum up, the frames under examination are selected based on the frequency of the frame, and the sentences including the frame are selected in the order in which they occur.

After picking 120 (6 x 20) sentences from both corpora, the correctness of the semantic labeler is manually checked. A linguist marks the correctness of both the frame and the frame element label. At this stage, the linguist does not consider the transferability of the frame, but merely checks the output of the automatic role labeler, marking the frame and the frame element either correct or incorrect. E.g problematic analyses caused by polysemous words are marked incorrect. We check the output of the labeler before analyzing the transferability of the frames because if the frame information is incorrect in the Swedish text to begin with, there is no point in transferring it to Finnish.

After checking the Swedish frame information, the Swedish–Finnish parallel sentences are compared. Two native Finnish speakers estimate, whether the frame and frame element label is transferable to Finnish or not. Because FrameNet is based on Frame Semantics (Fillmore, 1976), according to which the meanings of most words can best be understood by a description of a situation, the working hypothesis is that the semantic frames should be more or less language neutral. Hence, the semantic frame we assign for a certain situation in Swedish, should be transferable to Finnish.

In addition to the theoretical frame transferability, we also report the practical applicability of the transfer via the wordnet connections. We check whether the Swedish word is expressed in the Finnish parallel corpus with a word that has a direct link from the Swedish wordnet to the Finnish wordnet via the Princeton Wordnet. If there is no direct Wordnet link from the Swedish word to the Finnish one, we report whether the Finnish word used in the sentence and the Finnish word linked to the Swedish word via wordnets are in the same synset.

In sum, we manually evaluate whether the 20 most commonly occurring frames of the Swedish test sentences are the same in the equivalent Finnish sentences. After reporting whether the frames are equivalent in both languages, we evaluate, how many of the frame element labels can be transferred to Finnish.

3.2 The Test Corpora

Presumably, transferability of the frames between parallel corpora depends on the translation of the corpus. Our hypothesis is that if the translator follows the original expression very carefully, the frames can be more similar than in a more freely translated text. To see whether the transferability of the frames varies according to a corpus, we used two test corpora.

The test corpora consist of extracts from the JRC-Acquis Corpus (Steinberger et al., 2006) and the KOTUS Swedish–Finnish Parallel Corpus (Research Institute for the Languages of Finland, 2004). Both are Swedish–Finnish parallel corpora that are sentence aligned. In both corpora, the text type is formal: the former is a collection of legislative text and the latter consists of press releases of different Finnish companies.

4 Results

The evaluation consists of three parts: First and foremost, we concentrate on estimating whether the frame used in Swedish can be transferred to Finnish even in theory. These results are presented in Section 4.1. If the sentence is expressed using the same frames, we also report how many of the frame elements encoded correctly in Swedish are realized in Finnish (Section 4.2). In Section 4.3, we discuss the possibility of transferring the frames via the wordnet connections. The results for the two different corpora are presented separately enabling us to see whether the text type impacts frame transferring.

4.1 Possibility of Transferring Frames

In Tables 1 and 2, the first column lists the 20 most frequent frames of the evaluation corpora. The second column shows that for all 20 frames, we took the first six Swedish occurrences. The third column shows how many of the Swedish frame labels are correct. Finally, the right-most column portrays how many of the correct Swedish frames can be transferred to Finnish. The result we are mostly interested in is the difference between the third and the fourth columns.

As can be seen from Tables 1 and 2, most of the correct labels for Swedish are transferable to Finnish. In the JRC-Acquis corpus, the semantic labeler succeeded in 75%, and 72% of the frame labels can be transferred to Finnish. The corresponding success rates for the Kotus corpus are 80% and 72%.

Many of the words that are not correctly labeled in Swedish occur in idiomatic expressions, and by chance, some idioms are so frequent in the corpus that they end up to our evaluation corpus. E.g. the idiom *träda i kraft / astua voimaan / come into effect* is expressed in the same way in both Swedish and Finnish (lit. 'tread into force'). In both languages, a verb usually belonging to the frame SELF_MOTION is used in this idiom, but in the idiom, the meaning of it cannot be said to be expressing self motion.

Some sentences in which the frames are consid-

Frame	N	Correct in Swe	Correct in Fin
Being_necessary	6	6	6
Calendric_unit	6	6	6
Capability	6	3	3
Coming_to_believe	6	0	0
Commitment	6	6	6
Deciding	6	6	6
Dimension	6	5	4
Leadership	6	6	6
Part_orientational	6	4	4
Political_locales	6	6	6
Possession	6	2	1
Questioning	6	1	1
Removing	6	6	6
Request	6	6	6
Scrutiny	6	6	6
Self_motion	6	0	0
Substance	6	4	4
Suitability	6	6	5
Text	6	5	5
Using	6	6	5
Total (N)	120	90	86
Total (%)	100	75	72

Table 1: Frames from the JRC-Acquis Corpus

Frame	N	Correct in Swe	Correct in Fin
Assistance	6	6	6
Attempt_suasion	6	6	6
Becoming	6	6	3
Business	6	6	6
Calendric_unit	6	6	6
Capability	6	3	3
Change_position_on_a_scale_increase	6	6	5
Commitment	6	5	5
Create_physical_artwork	6	0	0
Create_representation	6	1	1
Deciding	6	6	6
Dimension	6	3	2
Employing	6	6	6
Leadership	6	4	4
Measure_duration	6	6	6
People	6	6	6
Possession	6	3	1
Relative_time	6	5	5
Supporting	6	6	2
Transfer	6	6	6
Total (N)	120	96	85
Total (%)	100	80	72

Table 2: Frames from the Kotus Corpus

ered non-transferable already on a theoretical level are expressed in Finnish completely without the frame, as demonstrated in Example (1) and (2).

(1) Tillväxten var dock mindre än det
growth was still smaller than the
ursprungliga målet.
original goal.
Still, growth was lower than what was the original goal.

(2) Se jäi kuitenkin alkuperäistä tavoitetta
it remained still original goal
heikommaksi.
weaker.
However, it remained weaker than what was the original goal.

In the Swedish example (1), the word *mindre* 'smaller' is used when expressing the decrease of economical growth. The word *mindre* fits the frame DIMENSION, but it is used in a figurative way. The Finnish parallel sentence could be expressed using the direct translation *pienempi* 'smaller' but the translation is different. *Mindre* in the Finnish Kotus corpus is translated as *heikompi* 'weaker', which is not expressing dimension even in a metaphorical way.

When focusing only on the correct Swedish labels, transferring frames seems to be beneficial, as reported in Table 3. The success rate of a theoretical possibility to use Swedish as a source language for Finnish frames is 92%.

	Correct Frames	Transferable Frames	Success %
Kotus	90	86	96%
JRC-A	96	85	89%
Total	186	171	92%

Table 3: The Success Rate of Frame Transfer

Table 3 sums up the comparison of the two corpora. The difference (7%) between the corpora is not remarkable, so based on these test corpora, the impact of the translation type is not big. In other words, in both corpora, the correct Swedish frames can be transferred to Finnish successfully.

4.2 Success of Transferring Frame Elements

When the sentence is expressed using the same frames in both languages, we also report, how many of the frame elements encoded correctly in Swedish are realized in Finnish. These results are presented in Tables 4 and 5. The numbers show how beneficial it is to transfer the frame element labels of the Swedish semantic labeler to Finnish.

The most common frame elements of the Swedish corpora are listed in the first column. We scrutinize such elements in detail which occur in the corpora at least four times. The rest are added up and presented on the last lines of the tables. The second column shows the frequency of the frame element, while the third column gives the number of correct frame element labels in the Swedish corpora. The last column shows the number of transferable frame elements.

As can be seen from Table 6 that sums up the results of the frame element transfer, frame element labels do not transfer from Swedish to Finnish as well as the frame labels. The success rate of the frame transfer is 92%, where as the frame elements can be successfully transferred in 83% of the cases.

In the Kotus corpus, 75% of the frame element labels are transferable. However, there is a difference between the two corpora: In the JRC-Acquis corpus, 91% of the elements can be transferred to Finnish.

4.3 Transferring Frames via Wordnets

Next we report how many of the Swedish frame-evoking words are expressed using such words that have the same wordnet identifier in Finnish. If the parallel sentences are not expressed using words that are equivalent in the wordnets, we examine whether the words are in equivalent synsets. This information is needed when estimating the usefulness of lexical resources and their internal links in the frame transferring.

In Tables 7 and 8, the first row displays the total number of frame-evoking words. The second row shows how many of the frames are transferable to Finnish even in theory. The numbers on the third row reflect the possibility of using the WordNet connections in frame transferring; this number shows how many of the words under examination are expressed both in Swedish and in Finnish with the equivalent wordnet words. The fourth row shows how many of the words are not directly linked with each other but are located in equivalent synsets. On the fifth row, we report how many of the words are

Frame Element	N	Correct in Swe	Correct in Fin
Entity	9	8	5
Speaker	8	2	2
Item	7	3	2
Theme	6	4	4
Supported	6	2	0
Recipient	6	5	5
Place	6	2	2
Whole	5	3	3
Landmark_occasion	5	5	5
Count	5	5	5
Content	5	4	4
Time_of_creation	4	0	0
Time	4	4	3
Supporter	4	1	1
Employer	4	0	0
Cognizer	4	4	4
Agent	4	2	2
Other (32 FEs)	60	35	20
Total (N)	152	89	67
Total (%)	100	59	44

Table 4: Frame Elements from the Kotus Corpus

Frame Element	N	Correct in Swe	Correct in Fin
Time	10	6	9
Speaker	9	2	2
Entity	9	7	5
Instrument	7	4	4
Theme	6	6	5
Evaluee	6	6	5
Ground	5	4	3
Final_category	5	5	4
Decision	5	2	2
Topic	4	0	0
Leader	4	2	2
Landmark_occasion	4	3	3
Dependent	4	4	3
Author	4	1	1
Other (32 FEs)	66	44	39
Total (N)	148	96	87
Total (%)	66	65	58

Table 5: Frame Elements from the JRC-Acquis Corpus

	Correct Frame E.	Transferable Frame E.	Success %
Kotus	89	67	75%
JRC-A	96	87	91%
Total	185	154	83%

Table 6: The Success Rate of Frame Element Transfer

Frame-evoking words	120
Transferable to Finnish	85
Same word as in FWN	37
In the same synset	2
Could be in the same synset	31

Table 7: Wordnet Links in the Kotus Corpus

Frame-evoking words	120
Transferable to Finnish	86
Same word as in FWN	41
In the same synset	0
Could be in the same synset	16

Table 8: Wordnet Links in the JRC-Acquis Corpus

synonyms of the word in question and could therefore be located in the same synset in the wordnets.

As can be seen in Tables 7 and 8, only 46% (37/85 and 41/86) of the theoretically transferable words can be transferred to Finnish directly using the wordnet links. Our hypothesis was that we could get better results when looking at all the words in a synset. This appears to be a wrong assumption: There are only 2 words that come from the same synset that are not equivalent words used in the translations.

The numbers on the fifth rows are remarkably big, especially when compared to the number of realized synonyms on the fourth row. These 47 words could (or should) be located in the same synset as the words in question. If the wordnets were complete, i.e. if all words that could be in the same synset were in the same synset, the theoretically transferable LUs would be 82% (70/85) and 65% (56/86).

5 Conclusion and Future Work

The main point of the experiment was to see if building a preliminary Finnish framenet and labeling semantic roles for Finnish using Swedish resources is feasible at all. In particular, we wanted to see whether the same situations are expressed using the same frames in both languages and whether it is possible to transfer the frames and frame elements with their lexical units from one language to the other.

In our experiment, we have evaluated how well the frames and frame elements can be transferred from a Swedish corpus to its Finnish parallel corpus. We have shown that in theory, 92% of the correct Swedish frame labels and 83% of the correct frame element labels can be transferred to Finnish.

We also investigated whether linked wordnets could be used for the transfer of frame-evoking words between Swedish and Finnish. The results here are more ambiguous, however. On the one hand, only about half of the words could be linked in this way. On the other hand, it turns out that this in part is because of many synsets being incomplete in these wordnets which are still under construction. Thus we should not dismiss out of hand the usefulness of lexical-semantic resources such as wordnets for the task of cross-language frame transfer, but rather explore further how the knowledge encoded in them could be best put to use.

The result of our experiment encourages us to find ways of performing frame transfer automatically. This can be accomplished using a word aligned parallel corpus for Swedish and Finnish. The automatic word alignment of Finnish is generally seen as a complicated task because of the free constituent order and rich morphology of Finnish. However, our future work is to examine the success of using automatic word alignment, e.g. Giza++, in automatically transferring the frame information from one language to another.

Acknowledgements

The research presented here was supported by the Swedish Research Council (the project *Swedish Framenet++*, VR dnr 2010-6013) and by the University of Gothenburg through its support of the Centre for Language Technology and its support of Språkbanken (the Swedish Language Bank). The work on linking the Swedish wordnet to the Princeton Core WordNet was conducted with funding by the European Commission through its support of the META-NORD project under the ICT PSP Programme, grant agreement no 270899. We would like to thank the anonymous reviewers for their constructive comments and Jyrki Niemi for his valuable help with FinnWordNet.

References

Emily M. Bender. 2011. On achieving and evaluating language-independence in NLP. *Linguistic Issues in Language Technology*, 6(3).

Lars Borin and Markus Forsberg. 2009. All in the family: A comparison of SALDO and WordNet. In *Proceedings of the Nodalida 2009 Workshop on WordNets and other Lexical Semantic Resources – between Lexical Semantics, Lexicography, Terminology and Formal Ontologies*, Odense, Denmark.

Lars Borin and Markus Forsberg. 2011. Swesaurus – ett svenskt ordnät med fria tyglar. *LexicoNordica*, 18:17–39.

Lars Borin, Markus Forsberg, and Lennart Lönngren. 2008. The hunting of the BLARK – SALDO, a freely available lexical database for Swedish language technology. In Joakim Nivre, Mats Dahllöf, and Beata Megyesi, editors, *Resourceful language technology. Festschrift in honor of Anna Sågvall Hein*, number 7 in Acta Universitatis Upsaliensis: Studia Linguistica Upsaliensia, pages 21–32. Uppsala University, Department of Linguistics and Philology, Uppsala.

Lars Borin, Dana Dannélls, Markus Forsberg, Maria Toporowska Gronostaj, and Dimitrios Kokkinakis. 2010. The past meets the present in the Swedish FrameNet++. In *Proc. of EURALEX*, pages 269–281, Leeuwarden. EURALEX.

Lars Borin, Markus Forsberg, and Johan Roxendal. 2012. Korp – the corpus infrastructure of Språkbanken. In *Proceedings of LREC 2012*.

Lars Borin. 2010. Med Zipf mot framtiden – en integrerad lexikonresurs för svensk språkteknologi. *LexicoNordica*, 17:35–54.

Aljoscha Burchardt, Katrin Erk, and Anette Frank. 2005. A WordNet detour to FrameNet. In *Proceedings of the GLDV 2005 workshop GermaNet II*, Bonn, Germany.

Christiane Fellbaum, editor. 1998. *WordNet: An Electronic Lexical Database*. Kluwer The MIT Press.

Charles J. Fillmore. 1976. Frame semantics and the nature of language. *Annals of the New York Academy of Sciences: Conference on the Origin and Development of Language and Speech*, 280(1):20–32.

Richard Johansson and Pierre Nugues. 2006. A FrameNet-based semantic role labeler for Swedish. In *Proc. of Coling/ACL*.

Richard Johansson and Pierre Nugues. 2007. Using WordNet to extend FrameNet coverage. In *Proceedings of the Workshop on Building Frame-semantic Resources for Scandinavian and Baltic Languages, at NODALIDA*, pages 27–30, Tartu, Estonia.

Richard Johansson, Karin Friberg Heppin, and Dimitrios Kokkinakis. 2012. Semantic role labeling with the Swedish FrameNet. In *Proceedings of LREC-2012*.

Krister Lindén and Lauri Carlson. 2010. FinnWordNet – WordNet på finska via översättning. *LexicoNordica – Nordic Journal of Lexicography*, 17:119–140.

Sebastian Padó and Mirella Lapata. 2005a. Cross-lingual bootstrapping for semantic lexicons: The case of Framenet. In *Proceedings of AAAI-05*, pages 1087–1092, Pittsburgh, United States.

Sebastian Padó and Mirella Lapata. 2005b. Cross-linguistic projection of role-semantic information. In *Proceedings of Human Language Technology Conference and Conference on Empirical Methods in Natural Language Processing*, pages 859–866, Vancouver, Canada.

Sebastian Padó. 2007. Translational equivalence and cross-lingual parallelism: The case of FrameNet frames. In *Proceedings of the NODALIDA Workshop on Building Frame Semantics Resources for Scandinavian and Baltic Languages*, Tartu, Estonia.

Research Institute for the Languages of Finland. 2004. KFSPC: KOTUS Swedish-Finnish Parallel Corpus. http://www.csc.fi/kielipankki.

Josef Ruppenhofer, Michael Ellsworth, Miriam R. L. Petruck, Christopher R. Johnson, and Jan Scheffczyk. 2006. FrameNet II: Extended theory and practice. *Unpublished Manuscript.*

Ralf Steinberger, Bruno Pouliquen, Anna Widiger, Camelia Ignat, Tomaž Erjavec, Dan Tufiş, and Dániel Varga. 2006. The JRC-Acquis: A multilingual aligned parallel corpus with 20+ languages. In *Proceedings of the Fifth International Conference on Language Resources and Evaluation (LREC)*, pages 2142–2147.

Piek Vossen, editor. 1998. *EuroWordNet: a multilingual database with lexical semantic networks for European Languages*. Kluwer Academic Publishers.

Unsupervised Induction of Frame-Semantic Representations

Ashutosh Modi **Ivan Titov** **Alexandre Klementiev**
Saarland University
Saarbrücken, Germany
{amodi|titov|aklement}@mmci.uni-saarland.de

Abstract

The frame-semantic parsing task is challenging for supervised techniques, even for those few languages where relatively large amounts of labeled data are available. In this preliminary work, we consider *unsupervised* induction of frame-semantic representations. An existing state-of-the-art Bayesian model for PropBank-style unsupervised semantic role induction (Titov and Klementiev, 2012) is extended to jointly induce semantic frames and their roles. We evaluate the model performance both quantitatively and qualitatively by comparing the induced representation against FrameNet annotations.

1 Introduction

Shallow representations of meaning, and semantic role labels in particular, have a long history in linguistics (Fillmore, 1968). In this paper we focus on frame-semantic representations: a *semantic frame* is a conceptual structure describing a situation (or an entity) and its participants (or its properties). Participants and properties are associated with *semantic roles* (also called *frame elements*). For example, following the FrameNet annotation guidelines (Ruppenhofer et al., 2006), in the following sentences:

(a) $[_{COOK}$ Mary$]$ cooks $[_{FOOD}$ the broccoli$]$ $[_{CONTAINER}$ in a small pan$]$.

(b) Sautee $[_{FOOD}$ the onions$]$ $[_{MANNER}$ gently $]$ $[_{TEMP\_SETTING}$ on low heat$]$.

the same semantic frame $Apply\_Heat$ is evoked by verbs *cook* and *sautee*, and roles $COOK$ and $FOOD$ in the sentence (a) are filled by *Mary* and *the broccoli*, respectively. Note that roles are specific to the frame, not to the individual *lexical units* (verbs *cook* and *sautee*, in the example).[1]

Most approaches to predicting these representations, called *semantic role labeling* (SRL), have relied on large annotated datasets (Gildea and Jurafsky, 2002; Carreras and Màrquez, 2005; Surdeanu et al., 2008; Hajič et al., 2009). By far, most of this work has focused on PropBank-style representations (Palmer et al., 2005) where roles are defined for each individual verb, or even individual senses of a verb. The only exceptions are modifiers and roles $A0$ and $A1$ which correspond to proto-agent (a doer, or initiator of the action) and proto-patient (an affected entity), respectively. However, the SRL task is known to be especially hard for the FrameNet-style representations for a number of reasons, including, the lack of cross-frame correspondence for most roles, fine-grain definitions of roles and frames in FrameNet, and relatively small amounts of statistically representative data (Erk and Pado, 2006; Das et al., 2010; Palmer and Sporleder, 2010; Das and Smith, 2011). Another reason for reduced interest in predicting FrameNet representations is the lack of annotated resources for most languages, with annotated corpora available or being developed only for English (Ruppenhofer et al., 2006), German (Burchardt et al., 2006), Spanish (Subirats, 2009) and Japanese (Ohara et al., 2004).

Due to scarcity of labeled data, purely unsupervised set-ups recently started to receive considerable attention (Swier and Stevenson, 2004; Grenager and Manning, 2006; Lang and Lapata, 2010; Lang and

[1] More accurately, FrameNet distinguishes core and non-core roles with non-core roles mostly corresponding to modifiers, e.g., $MANNER$ in sentence (b). Non-core roles are expected to generalize across frames.

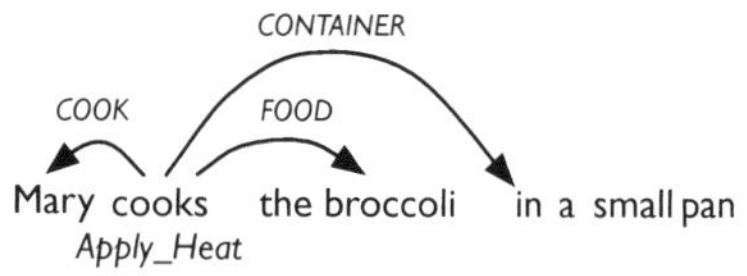

Figure 1: An example of a semantic dependency graph.

Lapata, 2011a; Lang and Lapata, 2011b; Titov and Klementiev, 2012). However, all these approaches have focused on PropBank-style representations. This may seem somewhat unnatural as FrameNet representations, though arguably more powerful, are harder to learn in the supervised setting, harder to annotate, and annotated data is available for a considerably fewer languages. This is the gap which we address in this preliminary study.

More specifically, we extend an existing state-of-the-art Bayesian model for unsupervised semantic role labeling and apply it to support FrameNet-style semantics. In other words, our method jointly induces both frames and frame-specific semantic roles. We experiment only with verbal predicates and evaluate the performance of the model with respect to some natural baselines. Though the scores for frame induction are not high, we argue that this is primarily due to very high granularity of FrameNet frames which is hard to reproduce for unsupervised systems, as the implicit supervision signal is not capable of providing these distinctions.

2 Task Definition

In this work, we use dependency representations of frame semantics. Dependency representations for SRL (Johansson and Nugues, 2008) were made popular by CoNLL-2008 and CoNLL-2009 shared tasks (Surdeanu et al., 2008; Hajič et al., 2009), but for English were limited to PropBank. Recently, English FrameNet was also released in the dependency format (Bauer et al., 2012). Instead of predicting argument spans, in dependency representation the goal is, roughly, to predict the syntactic head of the argument. The semantic dependency representation for sentence (a) is shown in Figure 1, labels on edges denote roles and labels on words denote frames. Note that in practice the structures can be more complex, as, for example, arguments can evoke their own frames or the same arguments can be shared by multiple predicates, as in right node raising constructions.

The SRL task, or more specifically frame-semantic parsing task consists, at least conceptually, of four stages: (1) identification of frame-evoking elements(FEE), (2) identification of arguments, (3) frame labeling and (4) role labeling. In this work, we focus only on the frame labeling and role labeling stages, relying on gold standard (i.e. the oracle) for FEEs and role identification. In other words, our goal is to label (or cluster) edges and nodes in the dependency graph, Figure 1. Since we focus in this study on verbal predicates only, the first stage would be trivial and the second stage could be handled with heuristics as in much of previous work on unsupervised SRL (Lang and Lapata, 2011a; Titov and Klementiev, 2012).

Additionally to considering only verbal predicates, we also assume that every verb belongs to a single frame. This assumption, though restrictive, may be reasonable in practice as (a) the distributions across frames (i.e. senses) are generally highly skewed, (b) current state-of-the-art techniques for word-sense induction hardly beat most-frequent-sense baselines in accuracy metrics (Manandhar et al., 2010). This assumption, or its minor relaxations, is relatively standard in work on unsupervised semantic parsing tasks (Poon and Domingos, 2009; Poon and Domingos, 2010; Titov and Klementiev, 2011). From the modeling prospective, there are no major obstacles to relaxing this assumption, but it would lead to a major explosion of the search space and, as a result, slow inference.

3 Model and Inference

We follow previous work on unsupervised semantic role labeling (Lang and Lapata, 2011a; Titov and Klementiev, 2012) and associate arguments with their frame specific syntactic signatures which we refer to as *argument keys*:

- Active or passive verb voice (`ACT/PASS`).
- Argument position relative to predicate (`LEFT/RIGHT`).
- Syntactic relation to its governor.
- Preposition used for argument realization.

Semantic roles are then represented as clusters of argument keys instead of individual argument occurrences. This representation aids our models in inducing high purity clusters (of argument keys) while reducing their granularity. Thus, if an argument key k is assigned to a role r ($k \in r$), all of its occurrences are labeled r.

3.1 A model for frame-semantic parsing

Our approach is similar to the models of Titov and Klementiev (2012; 2011). Please, see Section 5 for a discussion of the differences.

Our model encodes three assumptions about frames and semantic roles. First, we assume that the distribution of lexical units (verbal predicates) is sparse for each semantic frame. Second, we enforce the selectional restriction assumption: we assume that the distribution over potential argument fillers is sparse for every role, implying that 'peaky' distributions of arguments for each role r are preferred to flat distributions. Third, each role normally appears at most once per predicate occurrence. Our inference will search for a frame and role clustering which meets the above requirements to the maximal extent.

Our model associates three distributions with each frame. The first one (ϕ) models the selection of lexical units, the second (θ) governs the selection of argument fillers for each semantic role, and the third (ψ) models (and penalizes) duplicate occurrence of roles. Each frame occurrence is generated independently given these distributions. Let us describe the model by first defining how the set of model parameters and an argument key clustering are drawn, and then explaining the generation of individual frame instances. The generative story is formally presented in Figure 2.

For each frame, we begin by drawing a distribution of its lexical units from a DP prior $DP(\gamma, H^{(P)})$ with a small concentration parameter γ, and a base distribution $H^{(P)}$, pre-computed as normalized counts of all verbs in our dataset. Next, we generate a partition of argument keys B_f from CRP(α) with each subset $r \in B_f$ representing a single frame specific semantic role. The crucial part of the model is the set of selectional preference parameters $\theta_{f,r}$, the distributions of arguments x for each role r of frame f. We represent arguments by lemmas of their syntactic heads.[2] In order to encode the assumption about sparseness of the distributions $\theta_{f,r}$, we draw them from the DP prior $DP(\beta, H^{(A)})$ with a small concentration parameter β, the base probability distribution $H^{(A)}$ is just the normalized frequencies of arguments in the corpus. Finally, the geometric distribution $\psi_{f,r}$ is used to model the number of times a role r appears with a given frame occurrence. The decision whether to generate at least one role r is drawn from the uniform Bernoulli distribution. If 0 is drawn then the semantic role is not realized for the given occurrence, otherwise the number of additional roles r is drawn from the geometric distribution $Geom(\psi_{f,r})$. The Beta priors over ψ indicate the preference towards generating at most one argument for each role.

Now, when parameters and argument key clusterings are chosen, we can summarize the remainder of the generative story as follows. We begin by independently drawing occurrences for each frame. For each frame occurrence, we first draw its lexical unit. Then for each role we independently decide on the number of role occurrences. Then we generate each of the arguments (see **GenArgument** in Figure 2) by generating an argument key $k_{f,r}$ uniformly from the set of argument keys assigned to the cluster r, and finally choosing its filler $x_{f,r}$, where the filler is either a lemma or the syntactic head of the argument.

3.2 Inference

We use a simple approximate inference algorithm based on greedy search for the maximum a-posteriori clustering of lexical units and argument keys. We begin by assigning each verbal predicate to its own frame, and then iteratively choose a pair of frames and merge them. Note that each merge involves inducing a new set of roles, i.e. a re-clustering of argument keys, for the new merged frame. We use the search procedure proposed in (Titov and Klementiev, 2012), in order to cluster argument keys for each frame.

Our search procedure chooses a pair of frames to merge based on the largest incremental change to the objective due to the merge. Computing the change involves re-clustering of argument keys, so considering all pairs of initial frames containing single verbal predicates is computationally expensive. Instead, we

[2]For prepositional phrases, we take as head the head noun of the object noun phrase as it encodes crucial lexical information. However, the preposition is not ignored but rather encoded in the corresponding argument key.

```
Parameters:
for each frame f = 1, 2, . . . :
  φ_f ∼ DP(γ, H^(P))                      [distrib of lexical units]
  B_f ∼ CRP(α)                            [partition of arg keys]
  for each role r ∈ B_f:
    θ_{f,r} ∼ DP(β, H^(A))                [distrib of arg fillers]
    ψ_{f,r} ∼ Beta(η_0, η_1)              [geom distr for dup roles]
```

```
Data Generation:
for each frame f = 1, 2, . . . :
  for each occurrence of frame f:
    p ∼ φ_f                               [draw a lexical unit]
    for every role r ∈ B_f:
      if [n ∼ Unif(0, 1)] = 1:            [role appears at least once]
        GenArgument(f, r)                 [draw one arg]
        while [n ∼ ψ_{f,r}] = 1:          [continue generation]
          GenArgument(f, r)               [draw more args]
```

```
GenArgument(f, r):
  k_{f,r} ∼ Unif(1, . . . , |r|)          [draw arg key]
  x_{f,r} ∼ θ_{f,r}                       [draw arg filler]
```

Figure 2: Generative story for the frame-semantic parsing model.

prune the space of possible pairs of verbs using a simple but effective pre-processing step. Each verb is associated with a vector of normalized aggregate corpus counts of syntactic dependents of the verb (ignoring the type of dependency relation). Cosine similarity of these vectors are then used to prune the pairs of verbs so that only verbs which are distributionally similar enough are considered for a merge. Finally, the search terminates when no additional merges result in a positive change to the objective.

4 Experimental Evaluation

4.1 Data

We used the dependency representation of the FrameNet corpus (Bauer et al., 2012). The corpus is automatically annotated with syntactic dependency trees produced by the Stanford parser. The data consists of 158,048 sentences with 3,474 unique verbal predicates and 722 gold frames.

4.2 Evaluation Metrics

We cannot use supervised metrics to evaluate our models, since we do not have an alignment between gold labels and clusters induced in the unsupervised setup. Instead, we use the standard purity (PU) and collocation (CO) metrics as well as their harmonic mean (F1) to measure the quality of the resulting clusters. Purity measures the degree to which each cluster contains arguments (verbs) sharing the same gold role (gold frame) and collocation evaluates the degree to which arguments (verbs) with the same gold roles (gold frame) are assigned to a single cluster, see (Lang and Lapata, 2010). As in previous work, for role induction, the scores are first computed for individual predicates and then averaged with the weights proportional to the total number occurrences of roles for each predicate.

4.3 Model Parameters

The model parameters were tuned coarsely by visual inspection: $\alpha = 1.e\text{-}5$, $\beta = 1.e\text{-}4$, $\gamma = 1$, $\eta_0 = 100$, $\eta_1 = 1.e\text{-}10$. Only a single model was evaluated quantitatively to avoid overfitting to the evaluation set.

4.4 Qualitative Evaluation

Our model induced 128 multi-verb frames from the dataset. Out of 78,039 predicate occurrences in the data, these correspond to 18,963 verb occurrences (or, approximately, 25%). Some examples of the induced multi-verb frames are shown in Table 1. As we can observe from the table, our model clusters semantically related verbs into a single frame, even though they may not correspond to the same gold frame in FrameNet. Consider, for example, the frame *(ratify::sign::accede)*: the verbs are semantically related and hence they should go into a single frame, as they all denote a similar action.

Another result worth noting is that the model often clusters antonyms together as they are often used in similar context. For example, consider the frame *(cool::heat::warm)*, the verbs *cool*, *heat* and *warm*, all denote a change in temperature. This agrees well with annotation in FrameNet. Similarly, we cluster *sell* and *purchase* together. This contrasts with FrameNet annotation as FrameNet treats them not as antonyms but as different views on same situation and according to their guidelines, different frames are assigned to different views.

Often frames in FrameNet correspond to more fine-grained meanings of the verbs, as we can see in the example for *(plait::braid::dye)*. The three describe a similar activity involving hair but FrameNet

Induced frames	FrameNet frames corresponding to the verbs
(rush::dash::tiptoe)	rush : [Self_motion](150) [Fluidic_motion](19) dash : [Self_motion](100) tiptoe : [Self_motion](114)
(ratify::sign::accede)	ratify : [Ratification](41) sign : [Sign_agreement](81) [Hiring](18) [Text_Creation](1) accede : [Sign_Agreement](31)
(crane::lean::bustle)	crane : [Body_movement](26) lean: [Change_posture](70) [Placing](22) [Posture](12) bustle : [Self_motion](55)
(cool::heat::warm)	cool : [Cause_temperature_change](27) heat: [Cause_temperature_change](52) warm: [Cause_temperature_change](41) [Inchoative_change_of_temperature](16)
(want::fib::dare)	want : [Desiring](105) [Possession](44) fib : [Prevarication](9) dare : [Daring](21)
(encourage::intimidate::confuse)	encourage : [Stimulus_focus](49) intimidate : [Stimulus_focus](26) confuse: [Stimulus_focus](45)
(happen::transpire::teach)	happen : [Event](38) [Coincidence](21) [Eventive_affecting](1) transpire : [Event](15) teach : [Education_teaching](7)
(do::understand::hope)	do : [Intentionally_affect](6) [Intentionally_act](56) understand : [Grasp](74) [Awareness](57) [Categorization](15) hope : [Desiring](77)
(frighten::vary::reassure)	frighten : [Emotion_directed](44) vary : [Diversity](24) reassure : [Stimulus_focus](35)
(plait::braid::dye)	plait : [Hair_configuration](11) [Grooming](12) braid : [Hair_configuration](7) [Clothing_parts](6) [Rope_manipulation](4) dye : [Processing_materials](18)
(sell::purchase)	sell : [Commerce_sell](107) purchase : [Commerce_buy](93)
(glisten::sparkle::gleam)	glisten : [Location_of_light](52) [Light_movement](1) sparkle : [Location_of_light](23) [Light_movement](3) gleam : [Location_of_light](77) [Light_movement](4)
(forestall::shush)	forestall : [Thwarting](12) shush : [Silencing](6)

Table 1: Examples of the induced multi-verb frames. The left column shows the induced verb clusters and the right column lists the gold frames corresponding to each verb and the number in the parentheses are their occurrence counts.

gives them a finer distinction. Arguably, implicit supervision signal present in the unlabeled data is not sufficient to provide such fine-grained distinctions.

The model does not distinguish verb senses, i.e. it always assigns a single frame to each verb, so there is an upper bound on our clustering performance.

4.5 Quantitative Evaluation

Now we turn to quantitative evaluation of both frame and role induction.

Frame Labeling. In this section, we evaluate how well the induced frames correspond to the gold standard annotation. Because of the lack of relevant previous work, we use only a trivial baseline which places each verb in a separate cluster (*NoClustering*). The results are summarized in Table 3.

As we can see from the results, our model achieves a small, but probably significant, improvement in the F1-score. Though the scores are fairly low, note that, as discussed in Section 4.4, the model is severely penalized even for inducing semantically plausible frames such as the frame *(plait::braid::dye)*.

Role Labeling. In this section, we evaluate how well the induced roles correspond to the gold standard annotation. We use two baselines: one is the syntactic baseline *SyntF*, which simply clusters arguments according to the dependency rela-

	PU	CO	F1
Our approach	78.9	71.0	**74.8**
NoFrameInduction	79.2	70.7	**74.7**
SyntF	69.9	73.3	**71.6**

Table 2: Role labeling performance.

tion to their head, as described in (Lang and Lapata, 2010), and the other one is a version of our model which does not attempt to cluster verbs and only induces roles (*NoFrameInduction*). Note that the *NoFrameInduction* baseline is equivalent to the *factored* model of Titov and Klementiev (2012). The results are summarized in Table 2.

First, observe that both our full model and its simplified version *NoFrameInduction* significantly outperform the syntactic baseline. It is important to note that the syntactic baseline is not trivial to beat in the unsupervised setting (Lang and Lapata, 2010). Though there is a minor improvement from inducing frames, it is small and may not be significant.[3]

Another observation is that the absolute scores of all the systems, including the baselines, are significantly below the results reported in Titov and Klementiev (Titov and Klementiev, 2012) on the CoNLL-08 version of PropBank in a comparable setting (auto parses, gold argument identification): 73.9 % and 77.9 % F1 for *SyntF* and *NoFrameInduction*, respectively. We believe that the main reason for this discrepancy is the difference in the syntactic representations. The CoNLL-08 dependencies include function tags (e.g., *TMP*, *LOC*), and, therefore, modifiers do not need to be predicted, whereas the Stanford syntactic dependencies do not provide this information and the model needs to induce it.

It is clear from these results, and also from the previous observation that only 25% of verb occurrences belong to multi-verb clusters, that the model does not induce sufficiently rich clustering of verbs. Arguably, this is largely due to the relatively small size of FrameNet, as it may not provide enough evidence for clustering. Given that our method is quite efficient, a single experiment was taking around 8 hours on a single CPU, and the procedure is highly parallelizable, the next step would be to use a much larger and statistically representative corpus to induce the representations.

[3]There is no well-established methodology for testing statistical significance when comparing two clustering methods.

	PU	CO	F1
Our approach	77.9	31.4	**44.7**
NoClustering	80.8	29.0	**42.7**

Table 3: Frame labeling performance.

Additional visual inspection suggest that the data is quite noisy primarily due to mistakes in parsing. The large proportion of mistakes can probably be explained by the domain shift: the parser is trained on the WSJ newswire data and tested on more general BNC texts.

5 Related Work

The space constraints do not permit us to provide a comprehensive overview of related work. Aside from the original model of Titov and Klementiev (2012), the most related previous method is the Bayesian method of Titov and Klementiev (2011). In that work, along with predicate-argument structure, they also induce clusterings of dependency tree fragments (not necessarily verbs). However, their approach uses a different model for argument generation, a different inference procedure, and it has only been applied and evaluated on biomedical data. The same shallow semantic parsing task has also been considered in the work of Poon and Domingos (2009; 2010), but using a MLN model and, again, only on the biomedical domain. Another closely related vein of research is on semi-supervised frame-semantic parsing (Fürstenau and Lapata, 2009; Das and Smith, 2011).

6 Conclusions

This work is the first to consider the task of unsupervised frame-semantic parsing. Though the quantitative results are mixed, we showed that meaningful semantic frames are induced. In the future work, we intend to consider much larger corpora and to focus on a more general set-up by relaxing the assumption that frames are evoked only by verbal predicates.

Acknowledgements

The authors acknowledge the support of the MMCI Cluster of Excellence, and thank Caroline Sporleder, Alexis Palmer and the anonymous reviewers for their suggestions.

References

Daniel Bauer, Hagen Fürstenau, and Owen Rambow. 2012. The dependency-parsed framenet corpus. In *International conference on Language Resources and Evaluation (LREC)*, Istanbul, Turkey.

A. Burchardt, K. Erk, A. Frank, A. Kowalski, S. Pado, and M. Pinkal. 2006. The SALSA corpus: a german corpus resource for lexical semantics. In *LREC*.

Xavier Carreras and Lluís Màrquez. 2005. Introduction to the CoNLL-2005 Shared Task: Semantic Role Labeling. In *CoNLL*.

D. Das and N.A. Smith. 2011. Semi-supervised frame-semantic parsing for unknown predicates. In *Proceedings of the 49th Annual Meeting of the Association for Computational Linguistics: Human Language Technologies-Volume 1*, pages 1435–1444. Association for Computational Linguistics.

D. Das, N. Schneider, D. Chen, and N.A. Smith. 2010. Probabilistic frame-semantic parsing. In *Human Language Technologies: The 2010 Annual Conference of the North American Chapter of the Association for Computational Linguistics*, pages 948–956. Association for Computational Linguistics.

K. Erk and S. Pado. 2006. Shalmaneser–a toolchain for shallow semantic parsing. In *Proceedings of LREC*, volume 6. Citeseer.

Charles J. Fillmore. 1968. The case for case. In Bach E. and Harms R.T., editors, *Universals in Linguistic Theory*, pages 1–88. Holt, Rinehart, and Winston, New York.

Hagen Fürstenau and Mirella Lapata. 2009. Graph alignment for semi-supervised semantic role labeling. In *EMNLP*.

Daniel Gildea and Daniel Jurafsky. 2002. Automatic labelling of semantic roles. *Computational Linguistics*, 28(3):245–288.

Trond Grenager and Christoph Manning. 2006. Unsupervised discovery of a statistical verb lexicon. In *EMNLP*.

Jan Hajič, Massimiliano Ciaramita, Richard Johansson, Daisuke Kawahara, Maria Antònia Martí, Lluís Màrquez, Adam Meyers, Joakim Nivre, Sebastian Padó, Jan Štěpánek, Pavel Straňák, Mihai Surdeanu, Nianwen Xue, and Yi Zhang. 2009. The CoNLL-2009 shared task: Syntactic and semantic dependencies in multiple languages. In *Proceedings of the 13th Conference on Computational Natural Language Learning (CoNLL-2009), June 4-5*.

Richard Johansson and Pierre Nugues. 2008. Dependency-based semantic role labeling of PropBank. In *EMNLP*.

Joel Lang and Mirella Lapata. 2010. Unsupervised induction of semantic roles. In *ACL*.

Joel Lang and Mirella Lapata. 2011a. Unsupervised semantic role induction via split-merge clustering. In *ACL*.

Joel Lang and Mirella Lapata. 2011b. Unsupervised semantic role induction with graph partitioning. In *EMNLP*.

Suresh Manandhar, Ioannis P. Klapaftis, Dmitriy Dligach, and Sameer S. Pradhan. 2010. Semeval-2010 task 14: Word sense induction and disambiguation. In *Proceedings of the 5th International Workshop on Semantic Evaluation*.

K.H. Ohara, S. Fujii, T. Ohori, R. Suzuki, H. Saito, and S. Ishizaki. 2004. The japanese framenet project: An introduction. In *Proceedings of LREC-04 Satellite Workshop Building Lexical Resources from Semantically Annotated Corpora(LREC 2004)*, pages 9–11.

Alexis Palmer and Caroline Sporleder. 2010. Evaluating FrameNet-style semantic parsing: the role of coverage gaps in FrameNet. In *COLING*.

M. Palmer, D. Gildea, and P. Kingsbury. 2005. The proposition bank: An annotated corpus of semantic roles. *Computational Linguistics*, 31(1):71–106.

Hoifung Poon and Pedro Domingos. 2009. Unsupervised semantic parsing. In *EMNLP*.

H. Poon and P. Domingos. 2010. Unsupervised ontology induction from text. In *Proceedings of the 48th Annual Meeting of the Association for Computational Linguistics*, pages 296–305. Association for Computational Linguistics.

Josef Ruppenhofer, Michael Ellsworth, Miriam R. L. Petruck, Christopher R. Johnson, and Jan Scheffczyk. 2006. Framenet ii: Extended theory and practice. available at `http://framenet.icsi.berkeley.edu/index.php?option=com_wrapper&Itemid=126`.

C. Subirats. 2009. Spanish framenet: A frame-semantic analysis of the spanish lexicon. *Berlin/New York: Mouton de Gruyter*, pages 135–162.

Mihai Surdeanu, Adam Meyers Richard Johansson, Lluís Màrquez, and Joakim Nivre. 2008. The CoNLL-2008 shared task on joint parsing of syntactic and semantic dependencies. In *CoNLL 2008: Shared Task*.

Richard Swier and Suzanne Stevenson. 2004. Unsupervised semantic role labelling. In *EMNLP*.

Ivan Titov and Alexandre Klementiev. 2011. A Bayesian model for unsupervised semantic parsing. In *ACL*.

Ivan Titov and Alexandre Klementiev. 2012. A bayesian approach to semantic role induction. In *Proc. EACL*, Avignon, France.

Capitalization Cues Improve Dependency Grammar Induction

Valentin I. Spitkovsky
Stanford University and Google Inc.
valentin@cs.stanford.edu

Hiyan Alshawi
Google Inc., Mountain View, CA, 94043
hiyan@google.com

Daniel Jurafsky
Stanford University, Stanford, CA, 94305
jurafsky@stanford.edu

Abstract

We show that orthographic cues can be helpful for unsupervised parsing. In the Penn Treebank, transitions between upper- and lowercase tokens tend to align with the boundaries of base (English) noun phrases. Such signals can be used as partial bracketing constraints to train a grammar inducer: in our experiments, directed dependency accuracy increased by 2.2% (average over 14 languages having case information). Combining capitalization with punctuation-induced constraints in inference further improved parsing performance, attaining state-of-the-art levels for many languages.

1 Introduction

Dependency grammar induction and related problems of unsupervised syntactic structure discovery are attracting increasing attention (Rasooli and Faili, 2012; Mareček and Zabokrtský, 2011, *inter alia*). Since sentence structure is underdetermined by raw text, there have been efforts to simplify the task, via (i) pooling features of syntax across languages (Cohen et al., 2011; McDonald et al., 2011; Cohen and Smith, 2009); as well as (ii) identifying universal rules (Naseem et al., 2010) — such as verbocentricity (Gimpel and Smith, 2011) — that need not be learned at all. Unfortunately most of these techniques do not apply to plain text, because they require knowing, for example, which words are verbs.

As standard practice shifts away from relying on gold part-of-speech (POS) tags (Seginer, 2007; Ponvert et al., 2010; Søgaard, 2011b; Spitkovsky et al., 2011c, *inter alia*), lighter cues to inducing linguistic structure become more important. Examples of useful POS-agnostic clues include punctuation boundaries (Ponvert et al., 2011; Spitkovsky et al., 2011b; Briscoe, 1994) and various kinds of bracketing constraints (Naseem and Barzilay, 2011; Spitkovsky et al., 2010b; Pereira and Schabes, 1992). We propose adding capitalization to this growing list of sources of partial bracketings. Our intuition stems from English, where (maximal) spans of capitalized words — such as Apple II, World War I, Mayor William H. Hudnut III, International Business Machines Corp. and Alexandria, Va — tend to demarcate proper nouns.

Consider a motivating example (all of our examples are from WSJ) without punctuation, in which all (eight) capitalized word clumps and uncased numerals match base noun phrase constituent boundaries:

> [$_{NP}$ Jay Stevens] of [$_{NP}$ Dean Witter] actually cut his per-share earnings estimate to [$_{NP}$ $9] from [$_{NP}$ $9.50] for [$_{NP}$ 1989] and to [$_{NP}$ $9.50] from [$_{NP}$ $10.35] in [$_{NP}$ 1990] because he decided sales would be even weaker than he had expected.

and another (whose first word happens to be a leaf), where capitalization complements punctuation cues:

> [$_{NP}$ Jurors] in [$_{NP}$ U.S. District Court] in [$_{NP}$ Miami] cleared [$_{NP}$ Harold Hershhenson], a former executive vice president; [$_{NP}$ John Pagones], a former vice president; and [$_{NP}$ Stephen Vadas] and [$_{NP}$ Dean Ciporkin], who had been engineers with [$_{NP}$ Cordis].

Could such chunks help bootstrap grammar induction and/or improve the accuracy of already-trained unsupervised parsers? In answering these questions, we will focus predominantly on sentence-internal capitalization. But we will also show that first words — those capitalized by convention — and uncased segments — whose characters are not even drawn from an alphabet — could play a useful role as well.

2 English Capitalization from a Treebank

We began our study by consulting the 51,558 parsed sentences of the WSJ corpus (Marcus et al., 1993): 30,691 (59.5%) of them contain non-trivially capitalized *fragments* — maximal (non-empty and not

	Count	POS Sequence	Frac	Cum
1	27,524	NNP	44.6%	
2	17,222	NNP NNP	27.9	72.5
3	4,598	NNP NNP NNP	7.5	79.9
4	2,973	JJ	4.8	84.8
5	1,716	NNP NNP NNP NNP	2.8	87.5
6	1,037	NN	1.7	89.2
7	932	PRP	1.5	90.7
8	846	NNPS	1.4	92.1
9	604	NNP NNPS	1.0	93.1
10	526	NNP NNP NNP NNP NNP	0.9	93.9
WSJ	+3,753	*more with Count* ≤ 498	6.1%	

Table 1: Top 10 fragments of POS tag sequences in WSJ.

sentence-initial) consecutive sequences of words that each differs from its own lower-cased form. Nearly all — 59,388 (96.2%) — of the 61,731 fragments are dominated by noun phrases; slightly less than half — 27,005 (43.8%) — perfectly align with constituent boundaries in the treebank; and about as many — 27,230 (44.1%) are multi-token. Table 1 shows the top POS sequences comprising fragments.

3 Analytical Experiments with Gold Trees

We gauged the suitability of capitalization-induced fragments for guiding dependency grammar induction by assessing accuracy, in WSJ,[1] of parsing constraints derived from their end-points. Following the suite of increasingly-restrictive constraints on how dependencies may interact with fragments, introduced by Spitkovsky et al. (2011b, §2.2), we tested several such heuristics. The most lenient constraint, *thread*, only asks that no dependency path from the root to a leaf enter the fragment twice; *tear* requires any incoming arcs to come from the same side of the fragment; *sprawl* demands that there be exactly one incoming arc; *loose* further constrains any outgoing arcs to be from the fragment's head; and *strict* — the most stringent constraint — bans external dependents. Since only *strict* is binding for single words, we experimented also with *strict′*: applying *strict* solely to multi-token fragments (ignoring singletons). In sum, we explored six ways in which dependency parse trees can be constrained by fragments whose end-points could be defined by capitalization (or in other various ways, e.g., semantic annotations, punctuation or HTML tags in web pages).

[1]We converted labeled constituents into unlabeled dependencies using deterministic "head-percolation" rules (Collins, 1999), discarding any empty nodes, etc., as is standard practice.

	markup	punct.	capital	initial	uncased
thread	98.5	95.0	**99.5**	98.4	99.2
tear	97.9	94.7	**98.6**	98.4	98.5
sprawl	95.1	92.9	**98.2**	97.9	96.4
loose	87.5	74.0	**97.9**	96.9	96.4
strict′	32.7	35.6	38.7	40.3	**55.6**
strict	35.6	39.2	59.3	**66.9**	61.1

Table 2: Several sources of fragments' end-points and %-correctness of their derived constraints (for English).

For example, in the sentence about Cordis, the *strict* hypothesis would be wrong about five of the eight fragments: Jurors attaches in; Court takes the second in; Hershhenson and Pagones derive their titles, president; and (at least in our reference) Vadas attaches and, Ciporkin and who. Based on this, we would consider *strict* to be 37.5%-accurate. But *loose* — and the rest of the more relaxed constraints — would get perfect scores. (And *strict′* would retract the mistake about Jurors but also the correct guesses about Miami and Cordis, scoring only 20%.)

Table 2 (*capital*) shows scores averaged over the entire treebank. Columns *markup* (Spitkovsky et al., 2010b) and *punct* (Spitkovsky et al., 2011b) indicate that capitalization yields across-the-board more accurate constraints (for English) compared with fragments derived from punctuation or markup (i.e., anchor text, bold, italics and underline tags in HTML), for which such constraints were originally intended.

4 Pilot Experiments on Supervised Parsing

To further test the potential of capitalization-induced constraints, we applied them in the Viterbi-decoding phase of a simple (unlexicalized) supervised dependency parser — an instance of DBM-1 (Spitkovsky et al., 2012, §2.1), trained on WSJ sentences with up

	punct.:	thread	tear	sprawl	loose
	none: 71.8	74.3	74.4	74.5	73.3
capital:thread	72.3	74.6	74.7	74.9	73.6
tear	72.4	74.7	74.7	74.9	73.6
sprawl	72.4	74.7	74.7	74.9	73.4
loose	72.4	74.8	74.7	**74.9**	73.3
strict′	*71.4*	73.7	73.7	73.9	72.7
strict	*71.0*	73.1	73.1	73.2	72.1

Table 3: Supervised (directed) accuracy on Section 23 of WSJ using capitalization-induced constraints (vertical) jointly with punctuation (horizontal) in Viterbi-decoding.

CoNLL Year & Language	*Filtered Training* *Tokens*	/ *Sentences*	*none*	*thread*	*tear*	*sprawl*	*loose*	*strict′*	*strict*	*Fragments* *Multi*	*Single*
German 2006	139,333	12,296	36.3	36.3	36.3	**39.1**	*36.2*	36.3	*30.1*	3,287	30,435
Czech '6	187,505	20,378	51.3	51.3	51.3	51.3	**52.5**	**52.5**	51.4	1,831	6,722
English '7	74,023	5,087	29.2	*28.5*	*28.3*	*29.0*	**29.3**	*28.3*	*27.7*	1,135	2,218
Bulgarian '6	46,599	5,241	59.4	*59.3*	*59.3*	59.4	*59.1*	*59.3*	**59.5**	184	1,506
Danish '6	14,150	1,599	21.3	*17.7*	22.7	21.5	21.4	**31.4**	27.9	113	317
Greek '7	11,943	842	28.1	46.1	46.3	46.3	**46.4**	31.1	31.0	113	456
Dutch '6	72,043	7,107	**45.9**	*45.8*	45.9	*45.8*	*45.8*	*45.7*	*29.6*	89	4,335
Italian '7	9,142	921	41.7	52.6	**52.7**	52.6	44.2	52.6	45.8	41	296
Catalan '7	62,811	4,082	61.3	61.3	61.3	61.3	61.3	**61.3**	*36.5*	28	2,828
Turkish '6	17,610	2,835	32.9	32.9	*32.2*	33.0	33.0	33.6	**33.9**	27	590
Portuguese '6	24,494	2,042	68.9	*67.1*	69.1	**69.2**	68.9	68.9	*38.5*	9	953
Hungarian '7	10,343	1,258	43.2	43.2	*43.1*	43.2	43.2	**43.7**	*25.5*	7	277
Swedish '6	41,918	4,105	48.6	48.6	48.6	*48.5*	*48.5*	*48.5*	**48.8**	3	296
Slovenian '6	3,627	477	30.4	30.5	30.5	30.4	30.5	30.5	**30.8**	1	63
		Median:	42.5	46.0	**46.1**	46.0	45.0	44.7	*32.5*		
		Mean:	42.8	44.4	44.8	**45.0**	44.3	44.6	*36.9*		

Table 4: Parsing performance for grammar inducers trained with capitalization-based initial constraints, tested against 14 held-out sets from 2006/7 CoNLL shared tasks, and ordered by number of multi-token fragments in training data.

to 45 words (excluding Section 23). Table 3 shows evaluation results on held-out data (all sentences), using "add-one" smoothing. All constraints other than *strict* improve accuracy by about a half-a-point, from 71.8 to 72.4%, suggesting that capitalization is informative of certain regularities not captured by DBM grammars; moreover, it still continues to be useful when punctuation-based constraints are also enforced, boosting accuracy from 74.5 to 74.9%.

5 Multi-Lingual Grammar Induction

So far, we showed only that capitalization information can be helpful in parsing a very specific genre of English. Next, we tested its ability to generally aid dependency grammar induction, focusing on situations when other bracketing cues are unavailable.

We experimented with 14 languages from 2006/7 CoNLL shared tasks (Buchholz and Marsi, 2006; Nivre et al., 2007), excluding Arabic, Chinese and Japanese (which lack case), as well as Basque and Spanish (which are pre-processed in a way that loses relevant capitalization information). For all remaining languages we trained only on simple sentences — those lacking sentence-internal punctuation — from the relevant training sets (for blind evaluation).

Restricting our attention to a subset of the available training data serves a dual purpose. First, it allows us to estimate capitalization's impact where no other (known or obvious) cues could also be used. Otherwise, unconstrained baselines would not yield the strongest possible alternative, and hence not the most interesting comparison. Second, to the extent that presence of punctuation may correlate with sentence complexity (Frank, 2000), there are benefits to "starting small" (Elman, 1993): e.g., relegating full data to later stages helps training (Spitkovsky et al., 2010a; Cohn et al., 2011; Tu and Honavar, 2011).

Our base systems induced DBM-1, starting from uniformly-at-random chosen parse trees (Cohen and Smith, 2010) of each sentence, followed by inside-outside re-estimation (Baker, 1979) with "add-one" smoothing.[2] Capitalization-constrained systems differed from controls in exactly one way: each learner got a slight nudge towards more promising structures by choosing initial seed trees satisfying an appropriate constraint (but otherwise still uniformly).

Table 4 contains the stats for all 14 training sets, ordered by number of multi-token fragments. Final accuracies on respective (disjoint, full) evaluation sets are improved by all constraints other than *strict*, with the highest average performance resulting from *sprawl*: 45.0% directed dependency accuracy,[3] on average. This increase of about two points over the base system's 42.8% is driven primarily by improvements in two languages (Greek and Italian).

[2] We used "early-stopping lateen EM" (Spitkovsky et al., 2011a, §2.3) instead of thresholding or waiting for convergence.

[3] Starting from five parse trees for each sentence (using constraints *thread* through *strict′*) was no better, at 44.8% accuracy.

6 Capitalizing on Punctuation in Inference

Until now we avoided using punctuation in grammar induction, except to filter data. Yet our pilot experiments indicated that both kinds of information are helpful in the decoding stage of a supervised system.

We took trained models obtained using the *sprawl* nudge (from §5) and proceeded to again apply constraints in inference (as in §4). Capitalization alone increased parsing accuracy only slightly, from 45.0 to 45.1%, on average. Using punctuation constraints instead led to more improved performance: 46.5%. Combining both types of constraints again resulted in slightly higher accuracies: 46.7%. Table 5 breaks down our last average performance number by language and shows the combined approach to be competitive with state-of-the-art. We suspect that further improvements could be attained by also incorporating both constraints in training and with full data.

7 Discussion and A Few Post-Hoc Analyses

Our discussion, thus far, has been English-centric. Nevertheless, languages differ in how they use capitalization (and even the rules governing a given language tend to change over time — generally towards having fewer capitalized terms). For instance, adjectives derived from proper nouns are not capitalized in French, German, Polish, Spanish or Swedish, unlike in English (see Table 1: JJ). And while English forces capitalization of the first-person pronoun in the nominative case, I (see Table 1: PRP), in Danish it is the plural second-person pronoun (also I) that is capitalized; further, formal pronouns (and their case-forms) are capitalized in German (Sie and Ihre, Ihres...), Italian, Slovenian, Russian and Bulgarian.

In contrast to pronouns, single-word proper nouns — including personal names — are capitalized in nearly all European languages. Such shortest bracketings are not particularly useful for constraining sets of possible parse trees in grammar induction, however, compared to multi-word expressions; from this perspective, German appears less helpful than most cased languages, because of noun compounding, despite prescribing capitalization of all nouns. Another problem with longer word-strings in many languages is that, e.g., in French (as in English) lower-case prepositions may be mixed in with contiguous groups of proper nouns: even in surnames, the German particle von is not capitalized, although the Dutch van is, unless preceded by a given name or initial — hence Van Gogh, yet Vincent van Gogh.

CoNLL Year & Language		*this Work*	*State-of-the-Art Systems: POS- (i) Agnostic*		*(ii) Identified*	
Bulgarian	2006	**64.5**	44.3	$SCAJ_5$	**70.3**	S_{pt}
Catalan	'7	61.5	**63.8**	$SCAJ_5$	56.3	MZ_{NR}
Czech	'6	**53.5**	50.5	$SCAJ_5$	33.3*	MZ_{NR}
Danish	'6	20.6	**46.0**	RF	**56.5**	S_{ar}
Dutch	'6	**46.7**	32.5	$SCAJ_5$	**62.1**	MPH_{el}
English	'7	29.2	**50.3**	SAJ	45.7	MPH_{el}
German	'6	**42.6**	33.5	$SCAJ_5$	**55.8**	MPH_{nl}
Greek	'7	**49.3**	39.0	MZ	**63.9**	MPH_{en}
Hungarian	'7	**53.7**	48.0	MZ	48.1	MZ_{NR}
Italian	'7	50.5	**57.5**	MZ	**69.1**	MPH_{pt}
Portuguese	'6	**72.4**	43.2	MZ	**76.9**	S_{bg}
Slovenian	'6	**34.8**	33.6	$SCAJ_5$	34.6	MZ_{NR}
Swedish	'6	**50.5**	50.0	$SCAJ_6$	**66.8**	MPH_{pt}
Turkish	'6	34.4	**40.9**	SAJ	**61.3**	RF_{H1}
Median:		**48.5**	45.2		**58.9**	
Mean:		**46.7**	45.2		**57.2***	

Table 5: Unsupervised parsing with both capitalization- and punctuation-induced constraints in inference, tested against the 14 held-out sets from 2006/7 CoNLL shared tasks, and state-of-the-art results (all sentence lengths) for systems that: (i) are also POS-agnostic and monolingual, including SCAJ (Spitkovsky et al., 2011a, Tables 5–6) and SAJ (Spitkovsky et al., 2011b); and (ii) rely on gold POS-tag identities to (a) discourage noun roots (Mareček and Zabokrtský, 2011, MZ), (b) encourage verbs (Rasooli and Faili, 2012, RF), or (c) transfer delexicalized parsers (Søgaard, 2011a, S) from resource-rich languages with parallel translations (McDonald et al., 2011, MPH).

7.1 Constraint Accuracies Across Languages

Since even related languages (e.g., Flemish, Dutch, German and English) can have quite different conventions regarding capitalization, one would not expect the same simple strategy to be uniformly useful — or useful in the same way — across disparate languages. To get a better sense of how universal our constraints may be, we tabulated their accuracies for the full training sets of the CoNLL data, *after* all grammar induction experiments had been executed.

Table 6 shows that the less-strict capitalization-induced constraints all fall within narrow (yet high) bands of accuracies of just a few percentage points: 99–100% in the case of *thread*, 98–100% for *tear*, 95–99% for *sprawl* and 94–99% for *loose*. By contrast, the ranges for punctuation-induced constraints are all at least 10%. We do not see anything partic-

CoNLL Year & Language		*Total Training Tokens*	*/ Sentences*	*Capitalization-Induced Constraints*						*Punctuation-Induced Constraints*					
				thr-d	*tear*	*spr-l*	*loose*	*str.′*	*strict*	*thr-d*	*tear*	*spr-l*	*loose*	*str.′*	*strict*
Arabic	2006	52,752	1,460	—	—	—	—	—	—	89.6	89.5	*81.9*	61.2	29.7	33.4
	'7	102,375	2,912	—	—	—	—	—	—	90.9	90.6	83.1	*61.2*	29.5	35.2
Basque	'7	41,013	3,190	—	—	—	—	—	—	96.2	95.7	92.3	81.9	42.8	50.6
Bulgarian	'6	162,985	12,823	99.8	99.5	96.6	96.4	51.8	81.0	97.6	97.2	**96.1**	74.7	36.7	41.2
Catalan	'7	380,525	14,958	100	99.5	*95.0*	94.6	15.8	57.9	96.1	95.5	94.6	73.7	36.0	42.6
Chinese	'6	337,162	56,957	—	—	—	—	—	—	—	—	—	—	—	—
	'7	337,175	56,957	—	—	—	—	—	—	—	—	—	—	—	—
Czech	'6	1,063,413	72,703	99.7	98.3	96.2	95.4	42.4	68.0	*89.4*	*89.2*	87.7	68.9	37.2	41.7
	'7	368,624	25,364	99.7	98.3	96.1	95.4	42.6	67.6	89.5	89.3	87.8	69.3	37.4	41.9
Danish	'6	80,743	5,190	99.9	99.4	98.3	97.0	**59.0**	69.7	96.9	96.9	95.2	68.3	39.6	40.9
Dutch	'6	172,958	13,349	99.9	99.1	98.4	96.6	16.6	46.3	89.6	89.5	86.4	69.6	42.5	46.2
English	'7	395,139	18,577	*99.3*	98.7	98.0	96.0	17.5	*24.8*	91.5	91.4	90.6	76.5	39.6	42.3
German	'6	605,337	39,216	99.6	*98.0*	96.7	96.4	41.7	57.1	94.5	93.9	90.7	71.1	37.2	40.7
Greek	'7	58,766	2,705	99.9	99.3	98.5	96.6	13.6	50.1	91.3	91.0	89.8	75.7	43.7	47.0
Hungarian	'7	111,464	6,034	99.9	98.1	95.7	94.4	46.6	62.0	96.1	94.0	89.0	77.1	*28.9*	*32.6*
Italian	'7	60,653	3,110	99.9	99.6	**99.0**	98.8	*12.8*	68.2	97.1	96.8	96.0	77.8	44.7	47.9
Japanese	'6	133,927	17,044	—	—	—	—	—	—	**100**	**100**	95.4	**89.0**	**48.9**	**63.5**
Portuguese	'6	177,581	9,071	100	99.0	97.6	97.0	14.4	37.7	96.0	95.8	94.9	74.5	40.3	45.0
Slovenian	'6	23,779	1,534	**100**	99.8	98.9	**98.9**	52.0	**84.7**	93.3	93.3	92.6	72.7	42.7	45.8
Spanish	'6	78,068	3,306	—	—	—	—	—	—	96.5	96.0	95.2	75.4	33.4	40.9
Swedish	'6	163,301	11,042	99.8	99.6	99.0	97.0	24.7	58.4	90.8	90.4	87.4	66.8	31.1	33.9
Turkish	'6	48,373	4,997	**100**	99.8	96.2	*94.0*	22.8	42.8	99.8	99.7	95.1	76.9	37.7	42.0
	'7	54,761	5,635	**100**	**99.9**	96.1	94.2	21.6	42.9	99.8	99.7	94.6	76.7	38.2	42.8
			Max:	100	99.9	99.0	98.9	59.0	84.7	100	100	96.1	89.0	48.9	63.5
			Mean:	99.8	99.1	97.4	96.4	30.8	57.7	94.6	94.2	91.7	74.0	38.5	43.3
			Min:	99.3	98.0	95.0	94.0	12.8	24.8	89.4	89.2	81.9	61.2	28.9	32.6

Table 6: Accuracies for capitalization- and punctuation-induced constraints on all (full) 2006/7 CoNLL training sets.

ularly special about Greek or Italian in these summaries that could explain their substantial improvements (18 and 11%, respectively — see Table 4), though Italian does appear to mesh best with the *sprawl* constraint (not by much, closely followed by Swedish). And English — the language from which we drew our inspiration — barely improved with capitalization-induced constraints (see Table 4) and caused the lowest accuracies of *thread* and *strict*.

These outcomes are not entirely surprising: some best- and worst-performing results are due to noise, since learning via non-convex optimization can be chaotic: e.g., in the case of Greek, applying 113 constraints to initial parse trees could have a significant impact on the first grammar estimated in training — and consequently also on a learner's final, converged model instance. We expect the averages (i.e., means and medians) — computed over many data sets — to be more stable and meaningful than the outliers.

7.2 Immediate Impact from Capitalization

Next, we considered two settings that are less affected by training noise: grammar inducers immediately after an initial step of constrained Viterbi EM and supervised DBM parsers (trained on sentences with up to 45 words), for various languages in the CoNLL sets. Table 7 shows effects of capitalization to be exceedingly mild, both if applied alone and in tandem with punctuation. Exploring better ways of incorporating this informative resource — perhaps as soft features, rather than as hard constraints — and in combination with punctuation- and markup-induced bracketings could be a fruitful direction.

7.3 Odds and Ends

Our earlier analysis excluded sentence-initial words because their capitalization is, in a way, trivial. But for completeness, we also tested constraints derived from this source, separately (see Table 2: *initials*). As expected, the new constraints scored worse (despite many automatically-correct single-word fragments) except for *strict*, whose binding constraints over singletons drove *up* accuracy. It turns out, most first words in WSJ are leaves — possibly due to a dearth of imperatives (or just English's determiners).

We broadened our investigation of the "first leaf"

CoNLL Year & Language	*Evaluation Tokens*	*Evaluation Sents*	*Bracketings capital.*	*Bracketings punct.*	*Unsupervised Training init.*	*1-step*	*constrained*		*Supervised Parsing none*	*capital.*	*punct.*	*both*
Arabic 2006	5,215	146	—	101	18.4	20.6	—	—	59.8	—	—	—
'7	4,537	130	—	311	19.0	23.5	—	—	63.5	—	—	—
Basque '7	4,511	334	—	547	17.4	22.4	—	—	58.4	—	—	—
Bulgarian '6	5,032	398	44	552	19.4	28.9	28.4	-0.5	76.7	76.8	78.1	78.2
Catalan '7	4,478	167	24	398	18.0	25.1	25.4	+0.3	78.1	78.3	78.6	78.9
Chinese '6	5,012	867	—	—	23.5	27.2	—	—	83.7	—	—	—
'7	5,161	690	—	—	19.4	25.0	—	—	81.0	—	—	—
Czech '6	5,000	365	48	549	18.6	19.7	19.8	+0.1	64.9	64.8	67.0	66.9
'7	4,029	286	57	466	18.0	21.7	—	—	62.8	—	—	—
Danish '6	4,978	322	85	590	19.5	27.4	26.0	-1.3	71.9	72.0	74.2	74.3
Dutch '6	4,989	386	28	318	18.7	17.9	17.7	-0.1	*60.9*	*60.9*	*62.7*	*62.8*
English '7	4,386	214	151	423	17.6	24.0	21.9	*-2.1*	65.2	65.6	68.5	68.4
German '6	4,886	357	135	523	*16.4*	23.0	23.7	+0.7	70.7	70.7	71.5	71.4
Greek '7	4,307	197	47	372	17.1	*17.1*	*16.6*	-0.5	71.3	71.6	73.5	73.7
Hungarian '7	6,090	390	28	893	17.1	18.5	18.6	+0.1	67.3	67.2	69.8	69.6
Italian '7	4,360	249	71	505	18.6	**32.5**	**34.2**	**+1.7**	66.0	65.9	67.0	66.8
Japanese '6	5,005	709	—	0	26.5	36.8	—	—	85.1	—	—	—
Portuguese '6	5,009	288	29	559	19.3	24.2	24.0	-0.1	**80.5**	**80.5**	**81.6**	**81.6**
Slovenian '6	5,004	402	7	785	18.3	22.5	22.4	-0.1	67.5	67.4	70.9	70.9
Spanish '6	4,991	206	—	453	18.0	19.3	—	—	69.5	—	—	—
Swedish '6	4,873	389	14	417	20.2	31.4	31.4	+0.0	74.9	74.9	74.7	74.6
Turkish '6	6,288	623	18	683	**20.4**	26.4	26.7	+0.3	66.1	66.0	66.9	66.7
'7	3,983	300	4	305	20.3	24.8	—	—	67.3	—	—	—
				Max:	20.4	32.5	34.2	+1.7	80.5	80.5	81.6	81.6
(aggregated as in Tables 4 and 5)				*Mean:*	18.5	24.2	24.1	-0.1	70.1	70.2	71.8	71.8
				Min:	16.4	17.1	16.6	-2.1	60.9	60.9	62.7	62.8

Table 7: Unsupervised accuracies for uniform-at-random projective parse trees (init), also after a step of Viterbi EM, and supervised performance with induced constraints, on 2006/7 CoNLL evaluation sets (sentences under 145 tokens).

phenomenon and found that in 16 of the 19 CoNLL languages first words are more likely to be leaves than other words without dependents on the left;[4] last words, by contrast, are *more* likely to take dependents than expected. These propensities may be related to the functional tendency of languages to place old information before new (Ward and Birner, 2001) and could also help bias grammar induction.

Lastly, capitalization points to yet another class of words: those with identical upper- and lower-case forms. Their constraints too tend to be accurate (see Table 2: *uncased*), but the underlying text is not particularly interesting. In WSJ, caseless multi-token fragments are almost exclusively percentages (e.g., the two tokens of 10%), fractions (e.g., 1 1/4) or both. Such boundaries could be useful in dealing with financial data, as well as for breaking up text in languages without capitalization (e.g., Arabic, Chinese and Japanese). More generally, transitions between different fonts and scripts should be informative too.

8 Conclusion

Orthography provides valuable syntactic cues. We showed that bounding boxes signaled by capitalization changes can help guide grammar induction and boost unsupervised parsing performance. As with punctuation-delimited segments and tags from web markup, it is profitable to assume only that a single word derives the rest, in such text fragments, without further restricting relations to external words — possibly a useful feature for supervised parsing models.

Our results should be regarded with some caution, however, since improvements due to capitalization in grammar induction experiments came mainly from two languages, Greek and Italian. Further research is clearly needed to understand the ways that capitalization can continue to improve parsing.

[4]Arabic, Basque, Bulgarian, Catalan, Chinese, Danish, Dutch, English, German, Greek, Hungarian, Italian, Japanese, Portuguese, Spanish, Swedish *vs.* Czech, Slovenian, Turkish.

Acknowledgments

Funded, in part, by Defense Advanced Research Projects Agency (DARPA) Machine Reading Program under Air Force Research Laboratory (AFRL) prime contract FA8750-09-C-0181. Any opinions, findings, and conclusions or recommendations expressed in this material are those of the authors and do not necessarily reflect the views of DARPA, AFRL, or the US government. We also thank Ryan McDonald and the anonymous reviewers for helpful comments on draft versions of this paper.

References

J. K. Baker. 1979. Trainable grammars for speech recognition. In *Speech Communication Papers for the 97th Meeting of the Acoustical Society of America*.

E. J. Briscoe. 1994. Parsing (with) punctuation, etc. Technical report, Xerox European Research Laboratory.

S. Buchholz and E. Marsi. 2006. CoNLL-X shared task on multilingual dependency parsing. In *CoNLL*.

S. B. Cohen and N. A. Smith. 2009. Shared logistic normal distributions for soft parameter tying in unsupervised grammar induction. In *NAACL-HLT*.

S. B. Cohen and N. A. Smith. 2010. Viterbi training for PCFGs: Hardness results and competitiveness of uniform initialization. In *ACL*.

S. B. Cohen, D. Das, and N. A. Smith. 2011. Unsupervised structure prediction with non-parallel multilingual guidance. In *EMNLP*.

T. Cohn, P. Blunsom, and S. Goldwater. 2011. Inducing tree-substitution grammars. *Journal of Machine Learning Research*.

M. Collins. 1999. *Head-Driven Statistical Models for Natural Language Parsing*. Ph.D. thesis, University of Pennsylvania.

J. L. Elman. 1993. Learning and development in neural networks: The importance of starting small. *Cognition*, 48.

R. Frank. 2000. From regular to context-free to mildly context-sensitive tree rewriting systems: The path of child language acquisition. In A. Abeillé and O. Rambow, editors, *Tree Adjoining Grammars: Formalisms, Linguistic Analysis and Processing*. CSLI Publications.

K. Gimpel and N. A. Smith. 2011. Concavity and initialization for unsupervised dependency grammar induction. Technical report, CMU.

M. P. Marcus, B. Santorini, and M. A. Marcinkiewicz. 1993. Building a large annotated corpus of English: The Penn Treebank. *Computational Linguistics*, 19.

D. Mareček and Z. Zabokrtský. 2011. Gibbs sampling with treeness constraint in unsupervised dependency parsing. In *ROBUS*.

R. McDonald, S. Petrov, and K. Hall. 2011. Multi-source transfer of delexicalized dependency parsers. In *EMNLP*.

T. Naseem and R. Barzilay. 2011. Using semantic cues to learn syntax. In *AAAI*.

T. Naseem, H. Chen, R. Barzilay, and M. Johnson. 2010. Using universal linguistic knowledge to guide grammar induction. In *EMNLP*.

J. Nivre, J. Hall, S. Kübler, R. McDonald, J. Nilsson, S. Riedel, and D. Yuret. 2007. The CoNLL 2007 shared task on dependency parsing. In *EMNLP-CoNLL*.

F. Pereira and Y. Schabes. 1992. Inside-outside reestimation from partially bracketed corpora. In *ACL*.

E. Ponvert, J. Baldridge, and K. Erk. 2010. Simple unsupervised identification of low-level constituents. In *ICSC*.

E. Ponvert, J. Baldridge, and K. Erk. 2011. Simple unsupervised grammar induction from raw text with cascaded finite state models. In *ACL-HLT*.

M. S. Rasooli and H. Faili. 2012. Fast unsupervised dependency parsing with arc-standard transitions. In *ROBUS-UNSUP*.

Y. Seginer. 2007. Fast unsupervised incremental parsing. In *ACL*.

A. Søgaard. 2011a. Data point selection for cross-language adaptation of dependency parsers. In *ACL-HLT*.

A. Søgaard. 2011b. From ranked words to dependency trees: two-stage unsupervised non-projective dependency parsing. In *TextGraphs*.

V. I. Spitkovsky, H. Alshawi, and D. Jurafsky. 2010a. From Baby Steps to Leapfrog: How "Less is More" in unsupervised dependency parsing. In *NAACL-HLT*.

V. I. Spitkovsky, D. Jurafsky, and H. Alshawi. 2010b. Profiting from mark-up: Hyper-text annotations for guided parsing. In *ACL*.

V. I. Spitkovsky, H. Alshawi, and D. Jurafsky. 2011a. Lateen EM: Unsupervised training with multiple objectives, applied to dependency grammar induction. In *EMNLP*.

V. I. Spitkovsky, H. Alshawi, and D. Jurafsky. 2011b. Punctuation: Making a point in unsupervised dependency parsing. In *CoNLL*.

V. I. Spitkovsky, A. X. Chang, H. Alshawi, and D. Jurafsky. 2011c. Unsupervised dependency parsing without gold part-of-speech tags. In *EMNLP*.

V. I. Spitkovsky, H. Alshawi, and D. Jurafsky. 2012. Three dependency-and-boundary models for grammar induction. In *submission to EMNLP*.

K. Tu and V. Honavar. 2011. On the utility of curricula in unsupervised learning of probabilistic grammars. In *IJCAI*.

G. Ward and B. J. Birner. 2001. Discourse and information structure. In D. Schiffrin, D. Tannen, and H. Hamilton, editors, *Handbook of Discourse Analysis*. Oxford: Basil Blackwell.

Toward Tree Substitution Grammars with Latent Annotations

Francis Ferraro and **Benjamin Van Durme** and **Matt Post**
Center for Language and Speech Processing, and
Human Language Technology Center of Excellence
Johns Hopkins University

Abstract

We provide a model that extends the split-merge framework of Petrov et al. (2006) to jointly learn latent annotations and Tree Substitution Grammars (TSGs). We then conduct a variety of experiments with this model, first inducing grammars on a portion of the Penn Treebank and the Korean Treebank 2.0, and next experimenting with grammar refinement from a single nonterminal and from the Universal Part of Speech tagset. We present qualitative analysis showing promising signs across all experiments that our combined approach successfully provides for greater flexibility in grammar induction within the structured guidance provided by the treebank, leveraging the complementary natures of these two approaches.

1 Introduction

Context-free grammars (CFGs) are a useful tool for describing the structure of language, modeling a variety of linguistic phenomena while still permitting efficient inference. However, it is widely acknowledged that CFGs employed in practice make unrealistic independence and structural assumptions, resulting in grammars that are overly permissive. One successful approach has been to refine the nonterminals of grammars, first manually (Johnson, 1998; Klein and Manning, 2003) and later automatically (Matsuzaki et al., 2005; Dreyer and Eisner, 2006; Petrov et al., 2006). In addition to improving parsing accuracy, the automatically learned *latent annotations* of these latter approaches yield results that accord well with human intuitions, especially at the lexical or preterminal level (for example, separating demonstrative adjectives from definite articles under the DT tag). It is more difficult, though, to extend this analysis to higher-level nonterminals, where the long-distance interactions among latent annotations of internal nodes are subtle and difficult to trace.

In another line of work, many researchers have examined the use of formalisms with an *extended domain of locality* (Joshi and Schabes, 1997), where the basic grammatical units are arbitrary tree fragments instead of traditional depth-one context-free grammar productions. In particular, Tree Substitution Grammars (TSGs) retain the context-free properties of CFGs (and thus the cubic-time inference) while at the same time allowing for the modeling of long distance dependencies. Fragments from such grammars are intuitive, capturing exactly the sorts of phrasal-level properties (such as predicate-argument structure) that are not present in Treebank CFGs and which are difficult to model with latent annotations.

This paper is motivated by the complementarity of these approaches. We present our progress in learning latent-variable TSGs in a joint approach that extends the split-merge framework of Petrov et al. (2006). We present our current results on the Penn and Korean treebanks (Marcus et al., 1993; Han et al., 2001), demonstrating that we are able to learn fragments that draw on the strengths of both approaches. Table 1 situates this work among other contributions.

In addition to experimenting directly with the Penn and Korean Treebanks, we also conducted two experiments in this framework with the Universal

	CFG	TSG
none	Charniak '97	Cohn et al. '09
manual	Klein & Manning '03	Bansal & Klein '10
automatic	Matsuzaki et al. '05 Petrov et al. '06 Dreyer & Eisner '06	*This paper*

Table 1: Representative prior work in learning refinements for context-free and tree substitution grammars, with zero, manual, or automatically induced latent annotations.

(a) A TSG fragment.

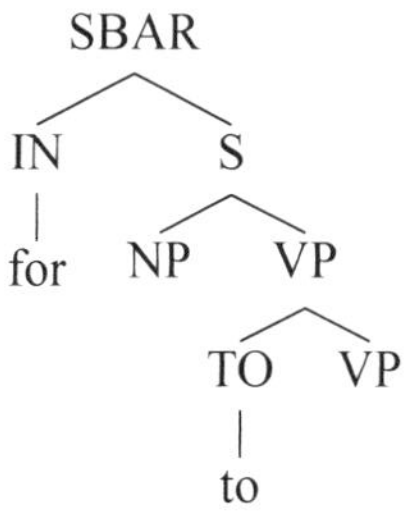

(b) Equivalent CFG rules.

SBAR → IN S
IN → for
S → NP VP
VP → TO VP
TO → to

Figure 1: Simple example of a TSG fragment and an equivalent representation with a CFG.

POS tagset (Petrov et al., 2011). First, we investigate whether the tagset can be automatically derived after mapping all nonterminals to a single, coarse nonterminal. Second, we begin with the mapping defined by the tagset, and investigate how closely the learned annotations resemble the original treebank. Together with our TSG efforts, this work is aimed at increased flexibility in the grammar induction process, while retaining the use of Treebanks for structural guidance.

2 Background

2.1 Latent variable grammars

Latent annotation learning is motivated by the observed coarseness of the nonterminals in treebank grammars, which often group together nodes with different grammatical roles and distributions (such as the role of NPs in subject and object position). Johnson (1998) presented a simple parent-annotation scheme that resulted in significant parsing improvement. Klein and Manning (2003) built on these observations, introducing a series of manual refinements that captured multiple linguistic phenomena, leading to accurate and fast unlexicalized parsing. Later, automated methods for nonterminal refinement were introduced, first splitting all categories equally (Matsuzaki et al., 2005), and later refining nonterminals to different degrees (Petrov et al., 2006) in a split-merge EM framework. This latter approach was able to recover many of the splits manually determined by Klein and Manning (2003), while also discovering interesting, novel clusterings, especially at the lexical level. However, phrasal-level analysis of latent-variable grammars is more difficult. (2006) observed that these grammars could learn long-distance dependencies through sequences of substates that place all or most of their weight on particular productions, but such patterns must be discovered manually via extensive analysis.

2.2 Tree substitution grammars

Tree substitution grammars (TSGs) allow for complementary analysis. These grammars employ an *extended domain of locality* over traditional context-free grammars by generalizing the atomic units of the grammar from depth-one productions to fragments of arbitrary size. An example TSG fragment along with equivalent CFG rules are depicted in Figure 1. The two formalisms are weakly equivalent, and computing the most probable derivation of a sentence with a TSG can be done in cubic time.

Unfortunately, learning TSGs is not straightforward, in large part because TSG-specific resources (e.g., large scale TSG-annotated treebanks) do not exist. One class of existing approaches, known as Data-Oriented Parsing, simply uses all the fragments (Bod, 1993, DOP). This does not scale well to large treebanks, forcing the use of implicit representations (Goodman, 1996) or heuristic subsets (Bod, 2001). It has also been generally observed that the use of all fragments results in poor, overfit grammars, though this can be addressed with held-out data (Zollmann and Sima'an, 2005) or statistical estimators to rule out fragments that are unlikely to generalize (Zuidema, 2007). More recently, a number of groups have found success employing Bayesian non-parametric priors (Post and Gildea, 2009; Cohn et al., 2010), which put a downward pressure on fragment size except where the data warrant the inclusion of larger fragments. Unfortunately, proper inference under these models is intractable, and though Monte Carlo techniques can provide an approximation, the samplers can be complex, difficult to code, and slow to converge.

This history suggests two approaches to state-split TSGs: (1) a Bayesian non-parametric sampling approach (incorporate state-splitting into existing TSG work), or (2) EM (incorporate TSG induction into existing state-splitting work). We choose the latter path, and in the next section will describe our approach which combines the simplicity of DOP, the intuitions motivating the Bayesian approach, and the efficiency of EM-based state-splitting.

In related work, Bansal and Klein (2010) combine (1996)'s implicit DOP representation with a number of the manual refinements described in Klein and Manning (2003). They achieve some of the best reported parsing scores for TSG work and demonstrate the complementarity of the tasks, but their approach is not able to learn arbitrary distributions over fragments, and the state splits are determined in a fixed pre-processing step. Our approach addresses both of these limitations.

3 State-Split TSG Induction

In this section we describe how we combine the ideas of dop, Bayesian-induced TSGs and Petrov et al. (2006)'s state-splitting framework.[1] We are able to do so by adding a **coupling** step to each iteration. That is, each iteration is of the form:

(1) **split** all symbols in two,

(2) **merge** 50% of the splits, and

(3) **couple** existing fragments.

Because every step results in a new grammar, production probabilities are fit to observed data by running at most 50 rounds of EM after every step listed above.[2] We focus on our contribution — the coupling step — and direct those interested in details regarding splitting/merging to (Petrov et al., 2006).

Let $\mathcal{T}$ be a treebank and let $\mathcal{F}$ be the set of all possible fragments in $\mathcal{T}$. Define a tree $T \in \mathcal{T}$ as a composition of fragments $\{F_i\}_{i=1}^{n} \subseteq \mathcal{F}$, with $T = F_1 \circ \cdots \circ F_n$. We use X to refer to an arbitrary fragment, with r_X being the root of X. Two fragments X and Y may compose (couple), which we denote by $X \circ Y$.[3] We assume that X and Y may couple only if $X \circ Y$ is an observed subtree.

3.1 Coupling Procedure

While Petrov et al. (2006) posit all refinements simulatenously and then retract half, applying this strategy to the coupling step would result in a combinatorial explosion. We control this combinatorial increase in three ways. First, we assume binary trees. Second, we introduce a constraint set $\mathcal{C} \subseteq \mathcal{F}$ that dictates what fragments are permitted to compose into larger fragments. Third, we adopt the iterative approach of split-merge and incrementally make our grammar more complex by forbidding a fragment from participating in "chained couplings:" $X \circ Y \circ Z$ is not allowed unless either $X \circ Y$ or $Y \circ Z$ is a valid fragment in the previous grammar (and the chained coupling is allowed by $\mathcal{C}$). Note that setting $\mathcal{C} = \emptyset$ results in standard split/merge, while $\mathcal{C} = \mathcal{F}$ results in a latently-refined dop-1 model.

We say that $\langle XY \rangle$ represents a valid coupling of X and Y only if $X \circ Y$ is allowed by $\mathcal{C}$, whereas $\overline{\langle XY \rangle}$ represents an invalid coupling if $X \circ Y$ is not allowed by $\mathcal{C}$. Valid couplings result in new fragments. (We describe how to obtain $\mathcal{C}$ in §3.3.)

Given a constraint set $\mathcal{C}$ and a current grammar $\mathcal{G}$, we construct a new grammar $\mathcal{G}'$. For every fragment $F \in \mathcal{G}$, hypothesize a fragment $F' = F \circ C$, provided $F \circ C$ is allowed by$\mathcal{C}$. In order to add F and F' to $\mathcal{G}'$, we assign an initial probability to both fragments (§3.2), and then use EM to determine appropriate weights. We do not explicitly remove smaller fragments from the grammar, though it is possible for weights to vanish throughout iterations of EM.

Note that a probabilistic TSG fragment may be uniquely represented as its constituent CFG rules: make the root of every internal depth-one subtree unique (have unit probability) and place the entirety of the TSG weight on the root depth-one rule. This representation has multiple benefits: it not only allows TSG induction within the split/merge framework, but it also provides a straight-forward way to use the inside-outside algorithm.

[1] Code available at `cs.jhu.edu/~ferraro`.

[2] We additionally apply Petrov et al. (2006)'s smoothing step between **split** and **merge**.

[3] Technically, the composition operator ($\circ$) is ambiguous if there is more than one occurrence of r_Y in the frontier of X. Although notation augmentations could resolve this, we rely on context for disambiguation.

3.2 Fragment Probability Estimation

First, we define a count function c over fragments by

$$c(X) = \sum_{T \in \mathcal{P}(\mathcal{T})} \sum_{\tau \in T} \delta_{X,\tau}, \quad (1)$$

where $\mathcal{P}(\mathcal{T})$ is a parsed version of $\mathcal{T}$, τ is a subtree of T and $\delta_{X,\tau}$ is 1 iff X matches τ.[4] We may then count fragment co-occurrence by

$$\sum_{Y} c(X \circ Y) = \sum_{Y:\overline{\langle XY \rangle}} c(X \circ Y) + \sum_{Y:\langle XY \rangle} c(X \circ Y).$$

Prior to running inside-outside, we must re-allocate the probability mass from the previous fragments to the hypothesized ones. As this is just a temporary initialization, can we allocate mass as done when splitting, where each rule's mass is uniformly distributed, modulo tie-breaking randomness, among its refinement offspring? Split/merge only hypothesizes that a node should have a particular refinement, but by learning subtrees our coupling method hypothesizes that deeper structure may better explain data. This leads to the realization that a symbol may both subsume, and be subsumed by, another symbol in the same coupling step; it is not clear how to apply the above redistribution technique to our situation.

However, even if uniform-redistribution could easily be applied, we would like to be able to indicate how much we "trust" newly hypothesized fragments. We achieve this via a parameter $\gamma \in [0, 1]$: as $\gamma \to 1$, we wish to move more of $\mathbf{P}[X \mid r_X]$ to $\mathbf{P}[\langle XY \rangle \mid r_X]$. Note that we need to know which fragments L couple below with X ($\langle XL \rangle$), and which fragments U couple above ($\langle UX \rangle$).

For reallocation, we remove a fraction of the number of occurrences of top-couplings of X:

$$\hat{c}(X) = 1 - \gamma \frac{\sum_{Y:\langle XY \rangle} c(X \circ Y)}{\sum_{Y} c(X \circ Y)}, \quad (2)$$

and some proportion of the number of occurrences of bottom-couplings of X:

$$\text{sub}(X) = \frac{\sum_{U:\langle UX \rangle} c(U \circ X)}{\sum_{\substack{U,L:\langle UL \rangle \\ r_X = r_L}} c(U \circ L)}. \quad (3)$$

[4] We use a parsed version because there are no labeled internal nodes in the original treebank.

To prevent division-by-zero (e.g., for pre-terminals), (2) returns 1 and (3) returns 0 as necessary.

Given any fragment X in an original grammar, let ρ be its conditional probability: $\rho = \mathbf{P}[X \mid r_X]$. For a new grammar, define the new conditional probability for X to be

$$\mathbf{P}[X \mid r_X] \quad \propto \quad \rho \cdot |\hat{c}(X) - \text{sub}(X)|, \quad (4)$$

and

$$\mathbf{P}[\langle XY \rangle \mid r_X] \quad \propto \quad \gamma \rho \frac{c(X \circ Y)}{\sum_{Y} c(X \circ Y)} \quad (5)$$

for applicable Y.

Taken together, equations (4) and (5) simply say that X must yield some percentage of its current mass to its hypothesized relatives $\langle XY \rangle$, the amount of which is proportionately determined by $\hat{c}$. But we may also hypothesize $\langle ZX \rangle$, which has the effect of removing (partial) occurrences of X.[5]

Though we would prefer posterior counts of fragments, it is not obvious how to efficiently obtain posterior "bigram" counts of arbitrarily large latent TSG fragments (i.e., $c(X \circ Y)$). We therefore obtain, in linear time, Viterbi counts using the previous best grammar. Although this could lead to count sparsity, in practice our previous grammar provides sufficient counts across fragments.

3.3 Coupling from Common Subtrees

We now turn to the question of how to acquire the constraint set $\mathcal{C}$. Drawing on the discussion in §2.2, the constraint set should, with little effort, enforce sparsity. Similarly to our experiments in classification with TSGs (Ferraro et al., 2012), we extract a list of the K most common subtrees of size at most R, which we refer to as $\mathcal{F}_{\langle R,K \rangle}$. Note that if $F \in \mathcal{F}_{\langle R,K \rangle}$, then all subtrees F' of F must also be in $\mathcal{F}_{\langle R,K \rangle}$.[6] Thus, we may incrementally build $\mathcal{F}_{\langle R,K \rangle}$ in the following manner: given r, for $1 \leq r \leq R$, maintain a ranking S, by frequency, of all fragments of size r; the key point is that S may be built from $\mathcal{F}_{\langle r-1,K \rangle}$. Once all fragments of size r have been considered, retain only the top K fragments of the ranked set $\mathcal{F}_{\langle r,K \rangle} = \mathcal{F}_{\langle r-1,K \rangle} \cup S$.

[5] If $\hat{c}(X) = \text{sub}(X)$, then define Eqn. (4) to be ρ.

[6] Analogously, if an n-gram appears K times, then all constituent m-grams, $m < n$, must also appear at least K times.

This incremental approach is appealing for two reasons: (1) practically, it helps temper the growth of intermediate rankings $\mathcal{F}_{\langle r,K\rangle}$; and (2) it provides two tunable parameters R and K, which relate to the base measure and concentration parameter of previous work (Post and Gildea, 2009; Cohn et al., 2010). We enforce sparsity by thresholding at every iteration.

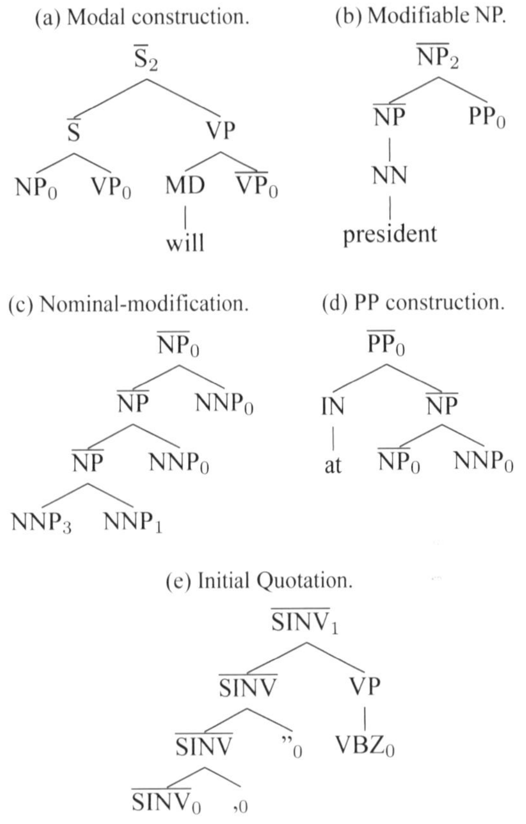

Figure 2: Example fragments learned on wsj2-3.

4 Datasets

We perform a qualitative analysis of fragments learned on datasets for two languages: the Korean Treebank v2.0 (Han and Ryu, 2005) and a comparably-sized portion of the WSJ portion of the Penn Treebank (Marcus et al., 1993). The Korean Treebank (KTB) has predefined splits; to be comparable for our analysis, from the PTB we used §2-3 for training and §22 for validation (we refer to this as wsj2-3). As described in Chung et al. (2010), although Korean presents its own challenges to grammar induction, the KTB yields additional difficulties by including a high occurrence of very flat rules (in 5K sentences, there are 13 NP rules with at least four righthand side NPs) and a coarser nonterminal set than that of the Penn Treebank. On both sets, we run for two iterations.

Recall that our algorithm is designed to induce a state-split TSG on a binarized tree; as neither dataset is binarized in native form we apply a left-branching binarization across all trees in both collections as a preprocessing step. Petrov et al. (2006) found different binarization methods to be inconsequential, and we have yet to observe significant impact of this binarization decision (this will be considered in more detail in future work).

Recently Petrov et al. (2011) provided a set of coarse, "universal" (as measured across 22 languages), part-of-speech tags. We explore here the interaction of this tagset in our model on wsj2-3: call this modified version uwsj2-3, on which we run three iterations. By further coarsening the PTB tags, we can ask questions such as: what is the refinement pattern? Can we identify linguistic phenomena in a different manner than we might without the universal tag set? Then, as an extreme, we replace all POS tags with the same symbol "X," to investigate what predicate/argument relationships can be derived: we call this set xwsj2-3 and run four times on it.[7]

5 Fragment Analysis

In this section we analyze hand-selected preliminary fragments and lexical clusterings our system learns.

WSJ, §2-3 As Figure 2 illustrates, after two iterations we learn various types of descriptive lexicalized and unlexicalized fragments. For example, Figure 2a concisely creates a four-step modal construction (*will*), while 2b demonstrates how a potentially useful nominal can be formed. Further, learned fragments may generate phrases with multiple nominal modifiers (2c), and lexicalized PPs (2d).

Note that phrases such as $\overline{\text{NP}}_0$ and $\overline{\text{VP}}_0$ are often lexicalized themselves (with determiners, common verbs and other constructions), though omitted due to space constraints; these lexicalized phrases could be very useful for 2a (given the incremental

[7]While the universal tag set has a Korean mapping, the symbols do not coincide with the KTB symbols.

(a) Common noun refinements.

	NNC		
0	경우 *case*	이날 *this day*	현재 *at the moment*
1	국제 *international*	경제 *economy*	세계 *world*
2	관련 *related*	발표 *announcement*	보도 *report*

(b) Verbal inflection. (c) Adjectival inflection.

Figure 3: Clusters and fragments for the KTB.

coupling employed, 2a could not have been further expanded in two iterations). Figure 2c demonstrates how TSGs and latent annotations are naturally complementary: the former provides structure while the latter describes lexical distributions of nominals.

Figure 2e illustrates a final example of syntactic structure, as we begin to learn how to properly analyze a complex quotation. A full analysis requires only five TSG rules while an equivalent CFG-only construction requires eight.

KTB2 To illustrate emergent semantic and syntactic patterns, we focus on common noun (NNC) refinements. As seen in Table 3a, top words from NNC_0 represent time expressions and planning-related. As a comparison, two other refinements, NNC_1 and NNC_2, are not temporally representative. This distinction is important as NNC_0 easily yields adverbial phrases, while the resultant adverbial yield for either NNC_1 or NNC_2 is much smaller.

Comparing NNC_1 and NNC_2, we see that the highest-ranked members of the latter, which include *report* and *announcement*, can be verbalized by appending an appropriate suffix. Nouns under NNC_1, such as *economy* and *world*, generally are subject to adjectival, rather than verbal, inflection. Figures 3b and 3c capture these verbal and adjectival inflections, respectively, as lexicalized TSG fragments.

WSJ, §2-3, Universal Tag Set In the preliminary work done here, we find that after a small number of iterations we can identify various cluster classifications for different POS tags. Figures 4a, 4b and 4c provide examples for NOUN, VERB and PRON, respectively. For NOUNs we found that refinements correspond to agentive entities (refinements 0, 1, e.g., corporations or governments), market or stock concepts (2), and numerically-modifiable nouns (7). Some refinements overlapped, or contained common nouns usable in many different contexts (3).

Similarly for VERBs (4b), we find suggested distinctions among action (1) and belief/cognition (2) verbs.[8] Further, some verb clusters are formed of eventive verbs, both general (3) and domain-specific (0). Another cluster is primarily of copula/auxiliary verbs (7). The remaining omitted categories appear to overlap, and only once we examine the contexts in which they occur do we see they are particularly useful for parsing FRAGs.

Though NOUN and VERB clusters can be discerned, there tends to be overlap among refinements that makes the analysis more difficult. On the other hand, refinements for PRON (4c) tend to be fairly clean and it is generally simple to describe each: possessives (1), personified *wh*-words (2) and general *wh*-words (3). Moreover, both subject (5) and object (6) are separately described.

Promisingly, we learn interactions among various refinements in the form of TSG rules, as illustrated by Figures 4d-4g. While all four examples involve VERBs it is enlightening to analyze a VERB's refinement and arguments. For example, the refinements in 4d may lend a simple analysis of financial actions, while 4e may describe different NP interactions (note the different refinement symbols). Different VERB refinements may also coordinate, as in 4f, where participle or gerund may help modify a main verb. Finally, note how in 4g, an object pronoun correctly occurs in object position. These examples suggest that even on coarsened POS tags, our method is able to learn preliminary joint syntactic and lexical relationships.

WSJ, §2-3, Preterminals as X In this experiment, we investigate whether the manual annotations of Petrov et al. (2011) can be re-derived through first reducing one's non-terminal tagset to the symbol X and splitting until finding first the coarse grain

[8] The next highest-ranked verbs for refinement 1 include *received*, *doing* and *announced*.

(a) Noun refinements.

	NOUN		
0	Corp	Big	Co.
1	Mr.	U.S.	New
2	Bush	prices	trading
3	Japan	September	Nissan
7	year	%	months

(b) Verb refinements.

	VERB				
0	says	said	sell	buy	rose
1	have	had	has	been	made
2	said	says	say	added	believe
3	sold	based	go	trading	filed
7	is	are	be	was	will

(c) Pronoun refinements.

	PRON		
1	its	his	your
2	who	whom	—
3	what	whose	What
5	it	he	they
6	it	them	him

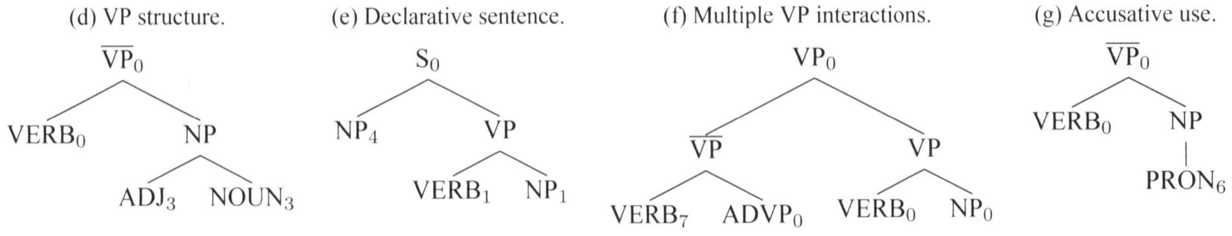

Figure 4: Highest weighted representatives for lexical categories (4a-4c) and learned fragments (4d-4g), for uwsj2-3.

	X			Universal Tag
0	two	market	brain	NOUN
1	's	said	says	VERB
2	%	company	year	NOUN
3	it	he	they	PRON
5	also	now	even	ADV
6	the	a	The	DET
7	10	1	all	NUM
9	.	–	...	.
10	and	or	but	CONJ
12	which	that	who	PRON
13	is	was	are	VERB
14	as	of	in	ADP
15	up	But	billion	ADP

Table 2: Top-three representatives for various refinements of X, with reasonable analogues to Petrov et al. (2011)'s tags. Universal tag recovery is promising.

tags of the universal set, followed by finer-grain tags from the original treebank. Due to the loss of lexical information, we run our system for four iterations rather than three.

As observed in Table 2, there is strong overlap observed between the induced refinements and the original universal tags. Though there are 16 refinements of X, due to lack of cluster coherence not all are listed. Those tags and unlisted refinements seem to be interwoven in a non-trivial way. We also see complex refinements of both open- and closed-class words occurring: refinements 0 and 2 correspond with the open-class NOUN, while refinements 3 and 12, and 14 and 15 both correspond with the closed classes PRON and ADP, respectively. Note that 1 and 13 are beginning to split verbs by auxiliaries.

6 Conclusion

We have shown that TSGs may be encoded and induced within a framework of syntactic latent annotations. Results were provided for induction using the English Penn, and Korean Treebanks, with further experiments based on the Universal Part of Speech tagset. Examples shown suggest the promise of our approach, with future work aimed at exploring larger datasets using more extensive computational resources.

Acknowledgements Thank you to the reviewers for helpful feedback, and to Johns Hopkins HLTCOE for providing support. We would also like to thank Byung Gyu Ahn for graciously helping us analyze the Korean results. Any opinions expressed in this work are those of the authors.

References

Mohit Bansal and Dan Klein. 2010. Simple, accurate parsing with an all-fragments grammar. In *Proceedings of ACL*, pages 1098–1107. Association for Computational Linguistics.

Rens Bod. 1993. Using an annotated corpus as a stochastic grammar. In *Proceedings of EACL*, pages 37–44. Association for Computational Linguistics.

Rens Bod. 2001. What is the minimal set of fragments that achieves maximal parse accuracy? In *Proceedings of ACL*, pages 66–73. Association for Computational Linguistics.

Eugene Charniak. 1997. Statistical parsing with a context-free grammar and word statistics. In *Proceedings of AAAI*, pages 598–603.

Tagyoung Chung, Matt Post, and Daniel Gildea. 2010. Factors affecting the accuracy of korean parsing. In *Proceedings of the NAACL HLT Workshop on Statistical Parsing of Morphologically-Rich Languages (SPMRL)*, pages 49–57, Los Angeles, California, USA, June.

Trevor Cohn, Sharon Goldwater, and Phil Blunsom. 2009. Inducing compact but accurate tree-substitution grammars. In *Proceedings of Human Language Technologies: The 2009 Annual Conference of the North American Chapter of the Association for Computational Linguistics*, pages 548–556, Stroudsburg, PA, USA. Association for Computational Linguistics.

Trevor Cohn, Phil Blunsom, and Sharon Goldwater. 2010. Inducing tree-substitution grammars. *Journal of Machine Learning Research*, 11:3053–3096, December.

Markus Dreyer and Jason Eisner. 2006. Better informed training of latent syntactic features. In *Proceedings of EMNLP*, pages 317–326, Sydney, Australia, July. Association for Computational Linguistics.

Francis Ferraro, Matt Post, and Benjamin Van Durme. 2012. Judging Grammaticality with Count-Induced Tree Substitution Grammars. In *Proceedings of the Seventh Workshop in Innovated Use of NLP for Building Educational Applications*.

Joshua Goodman. 1996. Efficient algorithms for parsing the dop model. In *Proceedings of EMNLP*, pages 143–152.

Na-Rae Han and Shijong Ryu. 2005. Guidelines for Penn Korean Treebank. Technical report, University of Pennsylvania.

Chung-hye Han, Na-Rae Han, and Eon-Suk Ko. 2001. Bracketing guidelines for penn korean treebank. Technical report, IRCS, University of Pennsylvania.

Mark Johnson. 1998. PCFG models of linguistic tree representations. *Computational Linguistics*, 24(4):613–632.

Aravind K. Joshi and Yves Schabes. 1997. Tree-adjoining grammars. In G. Rozenberg and A. Salomaa, editors, *Handbook of Formal Languages: Beyond Words*, volume 3, pages 71–122. Springer.

Dan Klein and Christopher D. Manning. 2003. Accurate unlexicalized parsing. In *Proceedings of the 41st Annual Meeting on Association for Computational Linguistics - Volume 1*, pages 423–430, Stroudsburg, PA, USA. Association for Computational Linguistics.

Mitchell P. Marcus, Mary Ann Marcinkiewicz, and Beatrice Santorini. 1993. Building a large annotated corpus of english: The Penn Treebank. *Computational linguistics*, 19(2):313–330.

Takuya Matsuzaki, Yusuke Miyao, and Jun'ichi Tsujii. 2005. Probabilistic cfg with latent annotations. In *Proceedings of ACL*, pages 75–82, Stroudsburg, PA, USA. Association for Computational Linguistics.

Slav Petrov, Leon Barrett, Romain Thibaux, and Dan Klein. 2006. Learning accurate, compact, and interpretable tree annotation. In *Proceedings of ACL-ICCL*, pages 433–440, Stroudsburg, PA, USA. Association for Computational Linguistics.

Slav Petrov, Dipanjan Das, and Ryan McDonald. 2011. A universal part-of-speech tagset. In *ArXiv*, April.

Matt Post and Daniel Gildea. 2009. Bayesian learning of a tree substitution grammar. In *Proceedings of ACL-IJCNLP (short papers)*, pages 45–48, Stroudsburg, PA, USA. Association for Computational Linguistics.

Andreas Zollmann and Khalil Sima'an. 2005. A consistent and efficient estimator for data-oriented parsing. *Journal of Automata Languages and Combinatorics*, 10(2/3):367.

Willem Zuidema. 2007. Parsimonious data-oriented parsing. In *Proceedings of EMNLP-CoNLL*, pages 551–560.

Exploiting Partial Annotations with EM Training

Dirk Hovy, Eduard Hovy
Information Sciences Institute
University of Southern California
4676 Admiralty Way, Marina del Rey, CA 90292

{dirkh, hovy}@isi.edu

Abstract

For many NLP tasks, EM-trained HMMs are the common models. However, in order to escape local maxima and find the best model, we need to start with a good initial model. Researchers suggested repeated random restarts or constraints that guide the model evolution. Neither approach is ideal. Restarts are time-intensive, and most constraint-based approaches require serious re-engineering or external solvers. In this paper we measure the effectiveness of very limited initial constraints: specifically, annotations of a small number of words in the training data. We vary the amount and distribution of initial partial annotations, and compare the results to unsupervised and supervised approaches. We find that partial annotations improve accuracy and can reduce the need for random restarts, which speeds up training time considerably.

1 Introduction

While supervised learning methods achieve good performance in many NLP tasks, they are incapable of dealing with missing annotations. For most new problems, however, missing data is the norm, which makes it impossible to train supervised models. Unsupervised learning techniques can make use of unannotated data and are thus well-suited for these problems.

For sequential labeling tasks (POS-tagging, NE-recognition), EM-trained HMMs are the most common unsupervised model. However, running vanilla forward-backward-EM leads to mediocre results, due to various properties of the training method (Johnson, 2007). Running repeated restarts with random initialization can help escape local maxima, but in order to find the global optimum, we need to run a great number (100 or more) of them (Ravi and Knight, 2009; Hovy et al., 2011). However, there is another solution. Various papers have shown that the inclusion of some knowledge greatly enhances performance of unsupervised systems. They introduce constraints on the initial model and the parameters. This directs the learning algorithm towards a better parameter configuration. Types of constraints include ILP-based methods (Chang et al., 2007; Chang et al., 2008; Ravi and Knight, 2009), and posterior regularization (Graça et al., 2007; Ganchev et al., 2010). While those approaches are powerful and yield good results, they require us to reformulate the constraints in a certain language, and either use an external solver, or re-design parts of the maximization step. This is time-consuming and requires a certain expertise.

One of the most natural ways of providing constraints is to annotate a small amount of data. This can either be done manually, or via simple heuristics, for example, if some words' parts of speech are unambiguous. This can significantly speed up learning and improve accuracy of the learned models. These *partial annotations* are a common technique for semi-supervised learning. It requires no changes to the general framework, or the use of external solvers.

While this well-known, it is unclear exactly how much annotation, and annotation of what, is most effective to improve accuracy. To our knowledge, no paper has investigated this aspect empirically. We

Inputs:	I went to the show
	walk on water
Partial Annotations:	I went to the:*DET* show:*NN*
	walk *on:sense*$_5$ water

Figure 1: In partial annotation, words are replaced by their label

explore the use of more unlabeled data vs. partial annotation of a small percentage. For the second case, we investigate how much annotation we need to achieve a particular accuracy, and what the best distribution of labels is. We test our approach on a POS-tagging and word sense disambiguation task for prepositions.

We find that using partial annotations improves accuracy and reduces the effect of random restarts. This indicates that the same accuracy can be reached with fewer restarts, which speeds up training time considerably.

Our contributions are:

- we show how to include partial annotations in EM training via parameter tying
- we show how the amounts and distribution of partial annotations influence accuracy
- we evaluate our method on an existing data set, comparing to both supervised and unsupervised methods on two tasks

2 Preliminaries

2.1 Partial Annotations

When training probabilistic models, more constraints generally lead to improved accuracy. The more knowledge we can bring to bear, the more we constrain the number of potential label sequences the training algorithm has to consider. They also help us to find a good initial model: it has to explain those fixed cases.

The purest form of unsupervised learning assumes the complete lack of annotation. However, in many cases, we can use prior knowledge to label words in context based on heuristics. It is usually not the case that all labels apply to all observations. If we know the alphabet of labels we use, we often also know which labels are applicable to which observations. This is encoded in a *dictionary*. For POS-tagging, it narrows the possible tags for each word–irrespective of context–down to a manageable set. Merialdo (1994) showed how the amount of available dictionary information is correlated with performance. However, dictionaries list all applicable labels per word, regardless of context. We can often restrict the applicable label for an observation in a specific context even more. We extend this to include constraints applied to some, but not all instances. This allows us to restrict the choice for an observation to one label. We substitute the word in case by a special token with just one label. Based on simple heuristics, we can annotate individual words in the training data with their label. For example, we can assume that "the" is always a determiner. This is a unigram constraint. We can expand those constraints to include a wider context. In a sentence like "I went to the show", we know that NN is the only applicable tag for "show", even if a dictionary lists the possible tags NN and VB. In fact, we can make that assumption for all words with a possible POS tag of NN that follow "the". This is an n-gram constraint.

Partial annotations provide local constraints. They arise from a number of different cases:

- simple heuristics that allow the disambiguation of some words in context (such as words after "the" being nouns)
- when we can leverage annotated data from a different task
- manual labeling of a few instances

While the technique is mainly useful for problems where only few labeled examples are available, we make use of a corpus of annotated data. This allows us to control the effect of the amount and type of annotated data on accuracy.

We evaluate the impact of partial annotations on two tasks: preposition sense disambiguation and POS tagging.

2.2 Preposition Sense Disambiguation

Prepositions are ubiquitous and highly ambiguous. Disambiguating prepositions is thus a challenging and interesting task in itself (see SemEval 2007 task,

(Litkowski and Hargraves, 2007)). There are three elements in the syntactic structure of prepositional phrases, namely the head word h (usually a noun, verb, or adjective), the preposition p, and the object of the preposition, o. The triple (h, p, o) forms a syntactically and semantically constrained structure. This structure is reflected in dependency parses as a common construction.

Tratz and Hovy (2009) show how to use the dependency structure to solve it. Their method outperformed the previous state-of-the-art (which used a window-based approach) by a significant margin. Hovy et al. (2011) showed how the sequential nature of the problem can be exploited in unsupervised learning. They present various sequential models and training options. They compare a standard bigram HMM and a very complex model that is designed to capture mutual constraints. In contrast to them, we use a trigram HMM, but move the preposition at the end of the observed sequence, to condition it on the previous words. As suggested there, we use EM with smoothing and random restarts.

2.3 Unsupervised POS-tagging

Merialdo (1994) introduced the task of unsupervised POS tagging using a dictionary. For each word, we know the possible labels in general. The model has to learn the labels in context. Subsequent work (Johnson, 2007; Ravi and Knight, 2009; Vaswani et al., 2010) has expanded on this in various ways, with accuracy between 86% and 96%. In this paper, we do not attempt to beat the state of the art, but rather test whether our constraints can be applied to a different task and data set.

3 Methodology

3.1 Data

For PSD, we use the SemEval task data. It consists of a training (16k) and a test set (8k) of sentences with sense-annotated prepositions following the sense inventory of *The Preposition Project*, TPP (Litkowski, 2005). It defines senses for each of the 34 most frequent English prepositions. There are on average 9.76 senses per preposition (between 2 and 25). We combine training and test and use the annotations from the training data to partially label our corpus. The test data remains unlabeled. We use the WordNet lexicographer senses as labels for the arguments. It has 45 labels for nouns, verbs, and adjectives and is thus roughly comparable to the prepositions sense granularity. It also allows us to construct a dictionary for the arguments from WordNet. Unknown words are assumed to have all possible senses applicable to their respective word class (i.e. all noun senses for words labeled as nouns, etc). We assume that pronouns other than "it" refer to people.

For the POS-tagged data, we use the Brown corpus. It contains $57k$ sentences and about $1, 16m$ words. We assume a simplified tag set with 38 tags and a dictionary that lists all possible tags for each word. For the partial annotations, we label every occurrence of "the", "a", and "an" as DET, and the next word with possible tag NN as NN. Additional constraints label all prepositions as "P" and all forms of "be" as "V". We train on the top two thirds and test on the last third.

For both data sets, we converted all words to lower case and replaced numbers by "@".

3.2 Models

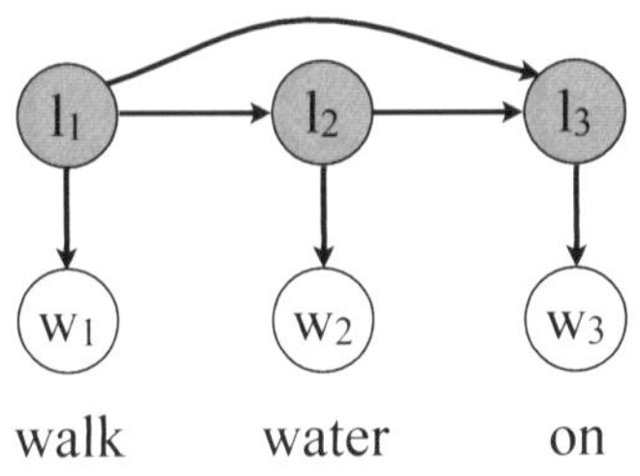

Figure 2: PSD: Trigram HMM with preposition as last element

For POS-tagging, we use a standard bigram HMM without back-off.

For PSD, we use a trigram HMM, but move the preposition at the end of the observed sequence, to condition it on the previous words (see Figure 2). Since not all prepositions have the same set of labels, we train individual models for each preposition. We can thus learn different parameter settings for the different prepositions.

We use EM with smoothing and random restarts to train our models. For smoothing, ϵ is added to each fractional count before normalization at each iteration to prevent overfitting (Eisner, 2002a). We set ϵ to 0.01. We stop training after 40 iterations, or if the perplexity change between iterations was less than 0.0001. We experimented with different numbers of random restarts (none, 10, 50, and 100).

3.3 Dealing with Partial Annotations

The most direct way to constrain a specific word to only one label is to substitute it for a special token that has only that label. If we have a partially annotated example "walk on-$sense_5$ water" as input (see Figure 1), we add an emission probability $P(word = label|tag = label)$ to our model.

However, this is problematic in two ways. Firstly, we have effectively removed a great number of instances where "on" should be labeled "$sense_5$" from our training data, and replaced them with another token: there are now fewer instances from which we collect $C(on|sense_5)$. The fractional counts for our transition parameters are not affected by this, but the counts for emission parameter are skewed. We thus essentially siphon probability mass from $P(on|sense_5)$ and move it to $P(on : sense_5|sense_5)$. Since the test data never contains labels such as $sense_5$, our partial annotations have moved a large amount of probability mass to a useless parameter: we are never going to use $P(on : sense_5|sense_5)$ during inference!

Secondly, since EM tends to find uniform distributions (Johnson, 2007), other, rarer labels will also have to receive some probability. The counts for labels with partial annotations are fixed, so in order to use the rare labels (for which we have no partial annotations), their emission counts need to come from unlabeled instances. Say $sense_1$ is a label for which we have no partial annotations. Every time EM collects emission counts from a word "on" (and not a labeled version "on:$sense_n$"), it assigns some of it to $P(on|sense_1)$. Effectively, we thus assign too much probability mass to the emission of the word from rare labels.

The result of these two effects is the inverse of what we want: our model will use the label with the *least* partial annotations (i.e., a rare label) disproportionately often during inference, while the labels for which we had partial annotations are rarely used. The resulting annotation has a low accuracy. We show an example of this in Section 5.

The solution to this problem is simple: *parameter tying*. We essentially have to link each partial annotation to the original word that we replaced. The observed word "on" and the partial annotation "$on : sense_5$" should behave the same way during training. This way, our emission probabilities for the word "on" given a label (say, "$sense_5$") take the information from the partial annotations into account. This technique is also described in Eisner (2002b) for a phonological problem with similar properties. Technically, the fractional counts we collect for $C(on : sense_5|sense_5)$ should also count for $C(on|sense_5)$. By tying the two parameters together, we achieve exactly that. This way, we can prevent probability mass from being siphoned away from the emission probability of the word, and an undue amount of probability mass from being assigned to rare labels.

4 Experiments

4.1 How Much Annotation Is Needed?

In order to test the effect of partial annotations on accuracy, we built different training sets. We varied the amount of partial annotations from 0 to 65% in increments of 5%. The original corpus we use contains 67% partial annotations, so we were unable to go beyond this number. We created the different corpora by randomly removing the existing annotations from our corpus. Since this is done stochastically, we ran 5 trials for each batch and averaged the results.

We also test the effect more unsupervised data has on the task. Theoretically, unsupervised methods should be able to exploit additional training data. We use 27k examples extracted from the prepositional attachment corpus from Ratnaparkhi et al. (1994).

4.2 What Kind of Annotation Is Needed?

We can assume that not only the quantity, but also the distribution of the partial annotations makes a difference. Given that we can only annotate a certain percentage of the data, how should we best distribute those annotations among instances to maximize accuracy? In order to test this, we hold the amount of annotated data fixed, but vary the labels we use. We choose one sense and annotate only the instances that have that sense, while leaving the rest unlabeled.

Ideally, one would like to examine all subsets of annotations, from just a single annotation to all but one instances of the entire training data. This would cover the spectrum from unsupervised to supervised. It is unlikely that there is a uniform best number that holds for all problems within this immense search space. Rather, we explore two very natural cases, and compare them to the unsupervised case, for various numbers of random restarts:

1. all partial annotations are of the same sense
2. one labeled example of each sense

5 Results

System	Acc. (%)
semi-supervised w/o param tying	4.73
MFS baseline	40.00
unsupervised (Hovy et al., 2011)	55.00
semi-supervised, no RR	63.18
semi-supervised, 10 RR	63.12
semi-supervised, 50 RR	63.16
semi-supervised, 100 RR	63.22
semi-supervised, addtl. data, no RR	62.67
semi-supervised, addtl. data, 10 RR	62.47
semi-supervised, addtl. data, 50 RR	62.58
semi-supervised, addtl. data, 100 RR	62.58
supervised (Hovy et al., 2010)	84.50

Table 1: Accuracy of various PSD systems. Baseline is most frequent sense.

Table 1 shows the results for the PSD systems we tested. Since not all test sets are the same size, we report the weighted average over all prepositions. For significance tests, we use two-tailed t-tests over the difference in accuracy at $p < 0.001$.

The difference between our models and the baseline as well as the best unsupervised models in Hovy et al. (2011) are significant. The low accuracy achieved without parameter tying underscores the importance of this technique. We find that the differences between none and 100 random restarts are not significant if partial annotations are used. Presumably, the partial annotations provide a strong enough constraint to overcome the effect of the random initializations. I.e., the fractional counts from the partial annotations overwhelm any initial parameter settings and move the model to a more advantageous position in the state space. The good accuracy for the case with no restarts corroborates this.

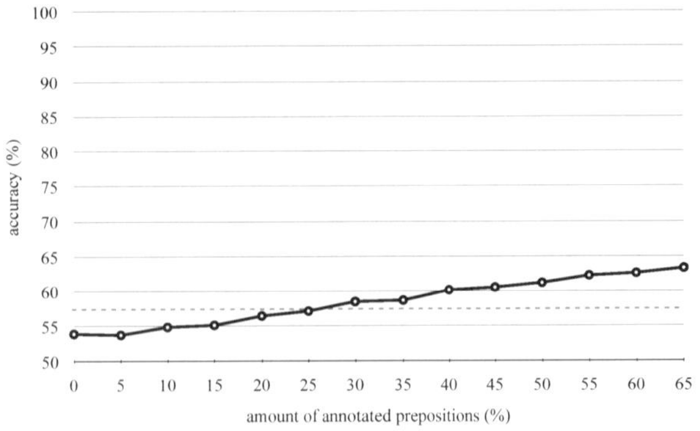

Figure 3: Accuracy for PSD systems improves linearly with amount of partial annotations. Accuracies above dotted line improve significantly (at $p < 0.001$) over unsupervised approach (Hovy et al., 2011)

Figure 3 shows the effect of more partial annotations on PSD accuracy. Using no annotations at all, just the dictionary, we achieve roughly the same results as reported in Hovy et al. (2011). Each increment of partial annotations increases accuracy. At around 27% annotated training examples, the difference starts to be significant. This shows that unsupervised training methods can benefit from partial annotations. When adding more unsupervised data, we do not see an increase in accuracy. In this case, the algorithm failed to make use of the additional training data. This might be because the two data sets were not heterogenous enough, or because the number of emission parameters grew faster than the amount of available training examples. A possible, yet somewhat unsatisfying explanation is that when we increase the overall training data, we reduce the percentage of labeled data (here to 47%; the result was comparable to the one observed in our ablation studies). It seems surprising, though, that the model does not benefit from the additional data[1]. More aggressive smoothing might help alleviate that problem.

The results on the distribution of partial annotation are shown in Figure 4. Using only the most

[1]Note that similar effects were observed by (Smith and Eisner, 2005; Goldwater and Griffiths, 2007).

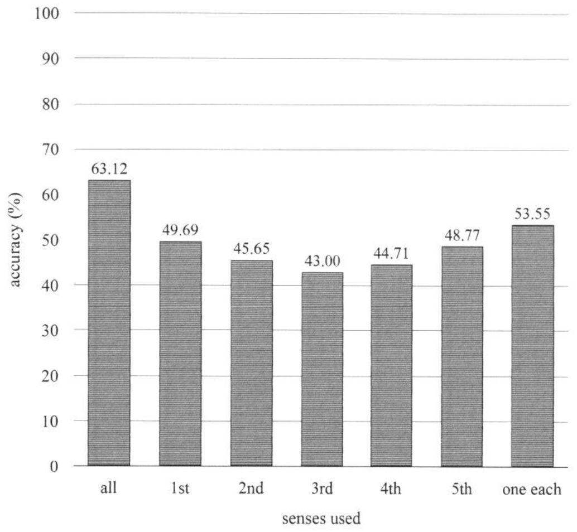

Figure 4: Labeling one example of each sense yields better results than all examples of any one sense. Senses ordered by frequency

frequent sense, accuracy drops to 49.69%. While this is better than the baseline which simply assigns this sense to every instance, it is a steep drop. We get better results using just one annotated example of each sense (53.55%).

System	Acc. (%)
(Merialdo, 1994)	86.60
random baseline	62.46
unsupervised, no RR	82.77
semi-supervised, DET+NN	88.51
semi-supervised, DET+NN+P	88.97
semi-supervised, DET+NN+P+V	87.07

Table 2: Accuracy of various POS systems. Random baseline averaged over 10 runs.

The results for POS tagging confirm our previous findings. The random baseline chooses for each word one of the possible tags. We averaged the results over 10 runs. The difference in accuracy between both the baseline and the unsupervised approach as well as the unsupervised approach and any of the partial annotations are significant. However, the drop in accuracy when adding the last heuristic points to a risk: partial annotation with heuristics can introduce errors and offset the benefits of the constraints. Careful selection of the right heuristics and the tradeoff between false positives they introduce and true positives they capture can alleviate this problem.

6 Related Research

Unsupervised methods have great appeal for resource-poor languages and new tasks. They have been applied to a wide variety of sequential labeling tasks, such as POS tagging, NE recognition, etc. The most common training technique is forward-backward EM. While EM is guaranteed to improve the data likelihood, it can get stuck in local maxima. Merialdo (1994) showed how the the initialized model influences the outcome after a fixed number of iterations. The importance is underscored succinctly by Goldberg et al. (2008). They experiment with various constraints.

The idea of using partial annotations has been explored in various settings. Druck et al. (2008) present an approach to label features instead of instances for discriminative probabilistic models, yielding substantial improvements. They also study the effectiveness of labeling features vs. labeling instances. Rehbein et al. (2009) study the utility of partial annotations as precursor to further, human annotation. Their experiments do not extend to unsupervised training. Tsuboi et al. (2008) used data that was not full annotated. However, their setting is in principle supervised, only few words are missing. Instead of no labels, those words have a limited number of possible alternatives. This works well for tasks with a small label alphabet or data where annotators left multiple options for some words. In contrast, we start out with unannotated data and assume that some words can be labeled. Gao et al. (2010) present a successful word alignment approach that uses partial annotations. These are derived from human annotation or heuristics. Their method improves BLEU, but requires some modification of the EM framework.

7 Conclusion and Future Work

It is obvious, and common knowledge, that providing some annotation to an unsupervised algorithm will improve accuracy and learning speed. Surprisingly, however, our literature search did not turn up any papers stating exactly how and to what degree the improvements appear. We therefore selected a very general training method, EM, and a simple approach to include partial annotations in it using parameter tying. This allows us to find more stable starting points for sequential labeling tasks than random or uniform initialization. We find that we would need a substantial amount of additional unlabeled data in order to boost accuracy. In contrast, we can get significant improvements by partially annotating some instances (around 27%). Given that we can only annotate a certain percentage of the data, it is best to distribute those annotations among all applicable senses, rather than focus on one. This obviates the need for random restarts and speeds up training.

This work suggests several interesting new avenues to explore. Can one integrate this procedure into a large-scale human annotation effort to obtain a kind of active learning, suggesting which instances to annotate next, until appropriate stopping criteria are satisfied (Zhu et al., 2008)? Can one determine upper bounds for the number of random restarts given the amount of annotations?

Acknowledgements

We would like to thank Victoria Fossum, Kevin Knight, Zornitsa Kozareva, and Ashish Vaswani for invaluable discussions and advice. We would also like to thank the reviewers who provided us with helpful feedback and suggestions. Research supported in part by Air Force Contract FA8750-09-C-0172 under the DARPA Machine Reading Program.

References

Ming-Wei Chang, Lev Ratinov, and Dan Roth. 2007. Guiding semi-supervision with constraint-driven learning. In *Proceedings of the 45th Annual Meeting of the Association of Computational Linguistics*, pages 280–287, Prague, Czech Republic. Association for Computational Linguistics.

Ming-Wei Chang, Lev Ratinov, Nicholas Rizzolo, and Dan Roth. 2008. Learning and inference with constraints. In *Proceedings of the 23rd national conference on Artificial intelligence*, pages 1513–1518.

Gregory Druck, Gideon Mann, and Andrew McCallum. 2008. Learning from labeled features using generalized expectation criteria. In *Proceedings of the 31st annual international ACM SIGIR conference on Research and development in information retrieval*, pages 595–602. ACM.

Jason Eisner. 2002a. An interactive spreadsheet for teaching the forward-backward algorithm. In *Proceedings of the ACL-02 Workshop on Effective tools and methodologies for teaching natural language processing and computational linguistics-Volume 1*, pages 10–18. Association for Computational Linguistics.

Jason Eisner. 2002b. Parameter estimation for probabilistic finite-state transducers. In *Proceedings of the 40th Annual Meeting on Association for Computational Linguistics*, pages 1–8. Association for Computational Linguistics.

Kuzman Ganchev, João Graça, Jennifer Gillenwater, and Ben Taskar. 2010. Posterior regularization for structured latent variable models. *The Journal of Machine Learning Research*, 11:2001–2049.

Qin Gao, Nguyen Bach, and Stephan Vogel. 2010. A semi-supervised word alignment algorithm with partial manual alignments. In *Proceedings of the Joint Fifth Workshop on Statistical Machine Translation and MetricsMATR*, pages 1–10. Association for Computational Linguistics.

Yoav Goldberg, Meni Adler, and Michael Elhadad. 2008. Em can find pretty good hmm pos-taggers (when given a good start). In *Proceedings of ACL*.

Sharon Goldwater and Thomas Griffiths. 2007. A fully bayesian approach to unsupervised part-of-speech tagging. In *ANNUAL MEETING-ASSOCIATION FOR COMPUTATIONAL LINGUISTICS*, volume 45, page 744.

João Graça, Kuzman Ganchev, and Ben Taskar. 2007. Expectation maximization and posterior constraints. *Advances in Neural Information Processing Systems*, 20:569–576.

Dirk Hovy, Stephen Tratz, and Eduard Hovy. 2010. What's in a Preposition? Dimensions of Sense Disambiguation for an Interesting Word Class. In *Coling 2010: Posters*, pages 454–462, Beijing, China, August. Coling 2010 Organizing Committee.

Dirk Hovy, Ashish Vaswani, Stephen Tratz, David Chiang, and Eduard Hovy. 2011. Models and training for unsupervised preposition sense disambiguation. In *Proceedings of the 49th Annual Meeting of the Association for Computational Linguistics: Human Language Technologies*, pages 323–328, Portland, Oregon, USA, June. Association for Computational Linguistics.

Mark Johnson. 2007. Why doesn't EM find good HMM POS-taggers. In *Proceedings of the 2007 Joint Conference on Empirical Methods in Natural Language Processing and Computational Natural Language Learning (EMNLP-CoNLL)*, pages 296–305.

Ken Litkowski and Orin Hargraves. 2007. SemEval-2007 Task 06: Word-Sense Disambiguation of Prepositions. In *Proceedings of the 4th International*

Workshop on Semantic Evaluations (SemEval-2007), Prague, Czech Republic.

Ken Litkowski. 2005. The preposition project. http://www.clres.com/prepositions.html.

Bernard Merialdo. 1994. Tagging English text with a probabilistic model. *Computational linguistics*, 20(2):155–171.

Adwait Ratnaparkhi, Jeff Reynar, and Salim Roukos. 1994. A maximum entropy model for prepositional phrase attachment. In *Proceedings of the workshop on Human Language Technology*, pages 250–255. Association for Computational Linguistics.

Sujith Ravi and Kevin Knight. 2009. Minimized models for unsupervised part-of-speech tagging. In *Proceedings of the Joint Conference of the 47th Annual Meeting of the ACL and the 4th International Joint Conference on Natural Language Processing of the AFNLP: Volume 1-Volume 1*, pages 504–512. Association for Computational Linguistics.

Ines Rehbein, Josef Ruppenhofer, and Caroline Sporleder. 2009. Assessing the benefits of partial automatic pre-labeling for frame-semantic annotation. In *Proceedings of the Third Linguistic Annotation Workshop*, pages 19–26. Association for Computational Linguistics.

Noah A. Smith and Jason Eisner. 2005. Contrastive estimation: Training log-linear models on unlabeled data. In *Proceedings of the 43rd Annual Meeting on Association for Computational Linguistics*, pages 354–362. Association for Computational Linguistics.

Stephen Tratz and Dirk Hovy. 2009. Disambiguation of Preposition Sense Using Linguistically Motivated Features. In *Proceedings of Human Language Technologies: The 2009 Annual Conference of the North American Chapter of the Association for Computational Linguistics, Companion Volume: Student Research Workshop and Doctoral Consortium*, pages 96–100, Boulder, Colorado, June. Association for Computational Linguistics.

Yuta Tsuboi, Hisashi Kashima, Hiroki Oda, Shinsuke Mori, and Yuji Matsumoto. 2008. Training conditional random fields using incomplete annotations. In *Proceedings of the 22nd International Conference on Computational Linguistics*, volume 1, pages 897–904. Association for Computational Linguistics.

Ashish Vaswani, Adam Pauls, and David Chiang. 2010. Efficient optimization of an mdl-inspired objective function for unsupervised part-of-speech tagging. In *Proceedings of the ACL 2010 Conference Short Papers*, pages 209–214. Association for Computational Linguistics.

Jingbo Zhu, Huizhen Wang, and Eduard Hovy. 2008. Multi-criteria-based strategy to stop active learning for data annotation. In *Proceedings of the 22nd International Conference on Computational Linguistics-Volume 1*, pages 1129–1136. Association for Computational Linguistics.

Using Senses in HMM Word Alignment

Douwe Gelling and **Trevor Cohn**
Department of Computer Science
University of Sheffield, UK
{d.gelling,t.cohn}@sheffield.ac.uk

Abstract

Some of the most used models for statistical word alignment are the IBM models. Although these models generate acceptable alignments, they do not exploit the rich information found in lexical resources, and as such have no reasonable means to choose better translations for specific senses.

We try to address this issue by extending the IBM HMM model with an extra hidden layer which represents the senses a word can take, allowing similar words to share similar output distributions. We test a preliminary version of this model on English-French data. We compare different ways of generating senses and assess the quality of the alignments relative to the IBM HMM model, as well as the generated sense probabilities, in order to gauge the usefulness in Word Sense Disambiguation.

1 Introduction

Modern machine translation is dominated by statistical methods, most of which are trained on word-aligned parallel corpora (Koehn et al., 2007; Koehn, 2004), which need to be generated separately. One of the most commonly used methods to generate these word alignments is to use the IBM models 1-5, which generate one-directional alignments.

Although the IBM models perform well, they fail to take into account certain situations. For example, if an alignment between two words f_1 and e_1 is considered, and f_1 is an uncommon translation for e_1, the translation probability will be low. It might happen, that an alignment to a different nearby word is preferred by the model. Consider for example the situation where f_1 is 'taal' (Dutch, meaning language), and e_1 is 'tongue'. The translation probability for this may be low, as 'tongue' usually translates as 'tong', meaning the body part. In this case the preference of the alignment model may dominate, leading to the wrong alignment.

Moreover, the standard tools for word alignment fail to make use of the lexical resources that already exist, and which could contribute useful information for the task. In particular, the ontology defined in WordNet (Miller, 1995) could be put to good use. Intuitively, the translation of a word should depend on the sense of the word being used. The current work seeks to explore this idea, by explicitly modeling the senses in the translation process. It does so, by modifying the HMM alignment model to include synsets as an intermediate stage of translation. This would facilitate sharing of translation distributions between words with similar senses that should generate the correct sense. In terms of the example above, one of the senses for 'tongue' will share the translation distribution with 'language', for which we will have more relevant translation probabilities.

As well as performing word alignment this model can be used to generate sense annotations on one side of a parallel corpus, given an alignment, or even generate sense annotations while aligning a corpus. Thus, the model could learn to align a corpus and do WSD at the same time. In this paper, the effect the usage of senses has on alignment is investigated, and the potential usefulness of the model for WSD is explored. In the next section related work is discussed, after which in section 3 the current model is discussed.

In section 4 the evaluation of the model is discussed, in two parts. In the first part, the model is evaluated for English-French on gold standard manually aligned data and compared to the results of the base HMM model. In the second part, the model is qualitatively evaluated by inspecting the senses and associated output distributions of selected words.

2 Previous Work

Although most researchers agree that Word Sense Disambiguation (WSD) is a useful field, it hasn't been shown to consistently help in related tasks. Machine Translation is no exception, and whether or not WSD systems can improve performance of MT systems is debated. Furthermore, it is unclear how parallel corpuses can be exploited for WSD systems. In this section we will present a brief overview of related work.

(Carpuat and Wu, 2007) report an improvement in translation quality by incorporating a WSD system directly in a phrase-based translation system. This is in response to earlier work done, where incorporating the output of a traditional WSD system gave disappointing results (Carpuat and Wu, 2005). The WSD task is redefined, to be similar to choosing the correct phrasal translation for a word, instead of choosing a sense from a sense inventory. This system is trained on the same data as the SMT system is.

The output of this model is incorporated into the machine translation system by providing the WSD probabilities for a phrase translation as extra features in a log-linear model (Carpuat and Wu, 2007). This system consistently outperforms the baseline system (the same system, but without WSD component), on multiple metrics, which seems to indicate that WSD can make a useful contribution to machine translation. However, the way the system is set up, it could also be viewed as a way of incorporating translation probabilities of other systems into the phrase-based translation model.

(Chan and Ng, 2007) introduce a system very similar to that of (Carpuat and Wu, 2007), but as applied to hierarchical phrase-based translation. They demonstrate modest improvements in BLEU score over the unmodified system, as well as some qualitative improvements in the output. Here again, the argument could be made that what is being done is not strictly word sense disambiguation, but augmenting the translation system with extra features for some of the phrase translations.

In (Tufiş et al., 2004) parallel corpora and aligned WordNets are exploited for WSD. This is done, by word aligning the parallel texts, and then for every aligned pair, generating a set of wordnet sense codes (ILI codes, or interlingual index codes) for either word, corresponding to the possible senses that word can take. As the wordnets for both languages are linked, if the ILI code of a sense is the same, the sense should be sufficiently similar. Thus, the intersection of both sets of ILI is taken to find an ILI code that is common to both pairs. If such a code is found, it represents the sense index of both words. Otherwise, the closest ILI code to the two most similar ILI codes is found, and that is taken as the sense for the word. The current work however only uses a lexical resource for one of the languages, and as such has fewer places to fail, and less demanding requirements.

Other similar work includes that in (Ng et al., 2003), where a sense-annotated corpus was automatically generated from a parallel corpus. This is done by word-aligning the parallel corpus, and then finding the senses according to WordNet given a list of nouns. Two senses are lumped together if they are translated into the same chinese word. The selection of correct translations is done manually. Only those occurrences of the chosen nouns that translate to one of the chosen chinese words are considered sense-tagged by the translation.

Although similar in approach to what the current system would do, this system uses a much more simple approach to generate sense annotations and it depends on a previously word-aligned corpus, whereas the current approach would integrate alignment and sense-tagging, whis may give a higher accuracy.

3 Senses Model

The current model is based on the HMM alignment model (Vogel et al., 1996), as it is a less complex model than IBM models 3 and above, but still finds acceptable alignments. The HMM alignment model is defined as a HMM model, where the observed

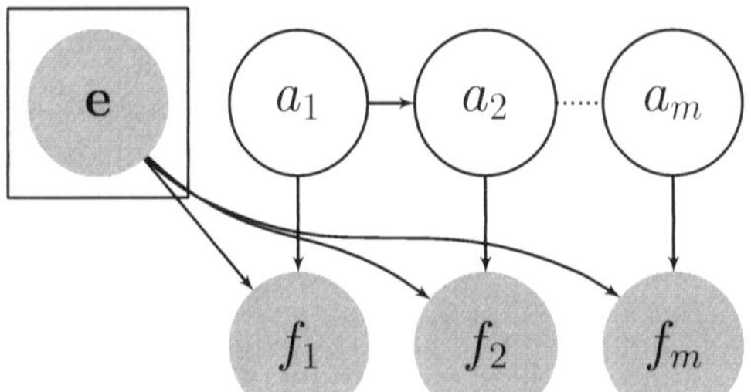

Figure 1: Diagram of HMM model. Arrows indicate dependencies, grey nodes indicate known values, white nodes indicate hidden variables.

variables are the words of a sentence in the French language **f**, and the hidden variables are alignments to words in the English sentence **e**, or to a null state. See figure 1 for a diagram of the standard HMM model. Under this model, French words can align to at most 1 English word. The transition probability is not dependent on the english words themselves, but on the size of jumps between alignments and the length of the English sentence. The probability of the French sentence given the English sentence is:

$$Pr(\mathbf{f}|\mathbf{e}) = \sum_{\mathbf{a}} \prod_{j=1}^{J} p(f_j|e_{a_j})p(a_j|a_{j-1}, I) \quad (1)$$

Here, **f** and **e** denote the French and English sentences, which have lengths J and I respectively, and **a** denotes an alignment of these two sentences. So, the states in the HMM assign a number from the range $[0, I]$ to each of the positions j in the French sentence, effectively assigning one English word e_{a_j} to each French word f_j, or a NULL translation e_0. The term $p(f_j|e_{a_j})$ is the translation probability of a pair of words, and $p(a_j|a_{j-1}, I)$ gives the transition probability in the HMM.

Here, i is the current state of the HMM, and i' is the previous state of the HMM, each being an index into the English sentence and $p(a_j|a_{j-1}, I)$ is defined as the probability of the gap between i and i'. So, if in an alignment French word 2 is aligned to the 3rd English word, and the next French Word (3) is aligned to the 5th English word, $p(a_j|a_{j-1}, I)$ isn't modelled directly as $p(5|3, I)$, but as $p(5-3|I)$.

To implement a dependency on senses in the model an extra hidden layer is added to the HMM model, representing the senses. The probability of a french word then depends on the generated sense, the probability of which depends on the English. The possible senses for a given English word is constrained by an external source, such as WordNet.

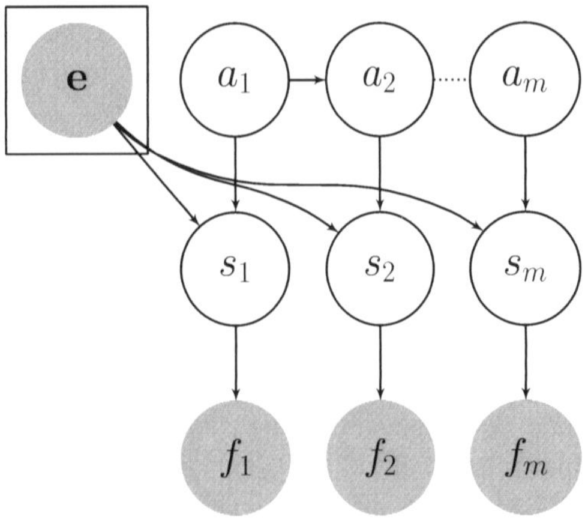

Figure 2: Diagram of SHMM model, with senses generated by the English words. Arrows indicate dependencies, grey nodes indicate known values, white nodes indicate hidden variables.

The probability under the model of a french sentence **f** given an English sentence **e** thus becomes:

$$Pr(\mathbf{f}|\mathbf{e}) = \sum_{\mathbf{a}} \prod_{j=1}^{J} p^*(f_j|e_{a_j})p(a_j|a_{j-1}, I) \quad (2)$$

where

$$p^*(f_j|e_{a_j}) = \sum_{k=1}^{K} p(f_j|s_k)p(s_k|e_{a_j}) \quad (3)$$

Here, K is the number of senses that english word associated with this translation pair. The senses will be constrained either by the English word e_{a_j} or by the French word f_j depending on which language the sense inventory is taken from. The first case, with senses constrained by the English, will be denoted with SHMM1, and the second with SHMM2. In this work, only SHMM1 is used.

If the amount of senses defined for each word is exactly 1 and this sense is different for each word, the model reduces to the HMM model (see Figure 2). However, if the sense inventory is defined such that for two different words with a sense that is similar, the same sense can be used, the model is able to use translation probabilities drawn from observations from both these words together. For example, in SHMM1, the words 'small' and 'little' may have the same sense listed in the sense inventory, which allows the model to learn a translation distribution to the French words that both these words often align to.

For training this model, as with the IBM models, Expectation-Maximization and initialisation are key. The more complex IBM models are initialised from simpler versions, so the complex models can start out with reasonable estimates, which allow it to find good alignments. Here, too, the same steps are used. The HMM model is initialised from Model 1, as described in citevogel:1996. From this, the SHMM models can be initialised.

For the SHMM1, given a translation probability for a french word given an english word under the HMM, $p(f|e)$, and a list of valid senses for that english word e, an equal portion of that translation probability is given to the new translation probability depending on the sense. This is done for all translation probabilities, and the translation table is then normalised. Probability of a sense given an english word is initialised to a uniform distribution over the valid senses.

For the SHMM2, the probability of french words given a sense is set to uniform over the words for which the sense is valid, and the probability of the sense given the english word is calculated analogous to the probability of the french word given the sense in the first case.

After initialisation, the expectation-maximisation algorithm can be used for training, as with the HMM model, using the forward-backward algorithm to find the posterior probabilities of the alignments. As the senses can be summed out during this phase, the algorithm can be used as-is, and afterwards the proportion of the partial count that should be assigned to each sense can be found. By summing out over the relevant senses and words, the two parts $c(f_j|q_k)$ and $c(q_k|e_i)$ can then be found.

3.1 Generating Senses for Words

In order to be able to use this model, an inventory of senses is needed for every word in the corpus, for one of the languages. The most obvious source for this is the English Wordnet (Miller, 1995), as it has a large inventory of senses. Note that, in this document, the words senses and synsets are used interchangeably.

The process of obtaining this inventory is explained from the viewpoint of using English WordNet, but the same basic conditions apply for any other lexicon, or language. The inventory of senses is obtained through the WordNet corpus in NLTK [1], which automatically stems the words that synsets are sought for.

In this model, two senses (synsets) are functionally equivalent, if the list of words that have them in their senselist is the same for both senses. That is to say, if the partial counts that will be added to either of the senses will be the same, there is no way of distinguishing between the two senses under this model. For example, in WordNet 3.0, among the synsets listed for the word 'small', there are 3 that have as constituent words only 'small' and 'little'. These 3 synsets would be functionally equivalent for our purposes. When this occurs, the senses that are equivalent are collated under one name, so that it's possible to find out which senses a particular sense is made up of.

At this point, there will be some words with only a sense that is unique to that word (such as those words that were not in the lexicon, which get a newly made sense), some words with only shared senses and some with a mix. We might want to enforce one of a few distinct options:

- All words have exactly 1 unique sense, and perhaps a few shared ones ('synthesis' condition)
- Some words have a unique sense, some don't ('merge' condition)
- No words have unique senses if they have at least 1 shared sense ('none' condition)

These conditions are generated by first finding the filtered list of senses for each word. At this point, some words have only unique senses, either because they didn't occur in WordNet, or because WordNet only listed unique senses for that word (the 'merge' condition. The 'synth' condition is made, by finding all words that have only shared senses, and adding a new sense, that is unique to that word. The 'none'

[1] http://www.nltk.org/

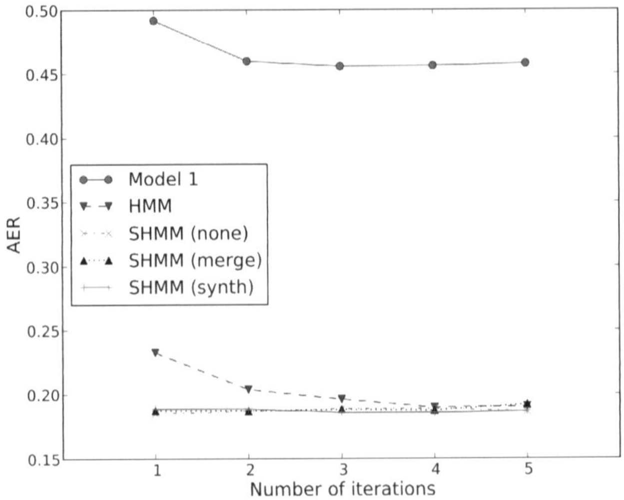

Figure 3: AER scores for Model 1, HMM, and 3 SHMM variations trained for 5 iterations each, lower is better.

condition then is found by doing the opposite: removing all unique senses from words that also have shared senses.

Under each of these 3 conditions, the model might work slightly differently. Under the 'synthesis' condition, it may generate the translation probabilities either directly, as in the HMM (which is what happens for any word with only 1 sense, which is unique for that word), or from the shared probabilities, through the senses. In the other models, the model is increasingly forced to use the shared translation probabilities.

4 Evaluation

We will evaluate the early results of this model against the HMM and Model 1 results, and will do a qualitative analysis of the distribution over senses and French words that the model obtains, in order to find out if reasonable predictions for senses are made.

The sense HMM model will be evaluated using the three sense inventories suggested in subsection 3.1. The dataset used was a 1 million sentence aligned English-French corpus, taken from the Europarl corpus (Koehn, 2005). The data was tokenised, length limited to a maximum length of 50, and lowercased. The results are evaluated on the test set from the ACL 2005 shared task, using Alignment Error Rate. The models are all trained for 5 iterations, and a pruning threshold is employed that removes probabilities from the translation tables if it is below $1.0 \cdot 10^{-6}$.

The results of training models based on senses generated in the 3 ways listed above is shown in Figure 3. The three SHMM models are compared against Model 1, and the standard HMM model, each of which is trained for 5 iterations. The HMM model is initialised from Model 1, and the SHMM models initialised from the HMM model. As the figure shows, the AER score for the last two iterations of the HMM model is very similar to the scores that the three variations of the SHMM model attain. The scores for the three HMM models range from 0.185 to 0.192

A possible reason for this performance is that the models didn't have enough sharing going on between the senses. The corpus contains 70700 unique words. Looking at the amount of senses that are found in the 'none' condition, meaning that all of the WordNet senses share output probabilities, there are 17194 words that have at least one of these senses listed, and there are 27120 distinct senses available in that setting. For the other 53500 senses, no sharing is going on whatsoever.

In the 'merge' and 'synth' conditions, there are more senses taken from WordNet (for a total from WordNet of 33133), but these don't add any shar-

Sense	Definition	$P(s\|e)$	Most likely French words in order
severe.s.06	very bad in degree or extent	0.4861	graves, sévères, des, sévère, grave, de, gravement, une, sérieuses, les
severe.s.04	unsparing and uncompromising in discipline or judgment	0.2358	graves, sévères, des, sévère, grave, de, gravement, une, sérieuses, les
dangerous.s.02	causing fear or anxiety by threatening great harm	0.1177	grave, des, graves, les, sérieux, très, sérieuses, une, importantes, sérieuse
austere.s.01	severely simple	0.1148	graves, des, grave, sévère, sévères, très, fortement, forte, rigoureuses, situation
hard.s.04	very strong or vigorous	0.035	dur, plus, importants, des, sévères, durement, son, une, difficile, très
severe.s.01	intensely or extremely bad or unpleasant in degree or quality	0.01055	terrible, terribles, des, grave, les, mauvais, dramatique, cette, aussi, terriblement

Table 1: Senses for the word 'severe' in the 'none' version of the SHMM model, their WordNet definition, the probability of the sense for the word severe, and the most likely French words for the senses given in order of likelihood.

ing. It might be then, that the model has insufficient opportunity to share output distributions, causing it to behave much as the HMM alignment model. Another possibility is, that the senses insufficiently well-defined, and share probabilities between words that are too dissimilar, negating any positive effect this may have and possibly pushing the model towards less sharing. We will suggest possibilities for dealing with this in section 5.

Regardless of the performance of the model in word alignment, if the model learns probabilities for senses that are reasonable, it can be used as a word sense disambiguation system for parallel corpora, with the candidate senses being made up from the senses out of WordNet. Those words not listed in WordNet, are treated as being monosemous words in this context. The 'merge' and 'none' conditions are most useful for this: if a WSD system chooses a sense that is not linked to a WordNet sense, it is not clearly defined which sense is meant here.

In order to find out if the model makes sensible distinctions between different senses, we have picked a random polysemous word, and looked at the senses associated with it in the 'none' condition. The word that was chosen is 'severe'. It has 6 possible senses, listed by main word and definition in Table 1, along with the probability of the senses, $p(s|e)$, and the 10 most likely French words for the senses.

Sense	Associated English words
severe.s.06	(only has basic 3 senses)
severe.s.04	spartan
dangerous.s.02	dangerous, grave, graver, gravest, grievous, life-threatening, serious
austere.s.01	austere, stark, starker, starkest, stern
hard.s.04	hard, harder, hardest
severe.s.01	terrible, wicked

Table 2: Senses for the word 'severe' in the 'none' version of the SHMM model and the English words apart from 'severe', 'severer' and 'severest' that have the sense in their senselist

As the table shows, the two most likely senses are quite similar. In fact, because words are stemmed before looking up suitable senses, all senses have at least the following 3 words associated with them: 'severe', 'severer' and 'severest'. The words that

Sense	Definition	P(s—e)	Most likely French words in order
rigorous.s.01	rigidly accurate; allowing no deviation from a standard	0.8962	rigoureuse, rigoureux, une, rigueur, rigoureuses, des, un, stricte, strict, strictes
rigorous.s.02	demanding strict attention to rules and procedures	0.1038	des, strictes, rigoureux, stricte, sévères, rigoureuses, stricts, rigoureuse, une, sévère

Table 3: Senses for the word 'rigorous' in the 'none' version of the SHMM model, their WordNet definition, the probability of the senses of the word 'rigorous', and the most likely French words for the senses given in order of likelihood.

cause the differences between the senses are listed in table 2. It can be seen that the only difference between severe.s.04 and severe.s.06 is the addition of the word 'spartan' for the first. As 'spartan' only occurs 67 times in the corpus, versus 484 for severe, it is possible that they are so similar, because the counts for 'spartan' get overshadowed.

For the other senses however, the most likely translations vary quite a bit. The sense 'hard.s.04', meaning very strong or vigorous, also includes translations to 'plus' and 'dur', which seems more likely given the sense. Given these translation probabilities though, it should at least be possible to distinguish between different senses of the word severe, given that it's aligned to a different french word.

One more example is listed in table 3, showing the probabilities for two different senses, and their most likely translations. The most likely sense for rigorous under the model is in the sense of 'allowing no deviation from a standard'. This is the only of the two senses that can translate to 'rigueur' in french, literally rigor. The other sense, meaning 'demanding strict attention to rules and procedures', is more likely to translate to 'strictes', 'stricte' and 'sévères', which reflects the WordNet definition.

The difference in contributing English words between these two senses can be found in Table 4. Interestingly, the three forms of the word strict are associated with the sense rigorous.s.01, even though the naive translations of these words into French are more likely for rigorous.s.02. Even so, the results match the WordNet definitions better.

These results show that useful translations are found, and the corresponding senses can be learned as well. For sense discrimination in parallel corpuses then, this model shows potential, and for

Sense	Associated English words
rigorous.s.01	rigorous strict stricter strictest
rigorous.s.02	rigorous stringent tight tighter tightest

alignment good alignments can be found, even with better abstraction in the model.

5 Conclusion

The results have shown that this may be a useful way to incorporate senses in a word alignment system. While the alignment results in themselves weren't significantly better, alignment probabilities to senses have been shown to be generated, which make it possible to distinguish between different senses. This could open the door to automatically sense annotating parallel corpora, using a predefined set of senses.

At this early point, several options lay open to improve upon the results so far. To improve the alignment results, more encompassing senses may be generated, for example by integrating similar synsets. At the same time, the list of synsets for each word may be improved upon, by filtering out very unlikely senses for a word.

It should also be possible to employ an already existing WSD system to annotate the parallel corpus, and use the counts of the annotated senses to better initialise the senses, rather than starting out assuming all are equaly likely for a given word. This may be used as well to initialise the translation probabilities for senses.

References

Marine Carpuat and Dekai Wu. 2005. Word sense disambiguation vs. statistical machine translation. In *Proceedings of the 43rd Annual Meeting on Association for Computational Linguistics*, ACL '05, pages 387–394, Stroudsburg, PA, USA. Association for Computational Linguistics.

Marine Carpuat and Dekai Wu. 2007. Improving statistical machine translation using word sense disambiguation. In *In The 2007 Joint Conference on Empirical Methods in Natural Language Processing and Computational Natural Language Learning (EMNLP-CoNLL 2007*, pages 61–72.

Yee Seng Chan and Hwee Tou Ng. 2007. Word sense disambiguation improves statistical machine translation. In *In 45th Annual Meeting of the Association for Computational Linguistics (ACL-07*, pages 33–40.

Philipp Koehn, Hieu Hoang, Alexandra Birch, Chris Callison-Burch, Marcello Federico, Nicola Bertoldi, Brooke Cowan, Wade Shen, Christine Moran, Richard Zens, Chris Dyer, Ondřej Bojar, Alexandra Constantin, and Evan Herbst. 2007. Moses: open source toolkit for statistical machine translation. In *Proceedings of the 45th Annual Meeting of the ACL on Interactive Poster and Demonstration Sessions*, ACL '07, pages 177–180, Stroudsburg, PA, USA. Association for Computational Linguistics.

Philipp Koehn. 2004. Pharaoh: a beam search decoder for phrase-based statistical machine translation models. In *Proceedings of AMTA 2004 (Conference of the Association for Machine Translation in the Americas)*, volume 3265, pages 115–124. Springer.

P. Koehn. 2005. Europarl: A Parallel Corpus for Statistical Machine Translation. In *Machine Translation Summit X*, pages 79–86, Phuket, Thailand.

George A. Miller. 1995. Wordnet: A lexical database for english. *Communications of the ACM*, 38:39–41.

Hwee Tou Ng, Bin Wang, and Yee Seng Chan. 2003. Exploiting parallel texts for word sense disambiguation: an empirical study. In *Proceedings of the 41st Annual Meeting on Association for Computational Linguistics - Volume 1*, ACL '03, pages 455–462, Stroudsburg, PA, USA. Association for Computational Linguistics.

Dan Tufiş, Radu Ion, and Nancy Ide. 2004. Fine-grained word sense disambiguation based on parallel corpora, word alignment, word clustering and aligned wordnets. In *Proceedings of the 20th international conference on Computational Linguistics*, COLING '04, Stroudsburg, PA, USA. Association for Computational Linguistics.

Stephan Vogel, Hermann Ney, and Christoph Tillmann. 1996. Hmm-based word alignment in statistical translation. In *Proceedings of the 16th conference on Computational linguistics - Volume 2*, COLING '96, pages 836–841, Stroudsburg, PA, USA. Association for Computational Linguistics.

Unsupervised Part of Speech Inference with Particle Filters

Gregory Dubbin and **Phil Blunsom**
Department of Computer Science
University of Oxford
Wolfson Building, Parks Road
Oxford, OX1 3QD, United Kingdom
Gregory.Dubbin@wolfson.ox.ac.uk Phil.Blunsom@cs.ox.ac.uk

Abstract

As linguistic models incorporate more subtle nuances of language and its structure, standard inference techniques can fall behind. Often, such models are tightly coupled such that they defy clever dynamic programming tricks. However, Sequential Monte Carlo (SMC) approaches, i.e. particle filters, are well suited to approximating such models, resolving their multi-modal nature at the cost of generating additional samples. We implement two particle filters, which jointly sample either sentences or word types, and incorporate them into a Gibbs sampler for part-of-speech (PoS) inference. We analyze the behavior of the particle filters, and compare them to a block sentence sampler, a local token sampler, and a heuristic sampler, which constrains inference to a single PoS per word type. Our findings show that particle filters can closely approximate a difficult or even intractable sampler quickly. However, we found that high posterior likelihood do not necessarily correspond to better Many-to-One accuracy. The results suggest that the approach has potential and more advanced particle filters are likely to lead to stronger performance.

1 Introduction

Modern research is steadily revealing more of the subtle structure of natural language to create increasingly intricate models. Many modern problems in computational linguistics require or benefit from modeling the long range correlations between latent variables, e.g. part of speech (PoS) induction (Liang et al., 2010), dependency parsing (Smith and Eisner, 2008), and coreference resolution (Denis and Baldridge, 2007). These correlations make inference difficult because they reflect the complicated effect variables have on each other in such tightly coupled models.

Sequential Monte Carlo (SMC) methods, like particle filters, are particularly well suited to estimating tightly coupled distributions (Andrieu et al., 2010). Particle filters sample sequences of latent variable assignments by concurrently generating several representative sequences consistent with a model's conditional dependencies. The sequential nature of the sampling simplifies inference by ignoring ambiguous correlations with unsampled variables at the cost of sampling the sequence multiple times. The few applications of particle filters in computational linguistics generally focus on the online nature of SMC (Canini et al., 2009; Borschinger and Johnson, 2011). However, batch applications still benefit from the power of SMC to generate samples from tightly coupled distributions that would otherwise need to be approximated. Furthermore, the time cost of the additional samples generated by SMC can be mitigated by generating them in parallel.

This report presents an initial approach to the integration of SMC and block sampling, sometimes reffered to as Particle Gibbs (PG) sampling (Andrieu et al., 2010). Unsupervised PoS induction serves as a motivating example for future extensions to other problems. Section 3 reviews the PYP-HMM model used for PoS inference. Section 4 explains the Sequential Importance Sampling (SIS) algorithm, a basic SMC method that generates samples for the block sampler. This approach yields two implementations: a simple sentence-based block sampler (4.1) and a more complicated type-based sampler (4.2). Finally, section 5 evaluates both implementations on a variety of unsupervised PoS inference tasks, analyzing the behavior of the SMC inference and comparing them to state-of-the-art approaches.

2 Background

SMC was introduced in 1993 as a Bayesian estimator for signal processing problems with strong non-linear conditional dependencies (Gordon et al., 1993). Since then, SMC methods have been adopted by many fields, including statistics, biology, economics, etc. (Jasra et al., 2008; Beaumont, 2003; Fernandez-Villaverde and Rubio-Ramirez, 2007). The SMC approach is the probabilisitic analogue of the beam search heuristic, where the beam width can be compared to the number of particles and pruning is analogous to resampling.

The basic SMC approach serves as the basis for several variants. Many SMC implementations resample the population of particles to create a new population that minimizes the effect of increasing sample variance with increasing sequence length (Kitagawa, 1996). Particle smoothing variants of SMC reduce the relative variance of marginals early in the sequence, as well improving the diversity of the final sample (Fearnhead et al., 2008). Particle Markov chain Monte Carlo (PMCMC) formally augments classic Markov chain Monte Carlo (MCMC) approaches, like Gibbs sampling, with samples generated by particle filters (Andrieu et al., 2010).

3 The PYP-HMM

The PYP-HMM model of PoS generation demonstrates the tightly coupled correlations that complicate many standard inference methods (Blunsom and Cohn, 2011). The model applies a hierarchical Pitman-Yor process (PYP) prior to a trigram hidden Markov model (HMM) to jointly model the distribution of a sequence of latent word classes, $\mathbf{t}$, and word tokens, $\mathbf{w}$. This model performs well on corpora in multiple languages, but the lack of a closed form solution for the sample probabilities makes it a strong canditate for PG sampling. The joint probability defined by a trigram HMM is

$$P_\theta(\mathbf{t}, \mathbf{w}) = \prod_{n=1}^{N+1} P_\theta(t_l | t_{n-1}, t_{n-2}) P_\theta(w_n | t_n)$$

where $N = |\mathbf{t}| = |\mathbf{w}|$ and the special tag \$ is added to the boundaries on the sentence. The model defines transition and emission distributions,

$$\begin{aligned} t_n | t_{n-1}, t_{n-2}, T \quad & \sim T_{t_{n-1}, t_{n-2}} \\ w_n | t_n, E \quad & \sim E_{t_n} \end{aligned}$$

The PYP-HMM smoothes these distributions by applying hierarchical PYP priors to them. The hierarchical PYP describes a back-off path of simpler PYP priors,

$$\begin{aligned} T_{ij} | a^T, b^T, B_i \quad & \sim \mathrm{PYP}(a^T, b^T, B_i) \\ B_i | a^B, b^B, U \quad & \sim \mathrm{PYP}(a^B, b^b, U) \\ U | a^U, b^U \quad & \sim \mathrm{PYP}(a^U, b^U, \mathrm{Uniform}). \\ E_i | a^E, b^E, C \quad & \sim \mathrm{PYP}(a^E, b^E, C_i), \end{aligned}$$

where T_{ij}, B_i, and U are trigram, bigram, and unigram transition distributions respectively and C_i is either a uniform distribution (PYP-HMM) or a bigram character language model emission distribution (PYP-HMM+LM, intended to model basic morphology).

Draws from the posterior of the hierarchical PYP can be calculated with a variant of the Chinese Restaraunt Process (CRP) called the Chinese Restaurant Franchise (CRF) (Teh, 2006; Goldwater et al., 2006). In the CRP analogy, each latent variable in a sequence is represented by a customer entering a restaurant and sitting at one of an infinite number of tables. A customer chooses to sit at a table in a restaurant according to the probability

$$P(z_n = k | \mathbf{z}_{1:n-1}) = \begin{cases} \frac{c_k^- - a}{n-1+b} & 1 \leq k \leq K^- \\ \frac{K^- a + b}{n-1+b} & k = K^- + 1 \end{cases} \quad (1)$$

where z_n is the index of the table chosen by the nth customer to the restaurant, $\mathbf{z}_{1:n-1}$ is the seating arrangement of the previous $n-1$ customers to enter, c_k^- is the count of the customers at table k, and K^- is the total number of tables chosen by the previous $n-1$ customers. All customers at a table share the same dish, representing the value assigned to the latent variables. When customers sit at an empty table, a new dish is assigned to that table according to the base distribution of the PYP. To expand the CRP analogy to the CRF for hierarchical PYPs, when a customer sits at a new table, a new customer enters the restaurant representing the PYP of the base distribution.

4 Sequential Monte Carlo

While MCMC approximates a distribution as the average of a sequence of samples taken from the posterior of the distribution, SMC approximates a distribution as the importance weighted sum of several sequentially generated samples, called particles. This article describes two SMC samplers that jointly sample multiple tag assignments: a sentence based block sampler (`sent`) and a word type based block sampler (`type`). The basics of particle filtering are outlined below, while the implementation specifics of the `sent` and `type` particle filters are described in secions 4.1 and 4.2, respectively.

SMC is essentially the probabilistic analogue of the beam search heuristic. SMC stores P sequences, analogous to beam width, and extends each incrementally according to a proposal distribution q_n, similar to the heuristic cost function in beam search. Many particle filtering implementations also include a resampling step which acts like pruning by reducing the number of unlikely sequences.

We implemented Sequential Importance Sampling (SIS), detailed by Doucet and Johansen (2009), to approximate joint samples from the sentence and word type distributions. This approach approximates a target distribution, $\pi_n(x_{1:n}) = \frac{\gamma_n(x_{1:n})}{Z_n}$, of the sequence, $x_{1:n}$, of n random variables, that is $\gamma_n(x_{1:n})$ calculates the unnormalized density of $x_{1:n}$.

SIS initilizes each particle $p \in [1, P]$ by sampling from the initial proposal distribution $q_1(x_1^p)$, where x_n^p is the value assigned to the n-th latent variable for particle p. The algorithm then sequentially extends each particle according to the conditional proposal distribution $q_n(x_n^p | x_{1:n}^p)$, where $x_{1:n}^p$ is the sequence of values assigned to the first n latent variables in particle p. After extending a particle p, SIS updates the importance weight $\omega_n^p = \omega_{n-1}^p * \alpha_n(x_{1:n}^p)$. The weight update, defined as

$$\alpha_n(x_{1:n}) = \frac{\gamma_n(x_{1:n})}{\gamma_{n-1}(x_{1:n-1}) q_n(x_n | x_{1:n-1})}, \quad (2)$$

accounts for the discrepancy between the proposal distribution, q_n, and the target distribution, π_n, without normalizing over $x_{1:n}$, which becomes intractable for longer sequences even in discrete domains. The normalizing constant of the target distribution is approximately $Z_n \approx \sum_{p=1}^{P} \omega_n^p$ and the unnormalized density is $\gamma_n(x_{1:n}) \approx \sum_{p=1}^{P} \omega_n^p \text{if} x_{1:n}^p = x_{1:n}$. The particles can also be used to generate an unbiased sample from π_n by choosing a particle p proportional to its weight ω_n^p.

Andrieu et al. (2010) shows that to ensure the samples generated by SMC for a Gibbs sampler has the target distribution as the invariant density, the particle filter must be modified to perform a *conditional SMC update*. This means that the particle filter guarantees that one of the final particles is assigned the same values as the previous Gibbs iteration. Our implementation of the conditional SMC update reserves one special particle, 0, for which the proposal distribution always chooses the previous iteration's value at that site.

4.1 Sentence Sampling

The `sent` particle filter samples blocks of tag assignments $\mathbf{t}_{1:n}^S$ for a sentence, S, composed of tokens, $\mathbf{w}_{1:n}^S$. Sampling an entire sentence minimizes the risk of assigning a tag with a high probability given its local context but minimal probability given the entire sentence. Sentences can be sampled by ignoring table counts while sampling a proposal sentence, incorporating them after the fact with a Metropolis-Hastings acceptance test (Gao and Johnson, 2008). The Metropolis-Hastings step simplifies the sentence block particle filter further by not requiring the conditional SMC update.

While there is already a tractable dynamic programming approach to sampling an entire sentence based on the Forward-Backward algorithm, particle filtering the sentences PYP-HMM model should prove beneficial. For the trigram HMM defined by the model, the forward-backward sampling approach has time complexity in $O(NT^3)$ for a sentence of length N with T possible tag assignments at each site. Particle filters with P particles can approximate these samples in $O(NTP)$ time, which becomes much faster as the number of tags, T, increases.

Sampling of sentence S begins by removing all of the transitions and emitions in S from the table counts, $\mathbf{z}$, resulting in the table counts $\mathbf{z}^{-S}$ of tag assignments $\mathbf{t}^{-S}$ the values assigned to the variables outside of S. For each site index $n \in [1, N]$ in the sentence, the particle filter chooses the new tag assignment, $t_n^{S,p}$, for each particle $p \in [1, P]$ from the sentence proposal distribution,

$$q_n^S(t_n^{S,p}|\mathbf{t}_{1:n-1}^{S,p}) \propto P(t_n^{S,p}|t_{n-2}^{S,p}, t_{n-1}^{S,p}, \mathbf{t}^{-S}, \mathbf{z}^{-S}) \times P(w_n^{S,p}|t_n^{S,p}, \mathbf{t}^{-S}, \mathbf{z}^{-S}, \mathbf{w}^{-S}).$$

After each new tag is assigned, the particle's weight is updated according to equation (2). The simplicity of the proposal density hints at the advantage of particle filtering over forward-backward sampling: it tracks only P histories and their weights rather than tracking the probability of over all possible histories. Once each particle has assigned a value to each site in the sentence, one tag sequence is chosen proportional to its particle weight, $\omega_N^{S,p}$.

4.2 Type Sampling

The type sampling case for the PYP-HMM is more complicated than the `sent` sampler. The long-range couplings defined by the hierarchical PYP priors strongly influence the joint distribution of tags assigned to tokens of the same word type (Liang et al., 2010). Therefore, the affects of the seating decisions of new customers cannot be postponed during filtering as in sentence sampling. To account for this, the `type` particle filter samples sequences of seating arrangements and tag assignments jointly, $\mathbf{x}_{1:n}^W = (\mathbf{t}_{1:n}^W, \mathbf{z}_{1:n}^W)$, for the word-type, W. The final table counts are resampled once a tag assignment has been chosen from the particles.

Tracking the seating arrangement history for each particle adds an additional complication to the `type` particle filter. The exchangeability of seating decisions means that only counts of customers are necessary to represent the history. Each particle represents both a tag sequence, $\mathbf{t}_{1:n}^{W,p}$, and the count deltas, $\mathbf{z}_{1:n}^{W,p}$. The count deltas of each particle are stored in a hash table that maps a dish in one of the CRF restaurants to the number of tables serving that dish and the total number of customers seated at those tables. The count delta hash table ensures that it has sufficient data to calculate the correct probabilities (per equation (1)) by storing any counts that are different from the base counts, $\mathbf{z}^{-W}$, and defering to the base counts for any counts it does not have stored.

At each token occurence n, the next tag assignment, $t_n^{W,p}$ for each particle $p \in [1, P]$ is chosen first according to the word type proposal distribution

$$\begin{aligned} q_n^W(t_n^{W,p}|\mathbf{t}_{1:n-1}^{W,p}, \mathbf{z}_{1:n-1}^{W,p}) \propto \\ P(t_n^{W,p}|c_n^{-2}, c_n^{-1}, \mathbf{t}_{1:n-1}^{-W,p}, \mathbf{z}_{1:n-1}^{-W,p}) \\ \times P(c_n^{+1}|c_n^{-1}, t_n^{W,p}, \mathbf{t}_{1:n-1}^{-W,p}, \mathbf{z}_{1:n-1}^{-W,p}) \\ \times P(c_n^{+2}|t_n^{W,p}, c_n^{+1}, \mathbf{t}_{1:n-1}^{-W,p}, \mathbf{z}_{1:n-1}^{-W,p}) \\ \times P(w_n^W|t_n^{W,p}, \mathbf{t}_{1:n-1}^{-W,p}, \mathbf{z}_{1:n-1}^{-W,p}, \mathbf{w}_{1:n-1}^{-W,p}). \end{aligned}$$

In this case, $c_n^{\pm k}$ represents a tag in the context of site t_n^W offset by k, while $\mathbf{t}_{1:n-1}^{-W,p}$, $\mathbf{z}_{1:n-1}^{W,p}$, and $\mathbf{w}_{1:n-1}^{-W,p}$ represent the tag assignments, table counts, and word token values chosen by particle p as well as the values at all of the sites where a word token of type W does not appear. This proposal distribution ignores changes to the seating arrangement between the three transitions involving the site n. The specific seating arrangement of a particle is chosen after the tag choice, at which point the weights are updated by the result of equation (2). As with the `sent` sampler, once all of the particles have been sampled, one of them is sampled with probability proportional to its weight. This final sample is a sample from the true target probability.

As mentioned earlier, the sequence of particle approximations do not have the target distribution as invariant unless they use the conditional SMC update. Therefore, a the special 0 particle is automatically assigned the value from the prior iteration of the Gibbs sampler at each site n, though the proposal probability $q_n^W(t_n^{W,0}|\mathbf{t}_{1:n-1}^{W,p}, \mathbf{z}_{1:n-1}^{W,p})$ still has to be calculated to update the weight $\omega_n^{W,p}$ properly. This ensures that the `type` sampler has a non-zero probability of reverting to the prior iteration's sequence.

5 Experiments and Results

We take two approaches to evaluating the SMC based samplers. The first approach is an analysis of the samplers as inference algorithms. The samplers should tend to maximize the posterior likelihood of the model over iterations, eventually converging to the mode. Section 5.1 analyzes the particle filter based samplers with various numbers of particles in an effort to understand how they behave.

Then, section 5.2 evaluates each of the proposed approaches on PoS inference tasks from several languages. These results allow a practical comparison with other PoS inference approaches.

5.1 SMC Analysis

Before comparing the performance of the SMC block samplers to other inference methods, we wish to learn more about the approaches themselves. It is not clear how well the benefits of block sampling transfer to SMC based approaches. Both the `sent` and `type` samplers are novel approaches to computational linguistics, and many of their properties are unclear. For example, the samples generated from the particle filter should have a higher variance than the target distribution. If the variance is too high, the sampler will be slower to converge. While additional particles lower the relative variance, they also increase the run time linearly. It is possible that there is a threshold of particles necessary to ensure that some are high likelihood sequences, beyond which inference gains are minimal the additional computational expense is wasted. All of the experiments in this section were run on the Arabic corpus from the CoNLL-X shared language task, which is small enough to quickly experiment with these issues (Buchholz and Marsi, 2006).

The sentence based sampler, `sent`, samples from a distribution that can be exactly computed, facilitating comparisons between the exact sampler and the SMC approach. Figure 5.1 compares the posterior log-likelihoods of the `sent` sampler and the exact sentence sampler over 200 iterations. As expected, the likelihoods of the particle filters approach that of the exact sentence sampler as the number of particles increases from 25 to 100, which completely overlaps the performance of the exact sampler by the 50th iteration. This is impressive, because even with 99 additional sequences sampled (one for each particle) each iteration the SMC approach is still faster than the exact sampler. Furthermore, the Arabic tagset has only 20 distinct tags, while other data sets, e.g. the WSJ and Bulgarian, use tagsets more than twice as large. The particle filter, which is linear in the number of tags, should take twice as long per token

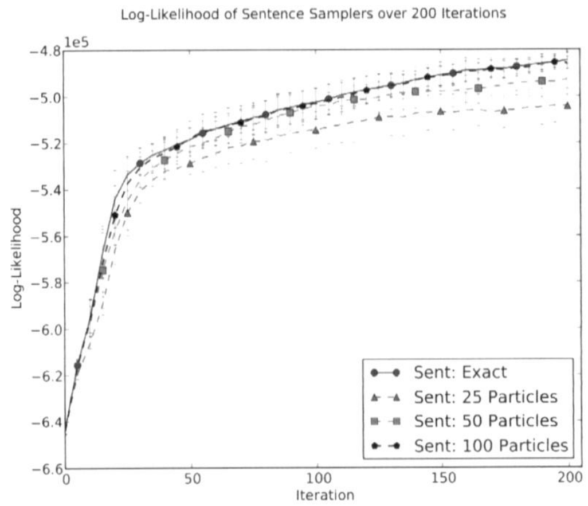

Figure 1: Posterior Log-Likelihood of PYP-HMM inference with exact as well as SMC sentence sampler with various numbers of particles. Error bars represent on standard deviation over three runs.

sampled on those data, relative to the arabic data. On the other hand, the forward-backward per token sample time, which is cubic in tagset size, should increase at least eightfold. So the time savings improve dramatically as the size of the tagset increases.

Figure 2 compares the table configuration log-likelihood of the 1HMM approximation implemented by Blunsom and Cohn (2011) with the `type` particle filter based sampler as well as the local, token-based sampler and the exact block sentence sampler. Unlike the sentence based block sampler, `type` sampler cannot be exactly calculated, even with the 1HMM approach of constraining inference to only consider sequences that assign the same tag to every token of the same word type. The 1HMM sampler approximates these probabilities using expected table counts. Theoretically, the `type` sampler should be a better approximation, being guaranteed to approach the true distribution as the number of particles increases. However, the `type` sampler does not constrain inference as the 1HMM does, slowing convergence by wasting particles on less likely tag sequences. As expected, the `type` sampler converges with the 1HMM sampler with sufficiently many particles in a few iterations. The exact block sentence sampler surpases approaches by iteration 75 and does not seem to have converged by the end of 200 iterations.

The local sampler samples a single site at a time with a standard, token-based Gibbs sampler. The

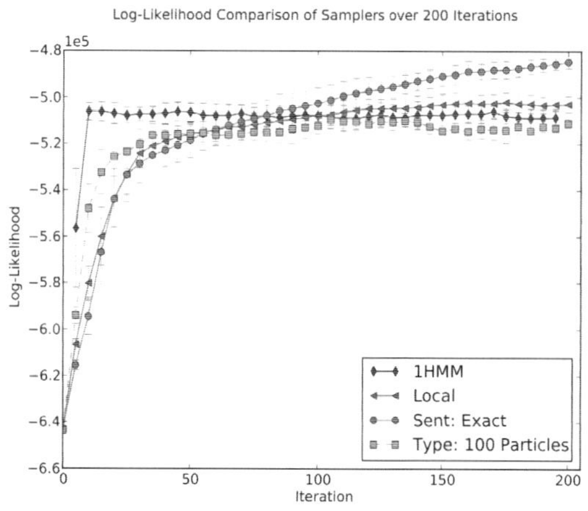

Figure 2: Posterior Log-Likelihood of PYP-HMM inference with particle filters, 1HMM approximation, and local samplers. Error bars represent one standard deviation over three runs.

local sampler performs surprisingly well, averaging a slightly higher likelihood than both the 1HMM and the `type` samplers. This may be an indication that the PYP-HMM model is not too tightly coupled for the local sampler to eventually migrate toward more likely modes. Note that both the `type` and 1HMM samplers initially take much larger steps, before eventually hitting a plateau. This suggests that some sort of mixed sampler may outperform its component samplers by only occasionally taking large steps.

5.2 Unsupervised Part-of-Speech Tagging

The samplers evaluated in section 5.1 induce syntactic categories analogous to PoS tags. However, to induce PoS tags, each syntactic category must be assigned to a PoS tag in the tagset. Each site in a corpus is assigned the most commonly visited syntactic category at that site over all iterations. The many-to-one (M-1) assignment for a category is the most common gold standard PoS tag of the tokens assigned to that category. While this assignment theoretically allows a perfect accuracy if each token is assigned to its own category, these experiments limit the number of induced categories to the size of the tagset. Table 1 compares the M-1 accuracy of the `sent` and `type` particle filter samplers, from sections 4.1 and 4.2, with 100 particles each. The particle filter based samplers rarely score a higher accuracy than even the local sampler, which completes 500 iterations before the particle filters complete 200.

While figure 2 shows that the sentence based block sampler eventually surpasses the 1HMM sampler in likelihood, the accuracies of the 1HMM and 1HMM-LM approximations remain well above the other approaches. The 1HMM sampler and the 100 particle `type` sampler have approximately the same likelihood, yet the M-1 accuracy of the 1HMM sampler is much higher. This suggests that there are high-likelihood assignments that produce lower accuracy results, presumably related to the fact that the `type` sampler is not restricted to assignments with exactly one tag for each word type. If the model assigns equal likelihood to these assignments, inference will not be able to distinguish between them. Perhaps a model that assigned higher likelihoods to tag sequences with fewer tags per word type would have a stronger correlation between likelihood and accuracy.

6 Future Work

While the results leave much room for improvement, the approach presented here is the most basic of particle methods. There has been considerable research in improvements to particle methods since their introduction in 1993 (Gordon et al., 1993). Two common approaches to improving particle filters are resampling and particle smoothing (Doucet and Johansen, 2009; Godsill and Clapp, 2001; Pitt, 2002). Resampling ensures that particles aren't wasted on unlikely sequences. Particle smoothing reduces the variability of the marginal distributions by combining the final particles.

7 Conclusion

This paper presented a preliminary approach to incorporating particle methods into computational linguistic inference applications. Such approaches show great potential for inference even in highly dependent distributions, but at a serious computational cost. However, the type particle filter itself can be largely run in parallel, only bottlenecking when the particle weights need to be normalized. Further expansion of the basic ideas presented will enable scalable inference in otherwise intractable models.

Language	Sent-100	Type-100	Local	1HMM	1HMM-LM	Tokens	Tag types
WSJ	69.8%	70.1%	70.2%	75.6%	77.5%	1,173,766	45
Arabic	53.5%	57.6%	56.2%	61.9%	62.0%	54,379	20
Bulgarian	64.8%	67.8%	67.6%	71.4%	76.2%	190,217	54
Czech	59.8%	61.6%	64.5%	65.4%	67.9%	1,249,408	12^c
Danish	65.0%	70.3%	69.1%	70.6%	74.6%	94,386	25
Dutch	61.6%	71.6%	64.1%	73.2%	72.9%	195,069	13^c
Hungarian	61.8%	61.8%	64.8%	69.6%	73.2%	131,799	43
Portuguese	59.4%	71.1%	68.1%	72.0%	77.1%	206,678	22

Table 1: Many-to-1 accuracies on CoNLL and Penn-Treebank Wall Street Journal corpora for sentence- (Sent) and type- (Type) based filtering. The table lists the average M-1 accuracy measured according to the maximum marginal tag assignments over 3 seperate runs after 200 iterations for the `sent`, `type`, 1HMM and 1HMM-LM samplers, and 500 iterations for the HMM local sampler. The 1HMM-LM model has been shown to achieve state-of-the-art unsupervised M-1 accuracies on these datasets. and thus represents the limit of unsupervised M-1 accuracy.

References

Christophe Andrieu, Arnaud Doucet, and Roman Holenstein. 2010. Particle markov chain monte carlo methods. *Journal Of The Royal Statistical Society Series B*, 72(3):269–342.

Mark A. Beaumont. 2003. Estimation of Population Growth or Decline in Genetically Monitored Populations. *Genetics*, 164(3):1139–1160, July.

Phil Blunsom and Trevor Cohn. 2011. A hierarchical pitman-yor process hmm for unsupervised part of speech induction. In *Proceedings of the 49th Annual Meeting of the Association for Computational Linguistics: Human Language Technologies*, pages 865–874, Portland, Oregon, USA, June. Association for Computational Linguistics.

Benjamin Borschinger and Mark Johnson. 2011. A particle filter algorithm for bayesian wordsegmentation. In *Proceedings of the Australasian Language Technology Association Workshop 2011*, pages 10–18, Canberra, Australia, December.

Sabine Buchholz and Erwin Marsi. 2006. Conll-x shared task on multilingual dependency parsing. In *Proceedings of the Tenth Conference on Computational Natural Language Learning*, CoNLL-X '06, pages 149–164, Morristown, NJ, USA. Association for Computational Linguistics.

Kevin R. Canini, Lei Shi, and Thomas L. Griffiths. 2009. Online inference of topics with latent Dirichlet allocation. In David van Dyk and Max Welling, editors, *Proceeings of the 12th International Conference on Artificial Intelligence and Statistics (AISTATS*09)*, pages 65–72.

Pascal Denis and Jason Baldridge. 2007. Joint determination of anaphoricity and coreference resolution using integer programming. In *Human Language Technologies 2007: The Conference of the North American Chapter of the Association for Computational Linguistics; Proceedings of the Main Conference*, pages 236–243, Rochester, New York, April. Association for Computational Linguistics.

Arnaud Doucet and Adam M. Johansen, 2009. *A Tutorial on Particle Filtering and Smoothing: Fifteen Years Later*. Oxford University Press.

Paul Fearnhead, David Wyncoll, and Jonathan Tawn. 2008. A sequential smoothing algorithm with linear computational cost. Technical report, Department of Mathematics and Statistics, Lancaster University.

Jesus Fernandez-Villaverde and Juan F. Rubio-Ramirez. 2007. Estimating macroeconomic models: A likelihood approach. *Review of Economic Studies*, 74(4):1059–1087, October.

Jianfeng Gao and Mark Johnson. 2008. A comparison of bayesian estimators for unsupervised hidden markov model pos taggers. In *Proceedings of the Conference on Empirical Methods in Natural Language Processing*, EMNLP '08, pages 344–352, Morristown, NJ, USA. Association for Computational Linguistics.

Simon Godsill and Tim Clapp. 2001. Improvement strategies for monte carlo particle filters. In A. Doucet, J. F. G. de Freitas, and N.J. Gordon, editors, *SEQUENTIAL MONTE CARLO METHODS IN PRACTICE*, pages 139–158. Springer-Verlag.

Sharon Goldwater, Tom Griffiths, and Mark Johnson. 2006. Interpolating between types and tokens by estimating power-law generators. In Y. Weiss, B. Schölkopf, and J. Platt, editors, *Advances in Neural Information Processing Systems 18*, pages 459–466. MIT Press, Cambridge, MA.

N. J. Gordon, D. J. Salmond, and A. F. M. Smith. 1993. Novel approach to nonlinear/non-Gaussian Bayesian state estimation. *Radar and Signal Processing, IEE Proceedings F*, 140(2):107–113, April.

A. Jasra, A. Doucet, D. Stephens, and C. Holmes. 2008. Interacting sequential Monte Carlo samplers for transdimensional simulation. *Computational Statistics & Data Analysis*, 52(4):1765–1791, January.

G Kitagawa. 1996. Monte carlo filter and smoother for non-gaussian nonlinear state space models. *Journal Of Computational And Graphical Statistics*, 5(1):1–25.

P. Liang, M. I. Jordan, and D. Klein. 2010. Type-based MCMC. In *North American Association for Computational Linguistics (NAACL)*.

Michael K Pitt. 2002. Smooth particle filters for likelihood evaluation and maximisation. The Warwick Economics Research Paper Series (TWERPS) 651, University of Warwick, Department of Economics, July.

David A. Smith and Jason Eisner. 2008. Dependency parsing by belief propagation. In *Proceedings of the Conference on Empirical Methods in Natural Language Processing*, EMNLP '08, pages 145–156, Stroudsburg, PA, USA. Association for Computational Linguistics.

Yee Whye Teh. 2006. A hierarchical bayesian language model based on pitman-yor processes. In *Proceedings of the 21st International Conference on Computational Linguistics and the 44th annual meeting of the Association for Computational Linguistics*, ACL-44, pages 985–992, Morristown, NJ, USA. Association for Computational Linguistics.

Nudging the Envelope of Direct Transfer Methods for Multilingual Named Entity Recognition

Oscar Täckström
SICS / Uppsala University
Sweden
oscar@sics.se

Abstract

In this paper, we study direct transfer methods for multilingual named entity recognition. Specifically, we extend the method recently proposed by Täckström et al. (2012), which is based on cross-lingual word cluster features. First, we show that by using multiple source languages, combined with self-training for target language adaptation, we can achieve significant improvements compared to using only single source direct transfer. Second, we investigate how the direct transfer system fares against a supervised target language system and conclude that between 8,000 and 16,000 word tokens need to be annotated in each target language to match the best direct transfer system. Finally, we show that we can significantly improve target language performance, even after annotating up to 64,000 tokens in the target language, by simply concatenating source and target language annotations.

1 Introduction

Recognition of named entities in natural language text is an important subtask of information extraction and thus bears importance for modern text mining and information retrieval applications. The need to identify named entities such as persons, locations, organizations and places, arises both in applications where the entities are first class objects of interest, such as in *Wikification* of documents (Ratinov et al., 2011), and in applications where knowledge of named entities is helpful in boosting performance, e.g., machine translation (Babych and Hartley, 2003) and question answering (Leidner et al., 2003). The advent of massive machine readable factual databases, such as Freebase[1] and the proposed Wikidata[2], will likely push the need for automatic extraction tools further. While these databases store information about entity *types* and the relationships between those types, the named entity recognition (NER) task concerns finding occurrences of named entities *in context*. This view originated with the Message Understanding Conferences (MUC) (Grishman and Sundheim, 1996).

As with the majority of tasks in contemporary natural language processing, most approaches to NER have been based on supervised machine learning. However, although resources for a handful of languages have been created, through initiatives such as MUC, the Multilingual Entity Task (Merchant et al., 1996) and the CoNLL shared tasks (Tjong Kim Sang, 2002; Tjong Kim Sang and De Meulder, 2003), coverage is still very limited in terms of both domains and languages. With fine-grained entity taxonomies such as that proposed by Sekine and Nobata (2004), who define over two hundred categories, we can expect an increase in the amount of annotated data required for acceptable performance, as well as an increased annotation cost for each entity occurrence. Although semi-supervised approaches have been shown to reduce the need for manual annotation (Freitag, 2004; Miller et al., 2004; Ando and Zhang, 2005; Suzuki and Isozaki, 2008; Lin and Wu, 2009; Turian et al., 2010; Dhillon et al., 2011; Täckström et al., 2012), these methods still require a substantial amount of manual annotation for each target language. Manually creating a sufficient amount of annotated resources for all entity types in all languages thus seems like an Herculean task.

In this study, we turn to direct transfer methods (McDonald et al., 2011; Täckström et al., 2012) as

[1]http://www.freebase.com

[2]http://meta.wikimedia.org/wiki/Wikidata

a way to combat the need for annotated resources in all languages. These methods allow one to train a system for a target language, using only annotations in some source language, as long as all source language features also have support in the target languages. Specifically, we extend the direct transfer method proposed by Täckström et al. (2012) in two ways. First, in §3, we use multiple source languages for training. We then propose a self-training algorithm, which allows for the inclusion of additional target language specific features, in §4. By combining these extensions, we achieve significant error reductions on all tested languages. Finally, in §5, we assess the viability of the different direct transfer systems compared to a supervised system trained on target language annotations, and conclude that direct transfer methods may be useful even in this scenario.

2 Direct Transfer for Cross-lingual NER

Rather than starting from scratch when creating systems that predict linguistic structure in one language, we should be able to take advantage of any corresponding annotations that are available in other languages. This idea is at the heart of both direct transfer methods (McDonald et al., 2011; Täckström et al., 2012) and of annotation projection methods (Yarowsky et al., 2001; Diab and Resnik, 2002; Hwa et al., 2005). While the aim of the latter is to transfer annotations across languages, direct transfer methods instead aim to transfer systems, trained on some source language, directly to other languages. In this paper, we focus on direct transfer methods, however, we briefly discuss the relationship between these approaches in §6.

Considering the substantial differences between languages at the grammatical and lexical level, the prospect of directly applying a system trained on one language to another language may seem bleak. However, McDonald et al. (2011) showed that a language independent dependency parser can indeed be created by training on a delexicalized treebank and by only incorporating features defined on universal part-of-speech tags (Das and Petrov, 2011).

Recently, Täckström et al. (2012) developed an algorithm for inducing cross-lingual word clusters and proposed to use these clusters to enrich the feature space of direct transfer systems. The richer set of cross-lingual features was shown to substantially improve on direct transfer of both dependency parsing and NER from English to other languages.

Cross-lingual word clusters are clusterings of words in two (or more) languages, such that the clusters are adequate in each language and at the same time consistent across languages. For cross-lingual word clusters to be useful in direct transfer of linguistic structure, the clusters should capture cross-lingual properties on both the semantic and syntactic level. Täckström et al. (2012) showed that this is, at least to some degree, achievable by coupling monolingual class-based language models, via word alignments. The basic building block is the following simple monolingual class-based language model (Saul and Pereira, 1997; Uszkoreit and Brants, 2008):

$$L(\boldsymbol{w}; \mathcal{C}) = \prod_{i=1}^{m} p(w_i | \mathcal{C}(w_i)) p(\mathcal{C}(w_i) | w_{i-1}) ,$$

where $L(\boldsymbol{w}; \mathcal{C})$ is the likelihood of a sequence of words, $\boldsymbol{w}$, and $\mathcal{C}$ is a (hard) clustering function, which maps words to cluster identities. These monolingual models are coupled through word alignments, which constrains the clusterings to be consistent across languages, and optimized by approximately maximizing the joint likelihood across languages. Just as monolingual word clusters are broadly applicable as features in monolingual models for linguistic structure prediction (Turian et al., 2010), the resulting cross-lingual word clusters can be used as features in various cross-lingual direct transfer models. We believe that the extensions that we propose are likely to be useful for other tasks as well, e.g., direct transfer dependency parsing, in this paper, we focus solely on discriminative direct transfer models for NER.

3 Multi-source Direct Transfer

Learning from multiple languages have been shown to be of benefit both in unsupervised learning of syntax and part-of-speech (Snyder et al., 2009; Berg-Kirkpatrick and Klein, 2010) and in transfer learning of dependency syntax (Cohen et al., 2011; McDonald et al., 2011). Here we perform a set of experiments where we investigate the potential of multi-source transfer for NER, in German (DE), English (EN), Spanish (ES) and Dutch (NL), using cross-lingual word clusters. For all experiments, we use the same

Source	DE	ES	NL
EN	39.7	62.0	63.7
EN + DE	–	61.8	65.5
EN + ES	39.3	–	65.6
EN + NL	**41.0**	62.5	–
ALL	**41.0**	**63.6**	**66.4**
↑ DEVELOPMENT SET ↓ TEST SET			
EN	37.8	59.1	57.2
EN + DE	–	59.4	57.9
EN + ES	35.9	–	59.1
EN + NL	**38.1**	59.7	–
ALL	36.4	**61.9**	**59.9**

Table 1: Results of multi-source direct transfer, measured with F_1-score on the CoNLL 2002/2003 development and test sets. ALL: all languages except the target language are used as source languages.

256 cross-lingual word clusters and the same feature templates as Täckström et al. (2012), with the exception that the transition factors are not conditioned on the input.[3] The features used are similar to those used by Turian et al. (2010), but include cross-lingual rather than monolingual word clusters. We remove the capitalization features when transferring to German, but keep them in all other cases, even when German is included in the set of source languages. We use the training, development and test data sets provided by the CoNLL 2002/2003 shared tasks (Tjong Kim Sang, 2002; Tjong Kim Sang and De Meulder, 2003). The multi-source training sets are created by concatenating each of the source languages' training sets. In order to have equivalent label sets across languages, we use the IO (inside/outside) encoding, rather than the BIO (begin/inside/outside) encoding, since the latter is available only for Spanish and Dutch. The models are trained using CRFSuite 0.12 (Okazaki, 2007), by running stochastic gradient descent for a maximum of 100 iterations.

Table 1 shows the result of using different source languages for different target languages. We see that multi-source transfer is somewhat helpful in general, but that the results are sensitive to the combination of source and target languages. On average, using all source languages only give a relative error reduction of about 3% on the test set. However, results for

[3]This is due to limitations in the sequence labeling software used and gives slightly lower results, across the board, than those reported by Täckström et al. (2012).

	DE	ES	NL	AVG
NATIVE CLUSTERS	71.2	80.7	82.5	*78.1*
X-LING CLUSTERS	68.9	78.8	80.9	*76.2*
NATIVE & X-LING CLUST.	72.5	81.2	83.6	*79.1*
↑ DEVELOPMENT SET ↓ TEST SET				
NATIVE CLUSTERS	72.2	81.0	83.0	*78.7*
X-LING CLUSTERS	71.0	80.2	80.7	*77.3*
NATIVE & X-LING CLUST.	73.5	81.8	83.7	*79.7*

Table 2: The impact of different word clusters in the supervised monolingual setting. Results are measured with F_1-score on the CoNLL 2002/2003 development and test sets. NATIVE/X-LING CLUSTERS: The cross-lingual/monolingual clusters from Täckström et al. (2012).

Spanish and Dutch are more promising, with relative reductions of 7% and 6%, respectively, when using all source languages. Using all available source languages gives the best results for both Spanish and Dutch, but slightly worse results for German. When transferring to Dutch, using more source languages consistently help, while Spanish and German are more sensitive to the choice of source languages. Based on the characteristics of these languages, this is not too surprising: while Dutch and German has the most similar vocabularies, Dutch uses similar capitalization rules to English and Spanish. Dutch should thus benefit from all the other languages, while Spanish may not bring much to the table for German and vice versa, given their lexical differences. Knowledge of such relationships between the languages, could potentially be used to give different weights to different source languages in the training objective, as was shown effective by Cohen et al. (2011) in the context of direct transfer of generative dependency parsing models. Although better results could be achieved by cherry-picking language combinations, since we do not have any general principled way of choosing/weighting source languages in discriminative models, we include all source languages with equal weight in all subsequent experiments where multiple source languages are used.

4 Domain Adaptation via Self-Training

Thus far, we have not made use of any information specific to the target language, except when inducing the cross-lingual word clusters. However, as shown in Table 2, which lists the results of experiments on

Algorithm 1 Self-Training for Domain Adaptation

$\mathcal{D}_s^l$: Labeled source domain data
$\mathcal{D}_t^l$: Labeled target domain data (possibly empty)
$\mathcal{D}_t^u$: Unlabeled target domain data
δ: Dominance threshold
T: Number of iterations
procedure SELFTRAIN($\mathcal{D}_s^l, \mathcal{D}_t^l, \mathcal{D}_t^u, \delta, T$)
    $\theta^0 \leftarrow$ LEARN($\mathcal{D}_s^l \cup \mathcal{D}_t^l$)   ▷ Train supervised model
    for $i \leftarrow 1$ **to** T **do**
        $P^i \leftarrow$ PREDICT($\mathcal{D}_t^u, \theta^{i-1}$)   ▷ Predict w/ curr. mod.
        $F^i \leftarrow$ FILTER(P^i, δ)   ▷ Filter $p_{\theta^{i-1}}(\boldsymbol{y}^*|\boldsymbol{x}) \le \delta$
        $S^i \leftarrow$ SAMPLE(F^i)   ▷ Pick $\sim p_{\theta^{i-1}}(\boldsymbol{y}|\boldsymbol{x})$. (†)
        $\theta^i \leftarrow$ LEARN($\mathcal{D}_s^l \cup \mathcal{D}_t^l \cup S^i$)   ▷ Retrain
    end for
    return θ^T ▷ Return adapted model
end procedure

† If LEARN(·) supports instance weighting, we could weight each instance $(\boldsymbol{x}, \boldsymbol{y}^*) \in F^i$ by $p_{\theta^{i-1}}(\boldsymbol{y}^*|\boldsymbol{x})$ in the training objective, rather than performing sampling according to the same distribution.

supervised target language models trained with different cluster features,[4] these clusters are not optimally adapted to the target language, compared to the monolingual *native* clusters that are induced solely on the target language, without any cross-lingual constraints. This is to be expected, as the probabilistic model used to learn the cross-lingual clusters strikes a balance between two language specific models. On the other hand, this suggests an opportunity for adapting to target language specific features through self-training. In fact, since the direct transfer models are trained using cross-lingual features, the target language can be viewed as simply representing a different domain from the source language.

Self-training has previously been shown to be a simple and effective way to perform domain adaptation for syntactic parsers and other tasks (McClosky et al., 2006; Chen et al., 2011). The idea of self-training for domain adaptation is to first train a supervised predictor on labeled instances from a source domain. This predictor is then used to label instances from some unlabeled target domain. Those instances for which the predictor is confident are added to the source training set, and the process is repeated until some stopping criterion is met. Recently, Daumé et al. (2010) and Chen et al. (2011) proposed more complex domain adaptation techniques, based on co-training. In this work, however, we stick with the simple single-view self-training approach just outlined. In the self-training for domain adaptation method, described by Chen et al. (2011), the top-k instances for which the predictor is most confident are added to the training set in each iteration. We instead propose to weight the target instances selected for self-training in each iteration proportional to the confidence of the classifier trained in the previous iteration.

In short, let $\boldsymbol{x} \in \mathcal{D}_t^u$ be an unlabeled target language input sequence (in our case a sentence) and $\boldsymbol{y}^* \in \mathcal{Y}_t(\boldsymbol{x})$ its top-ranked label sequence (in our case an IO sequence). In the first iteration, a predictor is trained on the labeled source language data, $\mathcal{D}_s^l$. In each subsequent iteration the sequences are scored according to the probabilities assigned by the predictor trained in the previous iteration, $p_{\theta^{i-1}}(\boldsymbol{y}^*|\boldsymbol{x})$. When constructing the training set for the next iteration, we first filter out all instances for which the top-ranked label sequence is not δ-dominating. That is, we filter out all instances $\boldsymbol{x} \in \mathcal{D}_u^t$ such that $p_{\theta^{i-1}}(\boldsymbol{y}^*|\boldsymbol{x}) < \delta$, for some user-specified δ. In this work, we set $\delta = 0.5$, since this guarantees that the output associated with each instance that is kept is assigned the majority of the probability mass. This is important, as we only consider the most likely output $\boldsymbol{y}^*$ for each input $\boldsymbol{x}$, so that sampling low-confidence instances will result in a highly biased sample. After filtering, we sample from the remaining instances, i.e. from the set of instances $\boldsymbol{x} \in \mathcal{D}_u^t$ such that $p_{\theta^{i-1}}(\boldsymbol{y}^*|\boldsymbol{x}) \ge \delta$, adding each instance $(\boldsymbol{x}, \boldsymbol{y}^*)$ to the training set with probability $p_{\theta^{i-1}}(\boldsymbol{y}^*|\boldsymbol{x})$. This procedure is repeated for T iterations as outlined in Algorithm 1. By using instance weighting rather than a top-k list, we remove the need to heuristically set the number of instances to be selected for self-training in each iteration. Further, although we have not verified this empirically, we hypothesize that using instance weighting is more robust than picking only the most confident instances, as it maintains diversity in the training set in the face of uncertainty. Note also that when we have access to target language test data during training, we can perform transductive learning by including the test set in the pool of unlabeled data. This gives the model the opportunity to adapt to the characteristics of the test domain.

Our use of self-training for exploiting features na-

[4]For these experiments, the same settings were used as in the multi-source transfer experiments in §3, with the difference that only target language training data was used.

	DE	ES	NL	AVG
SINGLE	39.7	62.0	63.7	*55.2*
MULTI	41.0	63.6	66.4	*57.0*
SINGLE + SELF	42.6	65.7	64.0	*57.4*
SINGLE + SELF/NATIVE	44.5	**66.5**	65.9	*59.0*
MULTI + SELF	48.4	64.7	68.1	*60.4*
MULTI + SELF/NATIVE	**49.5**	**66.5**	**69.7**	***61.9***
↑ DEVELOPMENT SET ↓ TEST SET				
SINGLE	37.8	59.1	57.2	*51.4*
MULTI	36.4	61.9	59.9	*52.8*
SINGLE + SELF	41.3	61.0	57.8	*53.3*
SINGLE + SELF/NATIVE	43.0	62.5	58.9	*54.8*
MULTI + SELF	45.3	62.3	61.9	*56.5*
MULTI + SELF/NATIVE	**47.2**	**64.8**	**63.1**	***58.4***

Table 3: Results of different extensions to direct transfer as measured with F_1-score on the CoNLL 2002/2003 development and test sets. SINGLE: single-source transfer, MULTI: multi-source transfer, SELF: self-training with only cross-lingual word clusters, SELF/NATIVE: self-training with cross-lingual and native word clusters.

tive to the target language resembles the way McDonald et al. (2011) re-lexicalize a delexicalized direct transfer parser. Both methods allow the model to move weights from shared parameters to more predictive target language specific parameters. However, rather than using the direct transfer parser's own predictions through self-training, these authors project head-modifier relations to the target language through loss-augmented learning (Hall et al., 2011). The bootstrapping methods for language independent NER of Cucerzan and Yarowsky (1999) have a similar effect. Our self-training approach is largely orthogonal to these approaches. We therefore believe that combining these methods could be fruitful.

4.1 Experiments

In these experiments we combine direct transfer with self-training using unlabeled target data. This is the transductive setting, as we include the test data (with labels removed, of course) in the unlabeled target data. We investigate the effect of adding self-training (SELF) to the single-source and multi-source transfer settings of §3, where only cross-lingual features are used (SINGLE and MULTI, respectively). We further study the effect of including native monolingual word cluster features in addition to the cross-lingual features (SELF/NATVE). The experimental settings and datasets used are the same as those described in §3. We performed self-training for $T = 5$ iterations for all languages, as preliminary experiments indicated that the procedure converges to a stable solution after this number of iterations. CRFSuite was used to compute all the required probabilities for the filtering and sampling steps.

The results of these experiments are shown in Table 3. By itself, self-training without target specific features result in an average relative error reduction of less than 4%, compared to the baseline direct transfer system. This is only slightly better than the improvement achieved with multi-source transfer. However, when adding target specific features, self-training works better, with a 7% reduction. Combining multi-source transfer with self-training, without target specific features, performs even better with a 10% reduction. Finally, combining multi-source transfer and self-training with target specific features, gives the best result across all three languages, with an average relative error reduction of more than 14%.

The results for German are particularly interesting, in that they highlight a rather surprising general trend. The relative improvement achieved by combining multi-source transfer and self training with native clusters is almost twice as large as that achieved when using only self-training with native clusters, despite the fact that multi-source transfer is not very effective on its own – in the case of German, multi-source transfer actually hurts results when used in isolation. One explanation for this behavior could be that the regularization imposed by the use of multiple source languages is beneficial to self-training, in that it generates better confidence estimates. Another, perhaps more speculative, explanation could be that each source language shares different characteristics with the target language. Even though the predictions on the target language are not much better on average in this case, as long as a large enough subset of the confident predictions are better than with single-source transfer, these predictions can be exploited during self-training.

In addition to using self-training with native word cluster features, we also experimented with creating target language specific versions of the cross-lingual features by means of the feature duplication trick (Daumé, 2007). However, preliminary experiments suggested that this is not an effective strategy in the

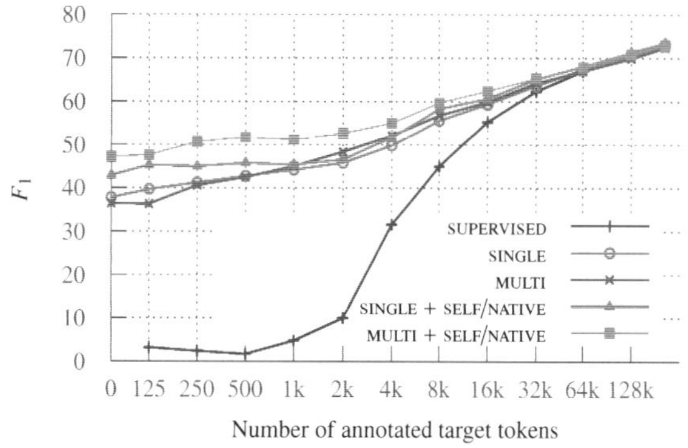

Figure 1: Learning curves for German.

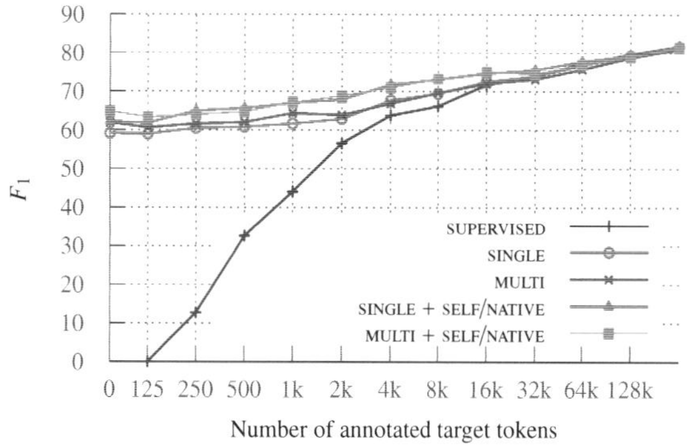

Figure 2: Learning curves for Spanish.

cross-lingual direct transfer scenario. It thus seems likely that the significant improvements that we observe are at least in part explained by the fact that the native features are distinct from the cross-lingual features and not mere duplicates.

5 Direct Transfer vs. Supervised Learning

Finally, we look at the relative performance of the different direct transfer methods and a target language specific supervised system trained with native and cross-lingual word cluster features. For these experiments we use the same settings as for the experiments in §3 and §4.1.

Figures 1–3 show the learning curves for the supervised system, as more and more target language annotations, selected by picking sentences at random from the full training set, are added to the training set, compared to the same system when combined with different direct transfer methods. From these curves, we can see that the purely supervised model

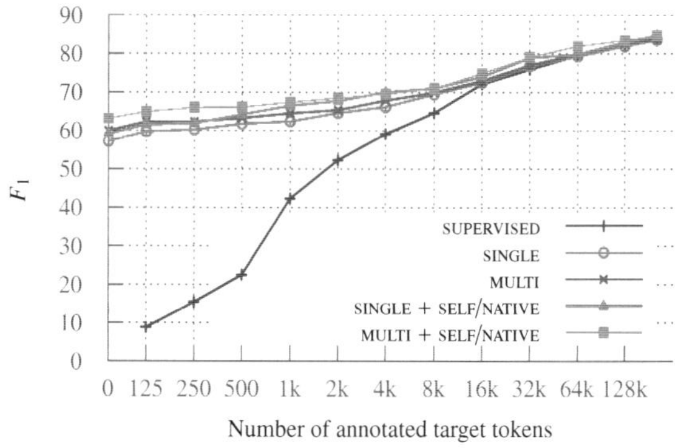

Figure 3: Learning curves for Dutch.

requires between 8,000 and 16,000 annotated word tokens (roughly corresponding to between 430 and 860 sentences) in each target language to match the best direct transfer system. The learning curves also show that adding source language data improves performance with as many as 64,000 annotated target language tokens.

Although we believe that the results on combining source and target data are interesting, in practice the marginal cost of annotation is typically quite low compared to the initial cost. Therefore, the cost of going from 125 to 64,000 annotated tokens is likely not too high, so that the benefit of cross-lingual transfer is small on the margin in this scenario. However, we believe that direct transfer methods can reduce the initial cost as well, especially when a larger label set is used, since a larger label set implies a larger cognitive load throughout annotation, but especially in the initial phase of the annotation.

Another aspect, which we were unable to investigate is the relative performance of these methods on domains other than news text. It is well known that the performance of supervised NER systems drop significantly when applied to data outside of the training domain (Nothman et al., 2008). Although the direct transfer systems in these experiments are also trained on news data, we suspect that the advantage of these methods will be more pronounced when applied to other domains, since the supervised target system runs a higher risk of overfitting to the characteristics of the target language training domain compared to the direct transfer system, which has already to some degree overfitted to the source language.

6 Discussion

We have focused on direct transfer methods that exploit cross-lingual word clusters, which are induced with the help of word alignments. A more common use of word alignments for cross-lingual linguistic structure prediction is for projecting annotations across languages (Yarowsky et al., 2001; Diab and Resnik, 2002; Hwa et al., 2005).

Apart from the algorithmic differences between these approaches, there are more fundamental differences in terms of the assumptions they make. Annotation projection relies on the construction of a mapping from structures in the source language to structures in the target language, $\mathcal{Y}_s \mapsto \mathcal{Y}'_t$. Based on the *direct correspondence assumption* (Diab and Resnik, 2002; Hwa et al., 2005), word alignments are assumed to be a good basis for this mapping. When projecting annotations, no consideration is taken to the source language input space, $\mathcal{X}_s$, nor to the target language input space, $\mathcal{X}_t$, except implicitly in the construction of the word alignments. The learning algorithm is thus free to use any parameters when training on instances from $\mathcal{X}_t \times \mathcal{Y}'_t$, but can at the same time not exploit any additional information that may be present in $\mathcal{X}_s \times \mathcal{Y}_s$ about $\mathcal{X}_t \times \mathcal{Y}_t$. Furthermore, word alignments are noisy and often only provide partial information about the target side annotations.

Direct transfer, on the other hand, makes a stronger assumption, as it relies on a mapping from the joint space of source inputs and output structures to the target language, $\mathcal{X}_s \times \mathcal{Y}_s \mapsto \mathcal{X}'_t \times \mathcal{Y}'_t$. Actually, the assumption is even stronger, since in order to achieve low error on the target language with a discriminative model, we must further assume that the conditional distribution $P(\mathcal{Y}'_t|\mathcal{X}'_t)$ does not diverge too much from $P(\mathcal{Y}_t|\mathcal{X}_t)$ in regions where $P(\mathcal{X}_t)$ is large. This suggests that direct transfer might be preferable when source and target languages are sufficiently similar so that a good mapping can be found.

These differences suggest that it may be fruitful to combine direct transfer with annotation projection. For example, direct transfer could be used to first map $\mathcal{X}_s \times \mathcal{Y}_s \mapsto \mathcal{X}'_t \times \mathcal{Y}'_t$, while annotation projection could be used to derive constraints on the target output space by means of a mapping $\mathcal{Y}_s \mapsto \mathcal{Y}''_t$. These constraints could perhaps be exploited in self-training, e.g., through posterior regularization (Ganchev et al., 2010), or be used for co-training (Blum and Mitchell, 1998).

7 Conclusions

We investigated several open questions regarding the use of cross-lingual word clusters for direct transfer named entity recognition. First, we looked at the scenario where no annotated resources are available in the target language. We showed that multi-source direct transfer and self-training with additional features, exclusive to the target language, both bring benefits in this setting, but that combining these methods provide an even larger advantage. We then examined the rate with which a supervised system, trained with cross-lingual and native word cluster features, approaches the performance of the direct transfer system. We found that on average between 8,000 and 16,000 word tokens need to be annotated in each target language to match our best direct transfer system. We also found that combining native and cross-lingual word clusters leads to improved results across the board. Finally, we showed that direct transfer methods can aid even in the supervised target language scenario. By simply mixing annotated source language data with target language data, we can significantly reduce the annotation burden required to reach a given level of performance in the target language, even with up to 64,000 tokens annotated in the target language. We hypothesize that more elaborate domain adaptation techniques, such as that proposed by Chen et al. (2011), can lead to further improvements in these scenarios.

Our use of cross-lingual word clusters is orthogonal to several other approaches discussed in this paper. We therefore suggest that such clusters could be of general use in multilingual learning of linguistic structure, in the same way that monolingual word clusters have been shown to be a robust way to bring improvements in many monolingual applications (Turian et al., 2010; Täckström et al., 2012).

Acknowledgments

This work benefited from discussions with Ryan McDonald and from comments by Joakim Nivre and three anonymous reviewers. The author is grateful for the financial support of the Swedish National Graduate School of Language Technology (GSLT).

References

Rie Kubota Ando and Tong Zhang. 2005. A high-performance semi-supervised learning method for text chunking. In *Proceedings of ACL*.

Bogdan Babych and Anthony Hartley. 2003. Improving machine translation quality with automatic named entity recognition. In *Proceedings of the EAMT workshop on Improving MT through other Language Technology Tools: Resources and Tools for Building MT*.

Taylor Berg-Kirkpatrick and Dan Klein. 2010. Phylogenetic grammar induction. In *Proceedings of ACL*.

Avrim Blum and Tom Mitchell. 1998. Combining labeled and unlabeled data with co-training. In *Proceedings of COLT*, COLT' 98, New York, NY, USA. ACM.

Minmin Chen, John Blitzer, and Kilian Q. Weinberger. 2011. Co-training for domain adaptation. In *Proceedings of NIPS*.

Shay B. Cohen, Dipanjan Das, and Noah A. Smith. 2011. Unsupervised structure prediction with non-parallel multilingual guidance. In *Proceedings of EMNLP*.

Silviu Cucerzan and David Yarowsky. 1999. Language independent named entity recognition combining morphological and contextual evidence. In *Proceedings of EMNLP-Very Large Corpora*.

Dipanjan Das and Slav Petrov. 2011. Unsupervised part-of-speech tagging with bilingual graph-based projections. In *Proceedings of ACL-HLT*.

Hal Daumé, III, Abhishek Kumar, and Avishek Saha. 2010. Frustratingly easy semi-supervised domain adaptation. In *Proceedings of the 2010 Workshop on Domain Adaptation for Natural Language Processing*.

Hal Daumé, III. 2007. Frustratingly easy domain adaptation. In *Proceedings of ACL*.

Paramveer Dhillon, Dean Foster, and Lyle Dean. 2011. Multi-view learning of word embeddings via cca. In *Proceedings of NIPS*.

Mona Diab and Philip Resnik. 2002. An unsupervised method for word sense tagging using parallel corpora. In *Proceedings of ACL*.

Dayne Freitag. 2004. Trained named entity recognition using distributional clusters. In *Proceedings of EMNLP*.

Kuzman Ganchev, João Graça, Jennifer Gillenwater, and Ben Taskar. 2010. Posterior regularization for structured latent variable models. *Journal of Machine Learning Research*.

Ralph Grishman and Beth Sundheim. 1996. Message understanding conference-6: a brief history. In *Proceedings of the 16th conference on Computational linguistics - Volume 1*.

Keith Hall, Ryan McDonald, Jason Katz-Brown, and Michael Ringgaard. 2011. Training dependency parsers by jointly optimizing multiple objectives. In *Proceedings of EMNLP*.

Rebecca Hwa, Philip Resnik, Amy Weinberg, Clara Cabezas, and Okan Kolak. 2005. Bootstrapping parsers via syntactic projection across parallel texts. *Natural Language Engineering*, 11(03):311–325.

Jochen L. Leidner, Gail Sinclair, and Bonnie Webber. 2003. Grounding spatial named entities for information extraction and question answering. In *Proceedings of HLT-NAACL-GEOREF*.

Dekang Lin and Xiaoyun Wu. 2009. Phrase clustering for discriminative learning. In *Proceedings of ACL-IJCNLP*, pages 1030–1038.

David McClosky, Eugene Charniak, and Mark Johnson. 2006. Effective self-training for parsing. In *Proceedings of NAACL-HLT*.

Ryan McDonald, Slav Petrov, and Keith Hall. 2011. Multi-source transfer of delexicalized dependency parsers. In *Proceedings of EMNLP*.

Roberta Merchant, Mary Ellen Okurowski, and Nancy Chinchor. 1996. The multilingual entity task (met) overview. In *Proceedings of a workshop on held at Vienna, Virginia: May 6-8, 1996*.

Scott Miller, Jethran Guinness, and Alex Zamanian. 2004. Name tagging with word clusters and discriminative training. In *Proceedings of HLT-NAACL*.

Joel Nothman, James R Curran, and Tara Murphy. 2008. Transforming wikipedia into named entity training data. In *Proceedings of the Australasian Language Technology Association Workshop 2008*, pages 124–132, Hobart, Australia, December.

Naoaki Okazaki. 2007. Crfsuite: a fast implementation of conditional random fields (crfs).

Lev Ratinov, Dan Roth, Doug Downey, and Mike Anderson. 2011. Local and global algorithms for disambiguation to wikipedia. In *Proceedings of ACL-HLT*.

Lawrence Saul and Fernando Pereira. 1997. Aggregate and mixed-order markov models for statistical language processing. In *Proceedings of EMNLP*, pages 81–89.

Satoshi Sekine and Chikashi Nobata. 2004. Definition, dictionaries and tagger for extended named entity hierarchy. In *Proceedings of LREC*.

Benjamin Snyder, Tahira Naseem, Jacob Eisenstein, and Regina Barzilay. 2009. Adding more languages improves unsupervised multilingual part-of-speech tagging: A bayesian non-parametric approach. In *Proceedings of NAACL*.

Jun Suzuki and Hideki Isozaki. 2008. Semi-supervised sequential labeling and segmentation using giga-word scale unlabeled data. In *Proceedings of ACL-HLT*.

Oscar Täckström, Ryan McDonald, and Jakob Uszkoreit. 2012. Cross-lingual word clusters for direct transfer of linguistic structure. In *Proceedings of NAACL-HLT*.

Erik F. Tjong Kim Sang and Fien De Meulder. 2003. Introduction to the conll-2003 shared task: Language-independent named entity recognition. In *Proceedings of CoNLL*.

Erik F. Tjong Kim Sang. 2002. Introduction to the conll-2002 shared task: Language-independent named entity recognition. In *Proceedings of CoNLL*.

Joseph Turian, Lev-Arie Ratinov, and Yoshua Bengio. 2010. Word representations: A simple and general method for semi-supervised learning. In *Proceedings of ACL*.

Jakob Uszkoreit and Thorsten Brants. 2008. Distributed word clustering for large scale class-based language modeling in machine translation. In *Proceedings of ACL-HLT*.

David Yarowsky, Grace Ngai, and Richard Wicentowski. 2001. Inducing multilingual text analysis tools via robust projection across aligned corpora. In *Proceedings of HLT*.

The PASCAL Challenge on Grammar Induction

Douwe Gelling and **Trevor Cohn**
Department of Computer Science
University of Sheffield, UK
{d.gelling,t.cohn}@sheffield.ac.uk

Phil Blunsom
Department of Computer Science
University of Oxford, UK
Phil.Blunsom@cs.ox.ac.uk

João Graça
L^2F Spoken Language Systems Laboratory
INESC ID Lisboa, Portugal
joao.graca@l2f.inesc-id.pt

Abstract

This paper presents the results of the PASCAL Challenge on Grammar Induction, a competition in which competitors sought to predict part-of-speech and dependency syntax from text. Although many previous competitions have featured dependency grammars or parts-of-speech, these were invariably framed as supervised learning and/or domain adaption. This is the first challenge to evaluate unsupervised induction systems, a sub-field of syntax which is rapidly becoming very popular. Our challenge made use of a 10 different treebanks annotated in a range of different linguistic formalisms and covering 9 languages. We provide an overview of the approaches taken by the participants, and evaluate their results on each dataset using a range of different evaluation metrics.

1 Introduction

Inducing grammatical structure from text has long been fundamental problem in Computational Linguistics and Natural Language Processing. In recent years interest has grown, spurred by advances in unsupervised statistical modelling and machine learning. The task has relevance to cognitive scientists and linguists attempting to gauge the learnability of natural language by human children, and also natural language processing researchers who seek syntactic representations for languages with few linguistic resources.

Grammar learning has been popular in previous challenges. For example the CoNLL shared tasks in 2006 and 2007 (Buchholz and Marsi, 2006; Nivre et al., 2007) involved supervised learning of dependency parsers across a wide range of different languages. Our challenge has many similarities to these, in that we focus on dependency grammars, however we seek to evaluate unsupervised algorithms only using syntactically annotated data for evaluation and not for training. Additionally we also consider the related task of part-of-speech (POS) induction, and the next logical challenge: the joint task of POS and dependency induction. Other related challenges can be found in the formal grammar community (e.g., the Omphalos[1] competition) in which competitors seek to learn synthetic languages. In contrast we seek to model natural language text, which entails many different challenges.

Research into unsupervised grammar and POS induction holds considerable promise, although current approaches are still a long way from solving the general problem. For example, the majority of recent research into dependency grammar induction has adopted the evaluation setting of Klein and Manning (2004) who learn grammars on strings of POS tags, rather than on words themselves. One aim of this challenge is to popularise the more difficult and ambitious task of inducing grammars directly from text, which can be viewed as integrating the POS and grammar induction tasks. A second aim is to foster grammar and POS induction research across a wider variety of languages, and improving the standard of evaluation.

We have collated data from existing treebanks in a variety of different languages, domains and linguistic formalisms. This gives a diverse range of

[1] See http://www.irisa.fr/Omphalos

data upon which to test induction algorithms, yielding a deeper insight into their strengths and shortcomings. One key problem in grammar induction research is how to evaluate the models' predictions given that often many different analyses are linguistically plausible, e.g., the choice of whether determiners or nouns should head noun phrases, or how to represent coordination. Simply comparing against a single gold standard often results in poor reported performance because the model has discovered a different analysis to that used when annotating the treebank. For this reason it has been popular to use lenient measures for comparing predicted trees to the treebank gold standard trees, such as undirected accuracy and the neutral edge distance (Schwartz et al., 2011). As well as evaluating using these popular metrics, we also propose a new method of evaluation which is also lenient in that it rewards different types of linguistically plausible output, but requires consistency in the output, something the previous methods cannot do.

The paper is organised as follows. Section 2 describes the tasks and our data format and section 3 outlines the different treebanks used for the challenge. The baselines, our own benchmark systems and the competitors entries are described in section 5. In section 6 we present and analyse the results for the three different tracks. Finally we conclude in section 7.

2 Task Definition

The three tracks of the WILS challenge are described below. First we describe the data format for the submissions common to the three tracks (POS induction, Dependency induction, and jointly inducing both), and then the three tracks are described along with the respective evaluation metrics.

2.1 Data format

All datasets were presented in a file format similar to that used in the CoNLL tasks, but with slight modifications. In particular the last two columns are removed, as no projective head or projective dependency relations were used, and an extra POS column was inserted at column 6 to accommodate the Universal POS tagset (Petrov et al., 2011). Each line in a file then either consists of 9 columns, separated by a tab character, or is an empty line. Empty lines separate sentences, and all other lines give the annotation for a single token in the sentence as follows:

1. ID: Token counter, gives the index of current word in the sentence. Indexing starts at 1.
2. FORM: Surface form of the token in the sentence.
3. LEMMA: Stemmed form of the word form if available.
4. CPOSTAG: Coarse-grained POS tag.
5. POSTAG: Fine-grained POS tag, or CPOSTAG again if not available.
6. UPOSTAG: Universal POS tag, based on the POSTAG and CPOSTAG.
7. FEATS: List of syntactic / morphological features, separated by a vertical pipe (|).
8. HEAD: Syntactic head of the token, with 0 indicating the root node.
9. DEPREL: The general type of the dependency relation, e.g., subject.

In this setup, the LEMMA, FEATS and DEPREL columns are optional, in which case an underscore (_) will be used as a placeholder. Each treebank was split into training, development and testing partitions. The HEAD and DEPREL entries were only supplied for the development and the final testing sets,[2] but not for the training partition. The competitors were encouraged to develop their unsupervised entries on the union of the three partitions, and make sparse use of the development set, i.e., for sanity checking more than model fitting in order to minimise the extent of supervision.

2.2 POS induction

In the POS induction track, participants developed systems to induce the Part-of-Speech (POS) classes for each word in the testing corpus. In order to train the systems, the same training and development sets were used as for the other tracks. These corpora included manually supplied POS tags for each token,

[2]For the initial test set these fields were omitted.

which were not to be used for training, only evaluation. Participants submitted predicted tags for each token, which were scored against the gold-standard.

For evaluation, we used 4 different metrics. The first is the many-to-one metric (M-1) (also known as cluster purity), which is widely used for cluster evaluation as well as evaluation of POS induction. This metric assigns each word cluster to its most common tag, and then measures the proportion of correctly tagged words. The second metric is the one-to-one mapping (1-1), a constrained version of Many-to-one mapping in which each predicted tag is associated with only one gold-standard tag and vice versa (Haghighi and Klein, 2006). Word clusters are assigned greedily to tags, and in the event of there being more word classes than tags, some word classes will be left unassigned. Another metric that was used is Variation of information (VI) (Meila, 2003), which is based the conditional entropy of between the two different clusterings (Johnson, 2007). Lastly, we use the V-measure (VM) metric (Rosenberg and Hirschberg, 2007), which is another entropy-based measure, but defined in terms of a F score to balance precision and recall terms (we use equal weighting of the two factors). Please see Christodoulopoulos et al. (2010) for further details about these metrics.[3] For these metrics, a higher score is better, with the exception of VI.

For all these metrics, the induced tags are evaluated against the universal pos tags, as this means there are a consistent number of tags across the languages. Using these metrics, the results will vary as a result of predicting a different number of tags (in particular, more tags will mean a higher score for M-1, and the converse is true for 1-1). However, using the universal POS tags, we think will make results less sensitive to large differences in POS inventory between languages (such as for the Dutch dataset).

2.3 Dependency induction

For the Dependency induction track, the training data consisted of the original treebank data, but without dependency annotations. A development set was also provided, which included the dependency annotations, but this was meant mainly as a way to verify systems, as we mean to minimise the amount of supervision in the task. The participants were later supplied with test sets for which the systems could generate predictions. Only after the predictions were submitted were the fully annotated test sets released.

The dependency inductions were evaluated on 3 metrics: directed accuracy, undirected accuracy and Neutral Edge Detection (NED) (Schwartz et al., 2011). Directed accuracy is the ratio of correctly predicted dependencies (including direction) over total amount of predicted dependencies. Undirected accuracy is much the same, but also considers a predicted dependency correct if the direction of the dependency is reversed (e.g. if the predicted dependency is not $A \rightarrow B$, but $B \rightarrow A$). Lastly, the NED metric is a variant of undirected accuracy that also rewards cases where an edge-flip occurs, meaning that the predicted parent of a token is actually the grandparent of that same token in the gold-standard data. Note that before evaluating with these metrics punctuation was removed from all sentences, and any child words under a punctuation node were reattached to their nearest ancestor that wasn't punctuation.

The final 'joint' task consisted of inducing dependency structure from only the tokens in the corpus, without recourse to the gold POS tags. Where POS is predicted (e.g., in a pipeline), we included these in our general POS evaluation. The induced dependency trees were evaluated with the same metrics as in the dependency induction track, but are considered separately. We expect these systems to have lower scores overall due to the lack of gold-standard POS tags.

3 Treebanks

We selected a number of different treebanks for use in the challenge, aiming to represent a wide range of different languages, dialects and genres of text. In total we used ten different treebanked corpora in nine different languages. For the practical reasons of simplifying the administration of the challenge and allowing the data to be reused in future research, we chose corpora with licences allowing either free redistribution, or those held by the Linguis-

[3]Thanks to Christos Christodoulopoulos for sharing his implementation of the POS induction metrics, which we have used in our evaluation.

tic Data Consortium (LDC).[4] Many of these datasets have been used before in dependency grammar or part-of-speech research, particularly the shared tasks at CoNLL 2006 and 2007. For the purpose of the competition, we have updated these datasets to include any annotation updates or additional data, where available. It is important for unsupervised approaches to have sufficient amounts of data, especially given the common sentence length limitations imposed by most dependency grammar models. As described in section 2, we have included an extra field for the universal part-of-speech (UPOS) using Petrov et al. (2011)'s automatic conversion tool.[5]

Below we describe the different treebanks used, and the conversion process into our data format for the purpose of the competition. Please see Table 1 for statistics on each of the treebanks.

Dependency treebanks We used the following dependency treebanks: **Arabic** The Prague Arabic Dependency Treebank V1 (Hajič et al., 2004).[6] **Basque** The Basque 3lb dependency treebank (Aduriz et al., 2003). **Czech** The Prague Dependency Treebank 2.0 (Böhmová et al., 2001).[7] **Danish** The Copenhagen Dependency Treebank version 2 (Buch-Kromann et al., 2007). **English** The CHILDES `US/Brown` subcorpus (Sagae et al., 2007). **Slovene** The jos500k Treebank (Erjavec et al., 2010). [8] **Swedish** The Talbanken treebank (Nivre et al., 2006). The conversion of each of these treebanks was quite straightforward as they were already annotated for dependencies. Moreover, many of these corpora had been used previously in the CoNLL 2006 and 2007 shared tasks, and therefore we were able to reuse this data and/or their conversion scripts. In the case of Arabic and Swedish we used the exact same data, simply converting from CoNLL dependency format into our own format (removing redundant columns and adding a UPOS column). While many of the other corpora had also been used previously, our data is different, making use of subsequent corrections to these treebanks and additional annotated data now available.

First language acquisition provides an important motivation for grammar induction research, consequently we have included data from the CHILDES database of child-directed speech. We use the Brown sub-corpus, a longitudinal study of parent-child interactions for three children aged between 18 months and 5 years old. The corpus has been manually annotated with syntactic dependencies (Sagae et al., 2007) and morphology. From this we take all child-directed utterances, extracting word, morphology, part-of-speech and dependency markup, and developed our own conversion into UPOS. Our testing and development sets were drawn from the first 15 Eve files which were manually annotated for dependency structure. The rest of the corpus, which had not been manually annotated for syntax, was merged to form the training set.

Phrase-structure treebanks As well as dependency treebanks, we used three different phrase-structure treebanks: The **Dutch** Alpino treebank (Bouma et al., 2000), the **English** Penn Treebank V3 (Marcus et al., 1993),[9] and the **Portuguese** Floresta Sintá(c)tica treebank (Afonso et al., 2002). As these treebanks do not explicitly mark dependencies, we automatically extracted these using head finding heuristics. Thankfully the difficult work of creating such scripts has already been done as part of the CoNLL shared tasks. We have reused their scripts to create dependency representations of these treebanks, before converting into our file format and augmenting with UPOS annotation. In the case of Dutch, we have reused the same CoNLL 2006 data; note that this dataset includes predicted part-of-speech rather than gold standard annotation (Buchholz and Marsi, 2006). For the Portuguese, we used the same Bosque 7.3 sub-corpus[10] from CoNLL 2006, additionally including in our training set the recently-annotated Selva 1.0 subcorpus.

The Penn Treebank is the most common data set in parsing and grammar induction. We have patched

[4]In the following corpus descriptions, when not otherwise specified the corpus is freely available for research purposes.

[5]`http://code.google.com/p/universal-pos-tags`

[6]LDC catalogue number LDC2004T23.

[7]LDC catalogue number LDC2006T01.

[8]For the shared task, the annotation was converted to english using the tables found at the JOS website: `http://nl.ijs.si/jos/msd/html-en/index.html`

[9]LDC catalogue number LDC99T42.

[10]An updated version of this corpus is available, however the file format had changed significantly and we were unable to adapt the conversion scripts in time for the competition.

	ar	cs	da	en-childes	en-ptb	eu	nl	pt	sl	sv
annotation	d	d	d	d	p	d	p	p	d	d
Training data										
Tokens	106.6k	1.2M	68.5k	312.8k	1.1M	124.7k	192.2k	196.4k	193k	184.6k
Sentences	2.8k	68.5k	3.6k	57.4k	45.4k	9.1k	13k	8.7k	9.4k	10.7k
Tokens/sent	38.4	17.1	18.8	5.5	23.9	13.7	14.8	22.6	20.5	17.3
CPOSTAG	15	12	25	31	31	16	13	16	13	41
POSTAG	21	61	141	76	45	50	300	22	31	41
FEATS	22	75	338	29	0	269	310	146	46	0
Development data										
Tokens	5.1k	159k	17k	25.3k	32.9k	12.6k	2.9k	10.3k	20.2k	6.9k
Sentences	139	9.3k	1k	5k	1.3k	1k	386	400	1k	389
Tokens/sent	36.8	17.1	17	5.1	24.4	12.5	7.4	25.8	20.2	17.6
% New words	27.5	26	49.8	9.8	11.4	46.1	18.8	27.5	38.7	13.8
Test data										
Tokens	5.1k	173.6k	14.7k	28.4k	56.7k	14.3k	5.6k	5.9k	22.6k	5.7k
Sentences	131	10.1k	1k	5.2k	2.4k	1.1k	386	288	1k	389
Tokens/sent	39.1	17.1	14.7	5.4	23.5	12.7	14.5	20.4	22.6	14.5
% New words	24.3	25.3	43.7	9	12.1	51.5	40.5	25.2	37.1	34.6

Table 1: Properties of the treebanks. We report the linguistic annotation method (dependency vs. phrase-structure), the size of each treebank, the number of types for the different granularities of part-of-speech tags and morphological features (note that UPOS has a fixed set of 12 tags), and the proportion of word types that were not present in training.

the treebank to include NP-internal structure using Vadas and Curran's annotations (Vadas and Curran, 2007), which was then converted to dependency structures using the `penn-converter`[11] script (Johansson and Nugues, 2007). This tool has a number of options controlling the linguistic decisions in converting from phrase-structure to dependency trees, e.g., the treatment of coordination. We extracted five versions of the treebank, each encoding each different sets of linguistic assumptions (Tsarfaty et al., 2011).[12] These are denoted default, old-LTH, CoNLL-2007, functional and lexical; for the main results we used the standard options, we also report separately evaluations using each of the five variants. The treebank was partitioned into training (sections 0-22), development (sec. 24) and testing sets (sec. 23).

4 Baselines and Benchmarks

A number of standard baselines and previously published benchmark systems were implemented for each task in order to place the submitted systems in context.

[11] `http://nlp.cs.lth.se/software/treebank_converter`

[12] Note that Tsarfaty et al. (2011) also propose an evaluation metric for comparing dependency trees, which we have not used. Note however that it could, in principle, be used for similar evaluations.

The standard baseline for grammar induction models is to assume either left branching or right branching analyses (`LB`, `RB`). These capture the tendency for languages to favour one attachment direction over another. The most frequently cited and extended model for dependency induction is DMV (Klein and Manning, 2004). We provide results for this model trained on each of the coarse ($\texttt{DMV}^c$), fine ($\texttt{DMV}^p$), and universal ($\texttt{DMV}^u$) POS tag sets, all initialised with the original harmonic initialiser. As a further baseline we also evaluated the dependency trees resulting from directly using the harmonic initialiser without any training (`H`).

As a strong benchmark we include the results of the non-parametric Bayesian model previously published in Blunsom and Cohn (2010) (`BC`). The stated results are for the unlexicalised model described in that paper where the final analysis is formed by choosing the maximum marginal probability dependency links estimated from forty independent Gibbs sampler runs.

For part-of-speech tagging we include results from an implementation of the Brown word clustering algorithm (Brown et al., 1992) ($\texttt{B}^{c,p,u}$), and the `mkcls` tool written by Franz Och (Och, 1999) ($\texttt{MK}^{c,p,u}$). Both of these benchmarks were trained with the number of classes matching the number in the gold standard of each of the tagsets in turn: coarse (`c`), fine (`p`), and universal (`u`). A notable property of both of these word class models is that they enforce a one-tag-per-type restriction that ensures there is a one-to-one mapping between word types and classes.

For POS tagging we also provide benchmark results from two previously published models. The first of these is the Pitman-Yor HMM model described in (Blunsom and Cohn, 2011), which incorporates ta one-tag-per-type restriction (BC). This model was trained with the same number of tags as in the gold standard fine tag set for each corpus. The second benchmark is the HMM with Sparsity Constraints trained using Posterior Regularization (PR) described in (Graça et al., 2011). In this model the HMM emission probabilitiy distribution are estimated using small Maximum Entropy models (features set described in the original paper). The models were trained for 200 iterations of PR using both the same number of hidden states as the coarse G^c and universal G^u gold standard. All parameters were set to the values described in the original paper.

5 Submissions

The shared task received submissions covering a diverse range of approaches to the dependency and part-of-speech induction challenges. Encouragingly all of these submissions made significant departures from the benchmark HMM and DMV approaches which have dominated the published literature on these tasks in recent years. The submissions were characterised by varied choices of model structure, parameterisation, regularisation, and the degree to which light supervision was provided through constraints or the use of labelled tuning data. In the following sections we summarise the approaches taken by the systems submitted for each task.

5.1 Part-of-Speech Induction

The part-of-speech induction challenge received two submission, (Chrupała, 2012; Christodoulopoulos et al., 2012). Both of these submissions based their induction systems on LDA inspired models for clustering word types by the contexts in which they appear. Notably, the strongest of the provided benchmarks and the two submissions modelled part-of-speech tags at the type level, thus restricting all tokens of a given word type to share the same tag. Though clearly out of step with the gold standard tagging, this one-tag-per-type restriction has previously been shown to be a crude but effective way of regularising models towards a good solution. Below we summarise the approach of each submission, identified by the surname of the first author on the submitted system description.

Chrupała (2012) employed a two stage approach to inducing part-of-speech tags. The first stage used an LDA style probabilistic model to induce a distribution over possible tags for a given word type. These distributions were then hierarchically clustered and the final tags selected using the prefix of the path from the root node to the word type in the cluster tree. The length of the prefixes, and thus the number of tags, was tuned on the labelled development data.

The system of Christodoulopoulos et al. (2012) was based upon an LDA type model which included both contexts and other conditionally independent features (Christodoulopoulos et al., 2011). This base system was then iterated with a DMV system and with the resultant dependencies being repeatedly fed back into the POS model as features. This submission is notable for being one of the first to attempt joint POS and dependency induction rather than taking a pipeline approach.

5.2 Dependency Induction

The dependency parsing task saw a variety of approaches with only a couple based on the previously dominant DMV system. Two forms of light supervision were popular, the first being the inclusion of pre-specified constraints or rules for allowable dependency links, and the second being the tuning of model parameters or selecting between competing models on the labelled development data. Obviously the merits of such supervision would depend on the desired application for the induced parser. The direct comparison of models which include a form of universal prior syntactic information with those that don't does permit interesting development linguistic questions to be explored in future.

Bisk and Hockenmaier (2012) chose to induce a restricted form of Combinatory Categorial Grammar (CCG), the parses of which were then mapped to dependency structures. Restrictions on head-child dependencies were encoded in the allowable categories for each POS tag and the heads of sentences. Key features of their approach were a maximum likelihood objective function and an iterative procedure for generating composite categories from simple ones. Such composite categories allow the parameterisation of larger units than just head-child dependencies, improving over the more limited conditioning of DMV.

Maraček and Žabokrtský (2012) introduced a number of novel features in their dependency induction submission. Wikipedia articles were used to quantify the reducibility of word types, the degree to which the word could be removed from a sentence and grammaticality maintained. This metric was then used, along with a model of child fertility and dependency distance, within a probabilistic model. Inference was performed by using a local Gibbs sampler to approximate the marginal distribution over head-child links.

Søgaard (2012) presented two model-free heuristic algorithms. The first was based on heuristically adding dependency edges based on rules such as adjacency, function words, and morphology. The resulting structure is then run through a PageRank algorithm and another heuristic is used to select a tree from the resulting ranked dependency edges. The second approach takes the universal rules of Naseem et al. (2010) but rather than estimating a probabilistic model with these rules, a rule based heuristic is used to select a parse rather. This second model-free approach in particular provides a strong baseline for probabilistic models built upon hand-specified dependency rules.

Tu (2012) described a system based on an extended DMV model. Their work focussed on the exploration of multiple forms of regularisation, including Dirichlet priors and posterior regularisation, to favour both sparse conditional distributions and low ambiguity in the induced parse charts. While many previous works have included sparse priors on the conditional head-child distributions the additional regularisation of the ambiguity over parse trees is a novel and interesting addition. The labelled development sets were employed to both select between models employing different regularisation, and to tune model parameters.

5.3 POS and Dependency Induction

There was only a single submission for the task of inducing dependencies without gold standard part-of-speech tags supplied. Christodoulopoulos et al. (2012) submitted the same joint tagging and DMV system used for the POS induction task to the dependency induction task. Results on the development data indicated that this iterated joint training had a significant benefit for the induced tags and a smaller benefit for the dependency structures induced.

6 Results

The main results for the three tasks are shown in Tables 2, 3, and 4, for the POS induction, dependency induction and joint tasks, respectively.[13] We now present a detailed analysis of each of the three tasks.

6.1 POS induction

The main evaluation results for the POS induction task are shown in Table 2, which compares the induced clusters against the gold universal tags (UPOS).[14] Given the diversity of scenarions used by each system (e.g. number of hidden states, tuning on development data) a direct comparison between the systems can only be illustrative. A first observation is that depending on the particular evaluation metric employed the ranking of the systems changes substantially, for instance the G^u system is the best using the 1-1 and VI metric but is the worst of the entries (excepting the baselines) when using the other two metrics. Focusing on the VM metric, which was shown empirically not to have low bias with respect to the word classes (Christodoulopoulos et al., 2010), the best entry is the BC system which has the best performance in 9 out of 10 entries followed by the CGS and the C system. Note that this ranking holds also for the comparison against fine POS tags, shown in Table 7.

An interesting aspect is that almost all systems beat the strong Brown (B) and mkcls (MK) baseline across the different metrics when we restrict our attention to the cases where the same number

[13] Additional tables of results are in the appendix, and further results are online at `http://wiki.cs.ox.ac.uk/InducingLinguisticStructure`.

[14] See also Table 7 for the comparison against the fine POS tags; we base our analysis on UPOS instead as this tag set has a fixed size irrespective of the treebank.

M-1												
testset	BC	CGS	C^c	C^p	G^c	G^u	B^c	B^p	B^u	MK^c	MK^p	MK^u
arabic	**83.80**	N/A	83.33	83.33	65.05	66.61	66.20	69.89	66.22	71.08	72.72	68.03
basque	80.85	79.54	**86.67**	**86.67**	77.37	73.88	74.73	77.49	73.32	74.80	78.63	71.40
czech	**83.10**	66.78	72.27	77.97	N/A	N/A	60.85	75.57	60.42	65.43	79.35	57.16
danish	81.44	77.76	84.13	**84.92**	68.16	53.78	72.12	79.77	47.09	72.26	82.59	53.07
dutch	80.75	70.13	74.04	76.11	63.37	57.64	57.99	84.17	57.31	68.18	**84.78**	63.04
en-childes	90.36	85.42	**91.50**	**91.50**	N/A	N/A	82.65	89.70	70.12	86.27	91.44	75.63
en-ptb	**86.73**	81.93	78.11	84.35	77.14	71.10	77.29	80.88	63.74	79.99	83.88	63.34
portuguese	81.69	77.38	80.38	**81.90**	75.54	74.35	70.07	74.25	67.60	70.79	72.90	68.08
slovene	70.81	65.31	75.53	**75.92**	67.94	59.96	61.58	68.93	58.32	58.43	65.69	50.36
swedish	78.61	**80.45**	79.60	79.60	69.91	58.79	71.69	71.69	57.55	76.45	76.45	57.30
averages	81.82	76.08	80.56	**82.23**	70.56	64.51	69.52	77.23	62.17	72.37	78.84	62.74

1-1												
testset	BC	CGS	C^c	C^p	G^c	G^u	B^c	B^p	B^u	MK^c	MK^p	MK^u
arabic	53.67	N/A	39.44	39.44	39.83	**55.52**	40.55	33.57	43.31	51.54	40.24	51.58
basque	36.10	36.03	47.15	47.15	47.09	**54.70**	32.61	20.53	40.62	34.80	27.28	37.65
czech	31.82	**49.30**	30.49	27.20	N/A	N/A	46.19	26.66	45.10	43.70	24.48	39.25
danish	42.54	42.77	31.67	31.04	39.95	**45.58**	36.04	17.74	39.19	43.89	22.18	44.23
dutch	42.79	56.15	43.10	39.62	**56.45**	45.37	48.18	21.36	43.12	55.99	21.32	54.09
en-childes	38.79	42.57	43.76	43.76	N/A	N/A	40.78	35.54	57.71	43.45	32.00	**59.18**
en-ptb	41.55	39.57	43.86	31.56	42.07	**51.70**	39.79	33.90	46.50	40.55	36.22	51.17
portuguese	**59.66**	47.45	35.90	35.50	46.50	56.08	51.15	42.68	51.58	44.28	35.38	46.31
slovene	39.02	**53.04**	33.18	32.50	50.90	48.50	46.83	40.16	42.28	40.34	39.32	40.58
swedish	42.38	32.44	26.45	26.45	34.99	**54.92**	27.56	27.56	51.34	35.82	35.82	43.60
averages	42.83	44.37	37.50	35.42	44.72	**51.55**	40.97	29.97	46.07	43.44	31.42	46.76

VM												
testset	BC	CGS	C^c	C^p	G^c	G^u	B^c	B^p	B^u	MK^c	MK^p	MK^u
arabic	**61.75**	N/A	51.27	51.27	44.81	47.07	39.93	42.43	39.92	47.47	43.91	44.49
basque	42.17	41.52	**43.04**	**43.04**	40.86	40.05	34.85	33.33	36.08	36.32	34.35	33.42
czech	**52.26**	45.31	40.22	39.20	N/A	N/A	38.56	42.90	37.46	41.70	46.03	37.34
danish	**56.57**	54.63	52.46	52.32	47.26	41.96	47.89	44.37	35.13	50.52	48.17	39.96
dutch	**56.96**	53.35	54.87	52.90	48.57	45.80	43.34	49.33	43.67	51.37	50.11	47.20
en-childes	**64.53**	62.32	62.76	62.76	N/A	N/A	58.87	60.31	57.06	62.76	60.92	60.51
en-ptb	**60.73**	57.99	53.14	52.09	55.10	52.54	54.76	55.08	48.04	56.81	57.29	48.46
portuguese	**64.17**	58.41	52.54	52.32	55.96	58.14	52.09	53.18	50.32	52.48	50.87	50.18
slovene	51.15	**51.29**	46.60	46.50	50.98	45.98	44.49	45.80	38.61	36.79	43.43	36.43
swedish	**57.05**	54.21	47.08	47.08	48.89	45.73	45.87	45.87	40.84	49.77	49.77	42.83
averages	**56.73**	53.23	50.40	49.95	49.05	47.16	46.06	47.26	42.71	48.60	48.48	44.08

VI												
testset	BC	CGS	C^c	C^p	G^c	G^u	B^c	B^p	B^u	MK^c	MK^p	MK^u
arabic	2.48	N/A	3.70	3.70	3.39	2.98	3.78	3.94	3.53	3.31	3.82	3.30
basque	3.82	3.44	3.98	3.98	3.25	**2.82**	3.92	4.98	3.45	3.79	4.76	3.58
czech	3.83	3.41	4.92	5.77	N/A	N/A	3.70	4.76	3.69	3.63	4.53	3.83
danish	3.36	**3.34**	4.31	4.38	3.78	3.46	3.86	5.43	3.79	3.64	4.90	3.59
dutch	3.56	**3.13**	3.28	3.71	3.30	3.44	3.66	5.22	3.60	3.26	5.15	3.39
en-childes	2.81	2.86	3.06	3.06	N/A	N/A	3.13	3.34	2.59	2.84	3.33	2.50
en-ptb	3.18	3.28	3.67	4.36	3.34	**3.03**	3.46	3.62	3.36	3.36	3.52	3.28
portuguese	**2.47**	2.83	3.96	4.09	2.96	2.62	3.19	3.36	3.10	3.21	3.52	3.15
slovene	3.62	**3.14**	4.80	4.86	3.16	3.30	3.61	4.09	3.73	4.15	4.33	3.99
swedish	**3.31**	3.68	4.98	4.98	3.90	3.32	4.46	4.46	3.70	4.07	4.07	3.62
averages	3.24	3.23	4.07	4.29	3.39	**3.12**	3.68	4.32	3.45	3.53	4.19	3.42

Table 2: Results for the POS induction task, showing one-to-one, many-to-one, VM and VI scores, measured against the gold UPOS tags. Each system is shown in a column, where the title is an acronym of the authors' last names, or else the name of a benchmark system (B is the Brown clusterer and MK is mkcls). The superscripts c, p and u denote different applications of the same method with a number of word classes set to equal the true number of coarse tags, full tags or universal tags, respectively, for each treebank.

of hidden states are used (the exception being the G system which occasionally under-performed against MK). Interestingly the assumption of one-tag-per-word, made by all but the G system, works very well in practice leading to consistently strong results. This suggests that dealing with word ambiguity is still an unresolved issue in unsupervised POS induction.

Comparing the performance of the systems for different languages, as expected the languages for which we have a larger corpora (English CHILDES and PTB and Czech) tend to result in systems with better accuracies. An interesting future question is how do the propose methods scale when training on really large corpora (e.g., wikipedia) both in terms of performance (accuracy) but also in the resources they required.

Finally, the wild divergences in the system rankings when considering the different evaluation metrics calls for some sort of external evaluation using the induced clusters as features to other end systems, for instance semi-supervised tagging. The main question is if there will be a definitive ranking between systems for a diverse set of tasks, or if on the contrary the effectiveness of the output of each system will vary according to the task at hand.

6.2 Dependency induction

The main evaluation results for the dependency task are shown in Table 3. From this we make several observations.[15] Firstly, for almost all the corpora the participants systems have outperformed the simple baselines, and by a significant margin. There are three exceptions to this: for Arabic, Basque and Danish the left or right-branching baselines outperforms most or all of the competitors. This may indicate that these languages are inherently difficult, or may simply be a consequence of these three languages having the least data of all of our corpora. Basque and Dutch proved to be the hardest of the treebanks, with the lowest overall scores, and the CHILDES (English) and Portuguese were the easiest. The reasons for this are not immediately clear, although we speculate that Basque is difficult due to its dissimilarity from other European languages, and therefore may not match the assumptions underlying models developed primarily on English. Dutch is difficult as its annotation was non-projective, and it has a very large set of POS tags, while CHILDES is made easier due to its extremely short and simple sentences.

In terms of declaring a 'winner', it is clear that Tu's system ranks best under directed accuracy and NED, and a very narrow second (to the organisers' submission, BC) for undirected accuracy. Moreover Tu's system was a consistent performed across all corpora, with no single result well below the results of the other participants. Note that the three different metrics often predict the same winner across the different treebanks, however there are some large discrepancies, such as Portuguese and Dutch where the directed and undirected accuracy metrics concur, but NED produces a very different ranking. It is unclear which metric should be trusted more than another; this could only be assessed by correlating these metrics with some form of secondary evaluation, such as in a task based setting or obtaining human grammaticality judgements.[16]

The benchmark systems include DMV (Klein and Manning, 2004), which has historical importance in terms of being the first research systems to outperform simple baselines for dependency induction, and also the model upon which most recent dependency induction research is based, including many of the competitors in the competition. We observe that in most cases the competitors have outperformed the DMV models, in many cases by a large margin. In all cases DMV improved over its initialisation condition (the harmonic initialiser), although often this improvement was only slight, underscoring the importance of good initialisation. The effect of inducing DMV grammars from various different granularity of POS tags made little difference in most cases, although for Dutch[17] and the English PTB there change was more dramatic.

[15]Table 3 evaluates against the full test sets, however it is traditional to present results for short sentences mirroring the common training setup. See Tables 8 and 9 for results over sentences with 10 words or fewer, excluding punctuation. Note that our analysis is based on the results for the full test set.

[16]It was our intention to include a task-based evaluation for machine translation, but this proved impractical for the competition due to the volumes of data that we would require each participant to process.

[17]Note that for Dutch the full POS tags were not gold standard, but were system predictions.

Directed														
testset	BC	BH	MZ^c	MZ^p	MZ^u	S^1	S^2	Tu	DMV^c	DMV^p	DMV^u	H	LB	RB
arabic	61.1	47.2	15.7	64.8	64.8	47.2	54.6	**66.7**	46.3	45.4	50.0	42.6	9.3	64.8
basque	56.3	50.3	28.0	30.3	27.2	33.3	22.3	**58.6**	46.3	43.2	31.3	21.8	34.3	24.4
czech	50.0	48.5	**61.3**	57.5	57.7	45.5	51.2	59.0	30.1	31.2	31.8	24.7	28.9	34.3
danish	46.2	49.3	60.2	51.3	**61.4**	56.9	60.5	60.8	47.2	50.2	35.3	36.4	18.7	49.2
dutch	50.5	50.8	37.0	49.5	38.4	38.9	50.0	**51.7**	48.7	39.7	49.1	35.1	34.0	39.5
en-childes	48.1	**62.2**	56.8	47.2	51.8	50.5	53.5	56.0	51.7	51.9	39.0	31.7	36.0	23.3
en-ptb	72.1	73.7	58.9	67.4	52.2	44.8	61.0	**74.7**	31.7	44.7	30.6	35.2	40.4	19.9
portuguese	54.3	**76.3**	63.6	59.9	44.3	47.7	71.1	55.7	27.1	37.2	26.9	31.1	28.1	37.7
slovene	65.8	53.9	42.1	51.4	39.2	39.7	50.3	**67.7**	35.7	37.2	35.6	25.7	35.9	14.7
swedish	65.8	66.7	61.4	63.7	70.8	48.2	72.0	**76.5**	44.2	44.2	45.8	39.1	33.2	31.3
averages	57.0	57.9	48.5	54.3	50.8	45.3	54.7	**62.7**	40.9	42.5	37.5	32.3	29.9	33.9
Undirected														
testset	BC	BH	MZ^c	MZ^p	MZ^u	S^1	S^2	Tu	DMV^c	DMV^p	DMV^u	H	LB	RB
arabic	57.3	29.7	57.6	62.0	58.7	48.0	58.4	59.3	41.8	42.0	43.7	41.2	61.7	**63.9**
basque	**58.0**	47.2	43.3	45.0	43.2	47.5	24.3	53.3	48.1	47.7	40.3	37.6	53.9	53.1
czech	59.0	45.0	57.8	54.3	55.5	49.3	55.8	**61.4**	46.2	46.7	45.3	38.5	51.5	52.3
danish	60.8	50.7	60.7	56.1	60.3	56.6	60.5	**61.6**	55.1	54.1	51.6	46.0	58.7	59.9
dutch	**61.0**	45.0	47.5	51.5	48.9	46.8	51.4	54.6	52.2	45.0	52.2	37.2	50.1	50.8
en-childes	63.5	**68.4**	67.2	59.9	61.4	62.0	62.4	66.9	63.8	64.0	57.5	49.0	50.0	49.9
en-ptb	**66.2**	58.1	49.7	57.6	48.2	49.5	58.8	62.1	43.1	53.1	43.0	36.2	51.7	51.5
portuguese	56.6	**72.4**	61.4	61.9	49.8	52.6	66.9	61.4	44.3	48.1	43.6	41.2	55.7	56.8
slovene	58.1	47.9	45.2	49.1	44.5	42.4	53.5	**61.8**	42.1	40.6	42.1	32.5	40.8	41.1
swedish	**70.0**	58.5	58.8	59.3	60.4	53.5	65.2	66.9	51.1	51.1	53.3	44.5	53.0	53.2
averages	**61.0**	52.3	54.9	55.7	53.1	50.8	55.7	60.9	48.8	49.2	47.3	40.4	52.7	53.2
NED														
testset	BC	BH	MZ^c	MZ^p	MZ^u	S^1	S^2	Tu	DMV^c	DMV^p	DMV^u	H	LB	RB
arabic	63.6	37.3	59.2	67.1	63.2	56.5	65.8	64.1	48.9	48.0	48.8	47.5	62.7	**69.0**
basque	**69.6**	55.8	51.5	55.6	53.4	58.8	38.0	65.8	57.6	57.1	51.5	49.3	67.2	59.1
czech	71.0	55.7	70.2	65.2	67.3	63.2	69.7	**71.6**	53.2	52.9	54.1	47.6	56.3	68.6
danish	72.0	63.1	72.9	69.5	73.5	65.9	71.8	**76.4**	64.8	63.5	58.9	53.5	61.6	71.5
dutch	71.6	58.6	68.6	**72.0**	69.7	60.6	63.8	66.9	63.5	54.5	63.5	46.9	55.1	67.0
en-childes	80.9	79.6	82.8	74.1	72.7	77.1	**83.2**	80.4	78.1	78.3	77.5	67.2	61.0	75.2
en-ptb	**75.2**	69.8	69.4	73.8	67.2	64.1	71.6	69.8	49.8	67.0	49.6	44.8	53.9	68.1
portuguese	67.5	79.8	75.6	75.7	71.7	66.9	78.2	**80.4**	62.1	66.6	61.3	51.8	57.3	75.4
slovene	64.4	60.7	56.9	58.9	57.1	55.9	66.7	**68.7**	49.2	47.3	49.2	38.9	43.8	56.6
swedish	**80.1**	70.9	73.2	73.8	72.7	66.7	77.0	77.1	64.0	64.0	62.0	56.0	56.5	71.0
averages	71.6	63.1	68.0	68.6	66.9	63.6	68.6	**72.1**	59.1	59.9	57.6	50.3	57.6	68.1

Table 3: Directed accuracy, undirected accuracy and NED results for the dependency task (using supplied POS). The first column (BC) is our benchmark system, the next seven are participants systems, and the remaining columns consist of the DMV benchmark and various simple baselines. The superscripts c, p and u denote which type of POS was used, and S^1 and S^2 denote two different submissions for Søgaard (2012).

Overall the full POS tagset lead to the best performance over the coarse and universal tags (considering undirected accuracy or NED), which is to be expected as there is considerably more syntactic information contained in the full POS. This must be balanced against the additional model complexity from expanding its parameter space, which may explain why the difference in performance differences are so small. The same pattern can also be seen in Maraček and Žabokrtský (2012)'s submission, whose system using full POS (M^p) outperformed their other variants.

6.3 Joint task

As we had only one submission for the joint problem of POS and dependency induction, there are few conclusions we can draw for this joint task (see Table 4 for the results, and Table 9 for the short sentence evaluation). Compared to the dependency induction task using gold standard POS, as shown in Table 3, the accuracy for the joint models are lower. Interestingly, the DMV model performs best when using the same number of word clusters as there are POS tags, mirroring the findings reported

directed				
testset	CGS	DMV^c	DMV^p	DMV^u
arabic	N/A	35.3	**44.4**	34.2
basque	24.5	27.5	25.1	**28.7**
czech	24.7	19.9	**33.2**	20.0
danish	21.4	23.3	**31.9**	10.0
dutch	15.1	20.6	**33.7**	20.5
en-childes	29.9	38.6	**42.2**	40.3
en-ptb	21.5	22.5	**23.3**	17.2
portuguese	19.7	**28.5**	28.0	17.1
slovene	**19.2**	13.9	11.5	14.4
swedish	23.6	**26.4**	**26.4**	20.5
averages	22.2	25.7	**30.0**	22.3

undirected				
testset	CGS	DMV^c	DMV^p	DMV^u
arabic	N/A	45.5	**52.5**	45.0
basque	43.5	46.4	**47.3**	47.0
czech	38.9	37.5	**50.9**	38.5
danish	51.4	**52.2**	48.8	37.3
dutch	40.3	41.9	**48.6**	40.8
en-childes	54.9	59.2	**60.8**	58.1
en-ptb	43.4	45.4	**48.8**	39.4
portuguese	45.5	51.8	**52.7**	39.8
slovene	32.8	33.3	**36.7**	32.8
swedish	45.6	**48.9**	**48.9**	40.3
averages	44.0	46.2	**49.6**	41.9

NED				
testset	CGS	DMV^c	DMV^p	DMV^u
arabic	N/A	53.4	**57.6**	53.3
basque	**55.9**	55.6	54.4	54.7
czech	51.2	49.3	**63.4**	51.5
danish	**61.7**	60.3	60.4	46.3
dutch	47.2	**57.5**	56.8	55.2
en-childes	**78.2**	77.7	78.1	76.5
en-ptb	53.9	60.2	**63.5**	47.5
portuguese	50.0	69.4	**70.8**	57.9
slovene	40.7	38.7	**47.5**	40.3
swedish	54.5	**65.4**	**65.4**	54.3
averages	54.8	58.8	**61.8**	53.8

Table 4: Directed, undirected and NED accuracy results for evaluating the predicted dependency structures in the joint task (i.e., not using supplied POS tags). The first column is the participant's system and the next three are DMV models trained on the Brown word clusters (see section 6.1).

above with gold standard tags. The best joint system was the DMV^p model, which only marginally under-performed the equivalent DMV model trained on gold POS. This is an encouraging finding, suggesting that word clusters are able to represent important POS distinctions to inform deeper syntactic processing.

6.4 Analysis

Until now we have adopted the standard metrics in dependency evaluation: namely directed head attachment accuracy, and its more lenient counterparts, undirected accuracy and NED. The latter metrics reward structures that almost match the gold standard tree, by way of rewarding child-parent edges that are predicted in the reverse direction, i.e., attaching the child as the parent (NED takes this further, by also rewarding the grandparent-child edge when this occurs). This allows some degree of flexibility when considering various contentious linguistic decisions such as whether a preposition should head a preposition phrase, or the head of the child noun-phrase. This added leniency comes at a price, as shown in Table 3 where the undirected accuracy and NED results are considerably higher than directed accuracy, and display less spread of values (look in particular at the random trees, Ra). Is is unclear that the predicted trees are truly predicting linguistically plausible structures, but instead that the differences are due largely to chance. Moreover, systems that predict linguistic phenomena inconsistently between sentences or across types of related phenomena are rewarded under these lenient metrics.

For these reasons we also consider a different, less permissive, evaluation method, using multiple references of the treebank where each is annotated with different styles of dependency. As described in section 2, we processed the Penn treebank five times with different options to the LTH conversion tool. This affected the treatment of coordination, preposition phrases, subordinate clauses, infinitival clauses etc. Next we compare the directed accuracy of the systems against these five different 'gold standard' references, which are displayed in Table 5, alongside the maximum score for each system. Note that most systems performed well against the standard, conll2007 and functional references but poorly against the lexical and oldLTH references.[18] Considering the latter two references, a different system would be selected as the highest performing, namely Bisk and Hockenmaier (2012) (BH) over Blunsom and Cohn (2010) (BC) which wins in the other cases.

[18]The common difference here is that the latter two references do not treat prepositions as heads of PPs.

This evaluation method rewards many different linguistically plausible structures, but in such a way that the predictions must be consistent between different sentences in the testing set, and in their treatment of related linguistic phenomena. One caveat is that this method can only be used when there are many references, although in many cases different outputs can be generated automatically, e.g., by adjusting head-finding heuristics in converting between phrase-structure to dependency trees.

The previous analysis has rated each system in terms of overall performance against treebank trees, however this doesn't necessarily mean that the predictions of the best ranked system will be the most useful ones in a task-based setting. Take the example of information extraction, in which a central problem is to identify the arguments (subject, object *etc*) of a given verb. This setting gives rise to some types of dependency edges being more valuable than others. We present comparative results for the Penn treebank in Table 6 showing the directed accuracy for different types of dependency relations. Observe that there is a wide spread of accuracies for predicting the head word of the sentence (ROOT), and similarly for verbs' subject and object arguments. These scores are similar to the scores for the local modifiers shown, such as NMOD which describe the arguments of a noun. This is surprising as noun edges tend to be much shorter than for the arguments to a verb, and thus should be easier to predict. Also interesting are the spread of results for the CC edges (these link a coordinating conjunction to its head), suggesting that the systems learn to represent coordination in very different ways to the method used in the reference.

Figure 1 illustrates the directed accuracy over different lengths of dependency edge. For all systems the accuracy diminishes with edge length, however some fall at a much faster rate. The two best systems (Tu, BC) have similar overall accuracy results, but it is clear that Tu does better on short edges while BC does better on longer ones. The same pattern was also observed when considering the average accuracy over all treebanks (not shown), although the systems' results were closer together.

system	ROOT	SBJ	OBJ	PRD	NMOD	COORD	CC
Tu	71.0	64.8	**53.7**	49.4	56.9	36.8	11.4
LB	17.8	40.1	15.3	18.0	41.9	27.7	9.7
BC	**74.9**	**65.7**	53.0	50.2	56.8	36.3	**71.4**
DMV^c	17.0	11.7	16.0	31.3	27.8	25.7	9.2
DMV^u	17.6	9.3	16.4	25.0	27.8	25.7	8.6
BH	67.5	55.3	44.9	45.6	**58.6**	27.6	62.7
M^u	29.3	42.4	38.8	51.8	34.5	30.5	33.0
R	12.9	9.4	16.1	21.1	12.1	15.7	2.7
M^c	60.7	47.4	39.9	45.8	36.5	33.9	44.3
RB	17.9	12.4	26.2	36.5	15.3	25.4	1.1
H	19.4	29.3	12.2	22.2	17.3	20.9	10.3
DMV^p	54.7	42.0	30.7	30.1	28.9	25.4	24.3
S^2	45.2	41.9	44.2	49.8	39.7	25.4	63.8
M^p	67.8	54.3	49.6	**59.4**	47.7	**37.7**	49.7
S^1	43.1	47.9	36.3	46.7	27.9	23.5	7.6

Table 6: Directed accuracy results on the Penn treebank, stratified by dependency relation. For clarity, only 9 important relation types are shown. The vertical bars separate different groups of relations, from left to right, relating to the main verb, general modifiers and coordination.

7 Conclusion

This challenge set out to evaluate the state-of-the-art in part-of-speech and dependency grammar induction, promoting research in this field and, importantly, providing a fair means of evaluation. The participants submissions used a wide variety of different approaches, many of which we shown to have improved over competitive benchmark systems. While the results were overall very positive, it is fair to say that the tasks of part-of-speech and grammar induction are still very much open challenges, and that there is still considerable room for improvement. The data submitted to this evaluation campaign will provide a great resource for devising new methods of evaluation, and we plan to pursue this avenue in future work, in particular task-based evaluation such as in an information extraction or machine translation setting.

8 Acknowledgements

This challenge was funded by the PASCAL 2 (Pattern Analysis, Statistical Modelling and Computational Intelligence) European Network of Excellence. We would also like to thank the treebank providers for allowing us to use their resources, assisting us in converting these into our desired format, and helping to resolve various questions. In particular, special thanks to Zdenek Zabokrtsky and Jan (Czech and Arabic), Tomaz Erjavec (Slovene), and Eckhard Bick and Diana Santos (Portuguese). We are also indebted to the organisers of the previ-

testset	BC	BH	MZ^c	MZ^p	MZ^u	S^1	S^2	Tu	DMV^c	DMV^p	DMV^u	H	LB	RB
conll2007	**54.9**	51.7	40.4	49.2	36.8	32.2	41.7	54.2	20.9	33.2	20.4	18.0	30.1	20.3
functional	**59.6**	52.4	41.5	47.4	36.2	30.6	40.0	58.5	20.9	37.2	20.6	19.3	29.2	23.7
lexical	40.6	**41.9**	28.5	37.3	24.8	27.7	35.5	39.5	23.5	23.1	23.0	14.4	33.1	10.1
oldLTH	41.4	**43.6**	28.8	37.8	24.6	28.6	36.1	39.5	22.3	23.7	21.8	14.3	32.0	10.7
standard	**56.0**	50.4	41.0	50.3	37.5	32.8	42.5	55.5	22.3	33.5	21.8	18.4	31.4	20.4
best	**59.6**	52.4	41.5	50.3	37.5	32.8	42.5	58.5	23.5	37.2	23.0	19.3	33.1	23.7

Table 5: Directed accuracy results measured against different conversions of the Penn Treebank into dependency trees.

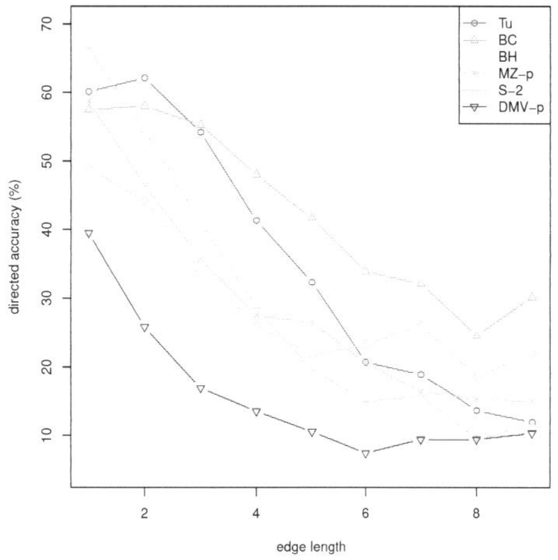

Figure 1: Directed accuracy on the Penn treebank stratified by dependency length. For clarity only a subset of the systems are shown, and edges of length 10 or more were omitted.

ous CoNLL 2006 and 2007 competitions, who contributed significant efforts into collating so many treebanks and developing treebank conversion tools, making our job much easier than it would otherwise have been. Thanks to Sebastian Reidel, Joakim Nivre and Sabine Buchholz for promptly answering our questions. We would like to thank the LDC, who allowed their licenced data to be used free of charge by the competitors, and Ilya Ahtaridis who administered the licencing and corpus distribution. Thanks also to Valentin Spitkovski and Christos Christodoulopoulos who kindly provided us with their evaluation scripts, and finally, the participants themselves for taking part.

References

I. Aduriz, M. J. Aranzabe, J. M. Arriola, A. Atutxa, A. Diaz de Ilarraza, A. Garmendia, and M. Oronoz. 2003. Construction of a Basque dependency treebank. In *Proceedings of the 2nd Workshop on Treebanks and Linguistic Theories (TLT)*.

Susana Afonso, Eckhard Bick, Renato Haber, and Diana Santos. 2002. Floresta sintá(c)tica: a treebank for Portuguese. In *Proceedings of the Third International Conference on Language Resources and Evaluation (LREC 2002)*, pages 1698–1703, May.

Yonatan Bisk and Julia Hockenmaier. 2012. Induction of linguistic structure with combinatory categorial grammars. In *Proceedings of the NAACL-HLT 2012 Workshop on Inducing Linguistic Structure Shared Task*, June.

Phil Blunsom and Trevor Cohn. 2010. Unsupervised induction of tree substitution grammars for dependency parsing. In *Proceedings of the 2010 Conference on Empirical Methods on Natural Language Processing (EMNLP)*, pages 1204–1213, Cambridge, MA, USA.

Phil Blunsom and Trevor Cohn. 2011. A hierarchical Pitman-Yor process HMM for unsupervised part of speech induction. In *Proceedings of the 49th Annual Meeting of the Association for Computational Linguistics: Human Language Technologies*, pages 865–874, Portland, Oregon, USA, June.

Alena Böhmová, Jan Hajič, Eva Hajičová, and Barbora Hladká. 2001. The Prague Dependency Treebank: A Three-Level Annotation Scenario. In Anne Abeillé, editor, *Treebanks: Building and Using Syntactically Annotated Corpora*, pages 103–127. Kluwer Academic Publishers.

Gosse Bouma, Gertjan van Noord, and Robert Malouf. 2000. Alpino: Wide coverage computational analysis of Dutch. In *Proceedings of Computational Linguistics in the Netherlands (CLIN 2000)*, pages 45–59.

Peter F. Brown, Peter V. deSouza, Robert L. Mercer, Vincent J. Della Pietra, and Jenifer C. Lai. 1992. Class-based n-gram models of natural language. *Comput. Linguist.*, 18:467–479, December.

Matthias Buch-Kromann, Jürgen Wedekind, and Jakob Elming. 2007. The Copenhagen Danish-English dependency treebank. `http://code.google.com/p/copenhagen-dependency-treebank`.

Sabine Buchholz and Erwin Marsi. 2006. CoNLL-X shared task on multilingual dependency parsing. In

Proceedings of the Tenth Conference on Computational Natural Language Learning (CoNLL-X), pages 149–164.

Christos Christodoulopoulos, Sharon Goldwater, and Mark Steedman. 2010. Two decades of unsupervised POS induction: how far have we come? In *Proceedings of the 2010 Conference on Empirical Methods in Natural Language Processing*, EMNLP '10, pages 575–584.

Christos Christodoulopoulos, Sharon Goldwater, and Mark Steedman. 2011. A Bayesian mixture model for PoS induction using multiple features. In *Proceedings of the 2011 Conference on Empirical Methods in Natural Language Processing*, pages 638–647, Edinburgh, Scotland, UK., July.

Christos Christodoulopoulos, Sharon Goldwater, and Mark Steedman. 2012. Turning the pipeline into a loop: Iterated unsupervised dependency parsing and pos induction. In *Proceedings of the NAACL-HLT 2012 Workshop on Inducing Linguistic Structure Shared Task*, June.

Grzegorz Chrupała. 2012. Hierarchical clustering of word class distributions. In *Proceedings of the NAACL-HLT 2012 Workshop on Inducing Linguistic Structure Shared Task*, June.

Tomaž Erjavec, Darja Fišer, Simon Krek, and Nina Ledinek. 2010. The JOS linguistically tagged corpus of Slovene. In *Proceedings of the Seventh International Conference on Language Resources and Evaluation (LREC'10)*.

João Graça, Kuzman Ganchev, Luísa Coheur, Fernando Pereira, and Benjamin Taskar. 2011. Controlling complexity in part-of-speech induction. *J. Artif. Intell. Res. (JAIR)*, 41:527–551.

Aria Haghighi and Dan Klein. 2006. Prototype-driven learning for sequence models. In *Proceedings of the main conference on Human Language Technology Conference of the North American Chapter of the Association of Computational Linguistics (HLT-NAACL '06)*, pages 320–327.

Jan Hajič, Otakar Smrž, Petr Zemánek, Jan Šnaidauf, and Emanuel Beška. 2004. Prague Arabic dependency treebank: Development in data and tools. In *Proceedings of the NEMLAR International Conference on Arabic Language Resources and Tools*, pages 110–117.

Richard Johansson and Pierre Nugues. 2007. Extended constituent-to-dependency conversion for English. In *Proceedings of the 16th Nordic Conference of Computational Linguistics (NODALIDA 2007)*.

Mark Johnson. 2007. Why doesn't EM find good hmm pos-taggers. In *Proceedings of the 2007 Joint Conference on Empirical Methods in Natural Language Processing and Computational Natural Language Learning*, EMNLP-CoNLL '07, pages 296–305.

Dan Klein and Christopher D. Manning. 2004. Corpus-based induction of syntactic structure: models of dependency and constituency. In *ACL '04: Proceedings of the 42nd Annual Meeting on Association for Computational Linguistics*, page 478.

David Maraček and Zdeněk Žabokrtský. 2012. Unsupervised dependency parsing using reducibility and fertility features. In *Proceedings of the NAACL-HLT 2012 Workshop on Inducing Linguistic Structure Shared Task*, June.

Mitchell P Marcus, Mary Ann Marcinkiewicz, and Beatrice Santorini. 1993. Building a large annotated corpus of English: the Penn treebank. *Computational Linguistics*, 19(2):313–330.

Marina Meila. 2003. Comparing Clusterings by the Variation of Information. *Learning Theory and Kernel Machines*, pages 173–187.

Tahira Naseem, Harr Chen, Regina Barzilay, and Mark Johnson. 2010. Using universal linguistic knowledge to guide grammar induction. In *Proceedings of the 2010 Conference on Empirical Methods in Natural Language Processing*, pages 1234–1244, October.

Joakim Nivre, Jens Nilsson, and Johan Hall. 2006. Talbanken05: A Swedish treebank with phrase structure and dependency annotation. In *Proceedings of the fifth international conference on Language Resources and Evaluation (LREC2006)*.

Joakim Nivre, Johan Hall, Sandra Kübler, Ryan McDonald, Jens Nilsson, Sebastian Riedel, and Deniz Yuret. 2007. The CoNLL 2007 shared task on dependency parsing. In *Proceedings of the CoNLL Shared Task Session of EMNLP-CoNLL 2007*, pages 915–932, June.

Franz Josef Och. 1999. An efficient method for determining bilingual word classes. In *Proceedings of the ninth conference on European chapter of the Association for Computational Linguistics*, pages 71–76.

Slav Petrov, Dipanjan Das, and Ryan T. McDonald. 2011. A universal part-of-speech tagset. *CoRR*, abs/1104.2086.

Andrew Rosenberg and Julia Hirschberg. 2007. V-measure: A conditional entropy-based external cluster evaluation measure. In *Proceedings of the 2007 Joint Conference on Empirical Methods in Natural Language Processing and Computational Natural Language Learning (EMNLP-CoNLL)*, pages 410–420.

K. Sagae, E. Davis, A. Lavie, B. MacWhinney, and S. Wintner. 2007. High-accuracy annotation and parsing of CHILDES transcripts. In *Proceedings of the ACL-2007 Workshop on Cognitive Aspects of Computational Language Acquisition.*, June.

Roy Schwartz, Omri Abend, Roi Reichart, and Ari Rappoport. 2011. Neutralizing linguistically problematic annotations in unsupervised dependency parsing evaluation. In *Proceedings of the 49th Annual Meeting of the Association for Computational Linguistics: Human Language Technologies*, pages 663–672.

Anders Søgaard. 2012. Two baselines for unsupervised dependency parsing. In *Proceedings of the NAACL-HLT 2012 Workshop on Inducing Linguistic Structure Shared Task*, June.

Reut Tsarfaty, Joakim Nivre, and Evelina Andersson. 2011. Evaluating dependency parsing: Robust and heuristics-free cross-annotation evaluation. In *Proceedings of the 2011 Conference on Empirical Methods in Natural Language Processing*, pages 385–396, Edinburgh, UK, July.

Kewei Tu. 2012. Combining the sparsity and unambiguity biases for grammar induction. In *Proceedings of the NAACL-HLT 2012 Workshop on Inducing Linguistic Structure Shared Task*, June.

David Vadas and James R. Curran. 2007. Adding noun phrase structure to the Penn Treebank. In *Proceedings of the 45th Annual Meeting of the Association for Computational Linguistics (ACL-07)*, pages 240–247, June.

Appendix

Directed				
testset	CGS	DMV^c	DMV^p	DMV^u
arabic	36.1	42.6	**51.9**	49.1
basque	28.4	28.9	27.1	**30.2**
czech	33.1	28.6	**38.2**	28.3
danish	27.9	36.4	**38.4**	18.2
dutch	31.0	39.0	**41.1**	40.3
en-childes	31.2	40.8	**44.3**	42.1
en-ptb	22.7	**25.1**	23.1	23.1
portuguese	26.7	**38.4**	34.5	31.1
slovene	**26.3**	20.6	19.2	22.6
swedish	29.0	**30.9**	**30.9**	26.5
averages	29.3	33.1	**34.9**	31.1
Undirected				
testset	CGS	DMV^c	DMV^p	DMV^u
arabic	58.3	52.8	58.3	**61.1**
basque	49.3	49.2	**50.5**	50.0
czech	48.7	45.9	**57.2**	47.9
danish	56.3	**60.9**	57.0	43.7
dutch	47.0	53.6	**57.2**	53.8
en-childes	56.3	61.0	**62.7**	59.9
en-ptb	50.7	52.9	**54.1**	46.9
portuguese	51.8	**61.1**	59.4	51.6
slovene	40.5	41.9	**45.3**	41.2
swedish	52.5	**57.1**	**57.1**	48.6
averages	51.1	53.6	**55.9**	50.5
NED				
testset	CGS	DMV^c	DMV^p	DMV^u
arabic	62.0	63.0	66.7	**67.6**
basque	**67.4**	62.8	62.5	62.3
czech	65.1	60.7	**72.0**	64.0
danish	72.0	72.4	**73.2**	60.3
dutch	57.7	64.9	**65.0**	64.7
en-childes	**79.9**	79.6	79.9	78.4
en-ptb	67.9	73.4	**74.3**	63.7
portuguese	58.2	**80.7**	79.5	72.6
slovene	55.7	52.3	**59.4**	51.9
swedish	64.8	**78.4**	**78.4**	65.7
averages	65.1	68.8	**71.1**	65.1

Table 9: Evaluation of the joint task on the dependency output using a maximum sentence length of 10.

M-1												
testset	BC	CGS	C^c	C^p	G^c	G^u	B^c	B^p	B^u	MK^c	MK^p	MK^u
arabic	75.06	N/A	**79.00**	**79.00**	62.20	62.24	61.81	64.60	61.55	65.69	67.82	63.23
basque	71.58	69.20	**75.23**	**75.23**	65.97	56.37	64.37	68.58	62.17	63.59	68.22	60.49
czech	74.84	61.53	66.97	**76.00**	N/A	N/A	55.60	72.51	55.01	60.38	73.38	51.96
danish	56.48	55.41	70.28	**71.62**	49.24	35.32	50.21	66.50	33.57	49.40	61.60	35.02
dutch	80.72	70.13	74.04	76.08	63.37	57.64	57.99	83.76	57.31	68.18	**84.64**	63.04
en-childes	84.23	77.57	85.35	85.35	N/A	N/A	76.34	85.11	59.75	77.55	**86.39**	59.55
en-ptb	**78.26**	72.26	62.86	73.46	63.15	56.32	65.10	68.10	48.76	70.31	73.96	47.91
portuguese	76.00	72.05	75.47	**77.13**	68.40	65.86	65.52	69.61	61.84	64.63	66.81	62.95
slovene	67.29	59.78	72.18	**72.71**	63.95	55.23	54.85	63.68	52.15	54.08	59.31	45.40
swedish	66.20	67.86	**73.55**	**73.55**	60.10	48.43	61.21	61.21	47.51	64.39	64.39	46.04
averages	73.07	67.31	73.49	**76.01**	62.05	54.68	61.30	70.37	53.96	63.82	70.65	53.56

1-1												
testset	BC	CGS	C^c	C^p	G^c	G^u	B^c	B^p	B^u	MK^c	MK^p	MK^u
arabic	50.90	N/A	39.15	39.15	41.49	**53.92**	39.89	34.23	40.63	50.53	41.98	50.27
basque	42.45	46.25	**52.38**	**52.38**	48.91	45.55	41.29	33.49	50.80	43.27	35.73	43.43
czech	31.45	**48.24**	32.18	31.74	N/A	N/A	43.12	33.55	41.94	38.93	28.33	35.31
danish	43.08	**43.64**	32.17	31.77	40.56	34.83	33.48	30.87	26.33	38.92	30.59	32.95
dutch	43.22	55.85	43.26	39.98	**56.45**	45.37	48.13	21.88	43.10	55.86	22.42	54.04
en-childes	64.10	63.62	**64.50**	**64.50**	N/A	N/A	59.96	56.87	59.75	63.43	53.40	57.68
en-ptb	**57.63**	56.02	45.52	41.35	48.95	53.15	55.43	49.60	47.57	54.10	51.80	45.43
portuguese	59.71	50.18	36.13	35.38	54.42	**60.08**	49.57	45.00	48.25	46.57	38.37	45.10
slovene	42.62	50.66	33.23	32.59	**56.55**	50.30	44.97	44.34	40.62	41.24	40.01	38.93
swedish	**48.76**	40.54	34.07	34.07	38.21	46.32	36.12	36.12	44.57	41.90	41.90	38.05
averages	48.39	**50.55**	41.26	40.29	48.19	48.69	45.20	38.59	44.36	47.48	38.45	44.12

VM												
testset	BC	CGS	C^c	C^p	G^c	G^u	B^c	B^p	B^u	MK^c	MK^p	MK^u
arabic	**61.59**	N/A	52.95	52.95	46.99	47.18	40.75	43.16	40.40	47.95	45.09	45.14
basque	53.83	51.34	**54.45**	**54.45**	49.34	44.26	44.18	45.46	45.37	45.02	44.90	42.76
czech	**56.80**	50.22	45.06	46.76	N/A	N/A	42.50	49.93	41.51	45.15	51.38	39.62
danish	61.57	59.00	63.39	**63.62**	53.35	43.20	51.83	58.38	33.46	52.52	58.44	39.46
dutch	**57.82**	53.94	55.01	53.40	48.99	46.26	44.08	50.49	44.37	52.02	51.33	47.99
en-childes	**80.17**	76.59	78.18	78.18	N/A	N/A	73.67	76.47	65.44	76.14	76.87	68.25
en-ptb	**71.44**	68.12	59.90	61.31	63.90	60.04	63.79	63.64	52.96	66.40	66.50	54.33
portuguese	**67.49**	60.37	54.61	54.74	58.91	59.58	53.30	54.99	50.26	53.15	52.67	50.76
slovene	**54.80**	52.13	51.85	51.88	52.99	48.55	45.33	48.33	40.13	39.25	45.73	38.68
swedish	**61.52**	58.23	56.09	56.09	55.02	48.69	51.76	51.76	43.39	54.28	54.28	44.51
averages	**62.70**	58.88	57.15	57.34	53.69	49.72	51.12	54.26	45.73	53.19	54.72	47.15

VI												
testset	BC	CGS	C^c	C^p	G^c	G^u	B^c	B^p	B^u	MK^c	MK^p	MK^u
arabic	2.65	N/A	3.76	3.76	3.47	3.19	3.96	4.12	3.73	3.49	3.96	3.48
basque	3.65	3.50	3.78	3.78	3.45	**3.36**	4.09	4.79	3.67	4.00	4.72	3.83
czech	3.80	3.49	4.96	5.48	N/A	N/A	3.92	4.57	3.91	3.85	4.46	4.17
danish	**3.76**	3.85	4.07	4.08	4.29	4.53	4.54	4.91	5.24	4.45	4.78	4.85
dutch	3.53	**3.14**	3.31	3.72	3.33	3.47	3.68	5.16	3.61	3.26	5.07	3.39
en-childes	1.86	2.12	2.11	2.11	N/A	N/A	2.39	2.32	2.59	2.17	2.31	2.47
en-ptb	**2.69**	2.90	3.67	4.03	3.16	3.08	3.24	3.41	3.66	3.05	3.19	3.50
portuguese	**2.40**	2.90	4.01	4.11	2.97	2.74	3.35	3.46	3.35	3.40	3.63	3.37
slovene	3.65	3.40	4.65	4.68	**3.34**	3.48	3.92	4.23	4.03	4.38	4.51	4.25
swedish	**3.36**	3.78	4.57	4.57	3.89	3.65	4.45	4.45	4.11	4.17	4.17	4.07
averages	**3.13**	3.23	3.89	4.03	3.49	3.44	3.75	4.14	3.79	3.62	4.08	3.74

Table 7: One to one, Many to one, VM and VI scores of POS induction results evaluated against fine POS tags (c.f., Table 2 which used UPOS).

Directed														
testset	BC	BH	MZ^c	MZ^p	MZ^u	S^1	S^2	Tu	DMV^c	DMV^p	DMV^u	H	LB	RB
arabic	61.1	47.2	15.7	64.8	64.8	47.2	54.6	**66.7**	46.3	45.4	50.0	42.6	9.3	64.8
basque	56.3	50.3	28.0	30.3	27.2	33.3	22.3	**58.6**	46.3	43.2	31.3	21.8	34.3	24.4
czech	50.0	48.5	**61.3**	57.5	57.7	45.5	51.2	59.0	30.1	31.2	31.8	24.7	28.9	34.3
danish	46.2	49.3	60.2	51.3	**61.4**	56.9	60.5	60.8	47.2	50.2	35.3	36.4	18.7	49.2
dutch	50.5	50.8	37.0	49.5	38.4	38.9	50.0	**51.7**	48.7	39.7	49.1	35.1	34.0	39.5
en-childes	48.1	**62.2**	56.8	47.2	51.8	50.5	53.5	56.0	51.7	51.9	39.0	31.7	36.0	23.3
en-ptb	72.1	73.7	58.9	67.4	52.2	44.8	61.0	**74.7**	31.7	44.7	30.6	35.2	40.4	19.9
portuguese	54.3	**76.3**	63.6	59.9	44.3	47.7	71.1	55.7	27.1	37.2	26.9	31.1	28.1	37.7
slovene	65.8	53.9	42.1	51.4	39.2	39.7	50.3	**67.7**	35.7	37.2	35.6	25.7	35.9	14.7
swedish	65.8	66.7	61.4	63.7	70.8	48.2	72.0	**76.5**	44.2	44.2	45.8	39.1	33.2	31.3
averages	57.0	57.9	48.5	54.3	50.8	45.3	54.7	**62.7**	40.9	42.5	37.5	32.3	29.9	33.9

Undirected														
testset	BC	BH	MZ^c	MZ^p	MZ^u	S^1	S^2	Tu	DMV^c	DMV^p	DMV^u	H	LB	RB
arabic	**69.4**	59.3	59.3	**69.4**	**69.4**	59.3	65.7	67.6	52.8	53.7	55.6	54.6	61.1	**69.4**
basque	65.6	59.5	49.8	50.1	48.4	54.3	32.8	**66.4**	60.1	58.1	48.5	42.2	56.4	53.9
czech	65.9	59.9	69.2	66.6	67.6	62.3	63.5	**70.1**	51.6	51.2	50.5	47.2	54.2	56.9
danish	67.9	63.5	70.6	64.4	**71.1**	67.9	70.7	70.2	65.0	64.3	60.0	56.4	59.7	63.9
dutch	63.2	59.9	57.5	**63.3**	58.0	58.5	58.5	60.5	62.7	56.7	62.9	51.1	56.3	60.7
en-childes	65.3	**70.6**	69.4	62.4	63.7	64.3	63.6	69.1	65.7	66.1	59.5	51.2	51.2	51.0
en-ptb	**79.4**	79.2	65.9	72.5	62.4	62.5	75.1	78.8	53.8	65.3	53.2	52.0	58.8	54.9
portuguese	66.3	**81.9**	71.6	70.2	62.3	65.8	78.5	72.1	54.0	60.9	54.3	53.3	56.7	63.8
slovene	70.6	63.7	56.3	59.1	55.1	54.8	63.7	**72.0**	46.4	53.1	46.3	44.9	45.5	46.0
swedish	82.3	73.5	70.1	71.1	75.4	66.5	77.3	**83.7**	64.5	64.5	66.1	59.2	59.2	59.5
averages	69.6	67.1	64.0	64.9	63.3	61.6	64.9	**71.0**	57.7	59.4	55.7	51.2	55.9	58.0

NED														
testset	BC	BH	MZ^c	MZ^p	MZ^u	S^1	S^2	Tu	DMV^c	DMV^p	DMV^u	H	LB	RB
arabic	**78.7**	68.5	66.7	75.9	75.9	68.5	72.2	71.3	61.1	63.0	63.0	63.0	64.8	75.9
basque	77.9	68.6	62.9	65.2	64.2	70.1	55.0	**79.5**	69.3	69.0	63.8	58.2	73.2	64.0
czech	79.9	72.6	**81.8**	78.6	79.9	76.0	78.1	81.2	62.9	61.7	63.6	60.3	63.2	73.8
danish	81.7	76.3	83.2	78.4	84.3	77.3	84.4	**85.0**	77.9	75.8	69.5	67.8	66.2	77.5
dutch	71.0	71.8	77.1	**78.4**	76.8	72.6	68.5	71.0	73.2	64.6	73.0	60.5	64.4	71.0
en-childes	82.4	81.6	84.5	76.7	74.8	79.0	**84.9**	82.5	79.9	80.4	79.9	70.1	63.2	76.9
en-ptb	86.7	**89.4**	87.5	88.4	84.0	78.7	87.1	84.3	64.0	80.7	64.2	64.3	65.2	75.0
portuguese	78.2	90.7	87.8	87.8	87.5	82.9	**91.9**	90.2	75.6	81.7	76.5	67.7	60.9	82.4
slovene	79.3	76.8	70.8	72.8	70.4	68.1	78.9	**79.8**	59.4	62.2	59.4	55.8	54.3	62.2
swedish	91.7	85.8	83.1	85.6	87.1	80.8	87.6	**92.1**	76.1	76.1	76.4	75.3	67.2	79.1
averages	80.8	78.2	78.5	78.8	78.5	75.4	78.9	**81.7**	69.9	71.5	68.9	64.3	64.3	73.8

Table 8: Evaluation of the dependency task using a maximum sentence length of 10. See also Table 3 which presents the same results with no length restriction.

Two baselines for unsupervised dependency parsing*

Anders Søgaard
Center for Language Technology
University of Copenhagen
DK-2300 Copenhagen S
soegaard@hum.ku.dk

Abstract

Results in unsupervised dependency parsing are typically compared to branching baselines and the DMV-EM parser of Klein and Manning (2004). State-of-the-art results are now well beyond these baselines. This paper describes two simple, heuristic baselines that are much harder to beat: a simple, heuristic algorithm recently presented in Søgaard (2012) and a heuristic application of the universal rules presented in Naseem et al. (2010). Our first baseline (RANK) outperforms existing baselines, including PR-DVM (Gillenwater et al., 2010), while relying *only on raw text*, but all submitted systems in the Pascal Grammar Induction Challenge score better. Our second baseline (RULES), however, outperforms several submitted systems.

1 RANK: a simple heuristic baseline

Our first baseline RANK is a simple heuristic baseline that does not rely on part of speech. It only assumes raw text. The intuition behind it is that a dependency structure encodes something related to the relatively salience of words in a sentence (Søgaard, 2012). It constructs a word graph of the words in a sentence and applies a random walk algorithm to rank the words by salience. The word ranking is then converted into a dependency tree using a simple heuristic algorithm.

The graph over the words in the input sentence is constructed by adding directed edges between the word nodes. The edges are not weighted, but multiple edges between nodes will make transitions between them more likely.

The edge template was validated on development data from the English Penn-III treebank (Marcus et al., 1993) and first presented in Søgaard (2012):

- *Short edges.* To favor short dependencies, we add links between all words and their neighbors. This makes probability mass flow from central words to their neighboring words.

- *Function words.* We use a keyword extraction algorithm without stop word lists to extract function or non-content words. The algorithm is a crude simplification of TextRank (Mihalcea and Tarau, 2004) that does not rely on linguistic resources, so that we can easily apply it to low-resource languages. Since we do not use stop word lists, highly ranked words will typically be function words. For the 50-most highly ranked words, we add additional links from their neighboring words. This will add additional probability mass to the function words. This is relevant to capture structures such as prepositional phrases where the function words take content words as complements.

- *Morphological inequality.* If two words w_i, w_j have different prefixes or suffixes, i.e. the first two or last three letters, we add an edge between them.

Given the constructed graph we rank the nodes using the algorithm in Page and Brin (1998), also known as PageRank. The input to the PageRank algorithm is any directed graph $G = \langle E, V \rangle$ and the output is an assignment $PR : V \rightarrow \mathbb{R}$ of a score, also referred to as PageRank, to each node in the graph, reflecting the probability of ending up in that node in a random walk.

*

from/to	The	finger-pointing	has	already	begun	.
The	0	3	2	2	3	2
finger-pointing	3	0	5	2	3	2
has	2	4	0	3	3	2
already	2	2	5	0	3	2
begun	2	3	3	3	0	3
.	2	2	3	2	4	0
PR(%)	13.4	17.4	21.2	15.1	19.3	13.6

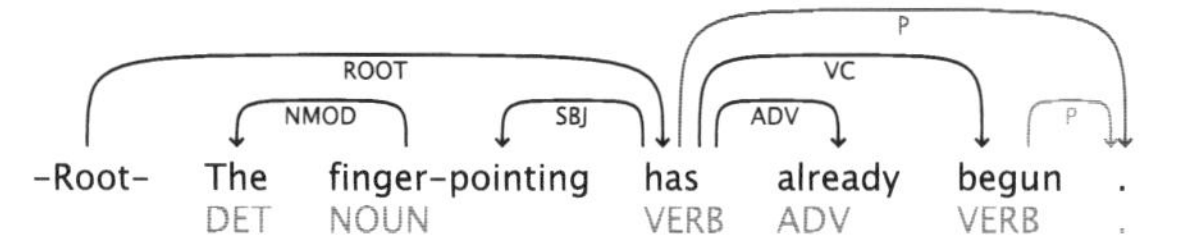

Figure 1: Graph, pagerank (PR) and predicted dependency structure for sentence 7 in PTB-III Sect. 23.

VERB⟶VERB VERB⟶NOUN VERB⟶ADV VERB⟶ADP VERB⟶CONJ VERB⟶DET VERB⟶NUM VERB⟶ADJ VERB⟶X	NOUN⟶ADJ NOUN⟶DET NOUN⟶NOUN NOUN⟶NUM
ADP⟶NOUN ADP⟶ADV	ADJ⟶ADV

Figure 2: Universal dependency rules (Naseem et al., 2010) wrt. universal tags.

The words are now ranked by their PageRank (Figure 1), and from the word ranking we derive a dependency tree. The derivation is very simple: We introduce a store of potential heads, initialized as a singleton containing the word with the highest PageRank (which is attached to the artificial root note). Each word is now assigned a syntactic head taken from all the words that were already assigned heads. Of these words, we simply select the closest possible head. In case of ties, we select the head with the highest PageRank.

2 RULES: a simple rule-based baseline

Our second baseline is even simpler than our first one, but makes use of input part of speech. In particular it builds on the idea that unsupervised parsing can be informed by universal dependency rules (Naseem et al., 2010). We reformulate the universal dependency rules used in Naseem et al. (2010) in terms of the universal tags provided in the shared task (Figure 2), but unlike them, we do not engage in grammar induction. Instead we simply present a straight-forward heuristic application of the universal dependency rules:

RULES finds the head of each word w by finding the nearest word w' such that POS(w')→POS(w) is a universal dependency rule. In case of ties, we select the left-most head in the candidate set. The head of the sentence is said to be the left-most verb. Note that we are not guaranteed to find a head satisfying a universal dependency rule. In fact when the dependent has part of speech AUX or '.' we will never find such a head. If no head is found, we attach the dependent to the artificial root node.

Note that like RANK, RULES would give us

	RANK	RULES	DMV	win	best
Arabic	0.340	0.465	0.274	0.541	0.573
Basque	0.255	0.137	0.321	0.440	0.459
Czech	0.329	0.409	0.276	0.488	0.491
Danish	0.424	0.451	0.395	0.502	0.502
Dutch	0.313	0.405	0.284	0.437	0.492
En-Childes	0.481	0.519	0.498	0.538	0.594
En-WSJ	0.328	0.425	0.335	0.555	0.560
Portuguese	0.371	0.546	0.240	0.418	0.652
Slovene	0.284	0.377	0.242	0.580	0.580
Swedish	0.375	0.551	0.290	0.573	0.573

the correct analysis of the sentence in Figure 1 (excl. punctuation). Surprisingly, RULES turns out to be a *very* competitive baseline.

3 Results

Shared task results were evaluated by the organizers in terms of directed accuracy (DA), also known as unlabeled attachment score, undirected accuracy (UA) and NED (Schwartz et al., 2011), both for short and full length sentences. We will focus on DA for full length sentences here, arguable the most widely accepted metric. Table 1 presents results for all 10 datasets, with DMV based on fine-grained native POS (which performs best on average compared to DMV-CPOS and DMV-UPOS),[1] and *Tu, standard* as the winning system ('win'). The 'best' result cherry-picks the best system for each dataset.

The first thing we note is that our two baselines

[1]In a way it would be fairer to *exclude* native POS and CPOS information, since native tag sets reflect language-specific syntax. Moreover, the validity of relying on manually labeled input is questionable.

are much better than the usual structural baselines. The macro-averages for the branching baselines are 0.252 (left) and 0.295 (right), but if we allow ourselves to cherry-pick the best branching baseline for each language the macro-average of that baseline is 0.352. This corresponds to the macro-average of RANK which is 0.350. The macro-average of RULES is 0.429.

Interestingly, RANK achieves better full length sentence DA than at least one of the submitted systems for each language, except English. The same holds for full length sentence NED. RULES is an even stronger baseline.

Most interestingly the two baselines are significantly better on average than *all* the baselines proposed by the organizers, including DMV-EM and DMV-PR. This is surprising in itself, since our two baselines are completely heuristic and require no training. It seems none of the baseline systems necessarily learn anything apart from simple, universal properties of linguistic trees that we could easily have spelled out in the first place.

More than half of the submitted systems are worse than RULES in terms of DA, but three systems also outperform our baselines by some margin (Bisk, Blunsom and Tu). Since our baselines are better than harmonic initialization, the obvious next step would be to try to initialize EM-based unsupervised parsers by the structures predicted by our baselines.

References

Jennifer Gillenwater, Kuzman Ganchev, Joao Graca, Fernando Pereira, and Ben Taskar. 2010. Sparsity in dependency grammar induction. In *ACL*.

Mitchell Marcus, Mary Marcinkiewicz, and Beatrice Santorini. 1993. Building a large annotated corpus of English: the Penn Treebank. *Computational Linguistics*, 19(2):313–330.

Rada Mihalcea and Paul Tarau. 2004. Textrank: bringing order into texts. In *EMNLP*.

Tahira Naseem, Harr Chen, Regina Barzilay, and Mark Johnson. 2010. Using universal linguistic knowledge to guide grammar induction. In *EMNLP*.

Larry Page and Sergey Brin. 1998. The anatomy of a large-scale hypertextual web search engine. In *International Web Conference*.

Roy Schwartz, , Omri Abend, Roi Reichart, and Ari Rappoport. 2011. Neutralizing linguistically problematic annotations in unsupervised dependency parsing evaluation. In *ACL*.

Anders Søgaard. 2012. Unsupervised dependency parsing without training. *Natural Language Engineering*, 18(1):187–203.

Unsupervised Dependency Parsing using Reducibility and Fertility features*

David Mareček and Zdeněk Žabokrtský
Charles University in Prague, Faculty of Mathematics and Physics
Institute of Formal and Applied Linguistics
Malostranské náměstí 25, Prague
{marecek,zabokrtsky}@ufal.mff.cuni.cz

Abstract

This paper describes a system for unsupervised dependency parsing based on Gibbs sampling algorithm. The novel approach introduces a fertility model and reducibility model, which assumes that dependent words can be removed from a sentence without violating its syntactic correctness.

1 Introduction

One of the traditional linguistic criteria for recognizing dependency relations (including their head-dependent orientation) is that stepwise deletion of dependent elements within a sentence preserves its syntactic correctness (Lopatková et al., 2005; Kübler et al., 2009; Gerdes and Kahane, 2011).[1] If a word can be removed from a sentence without damaging it, then it is likely to be dependent on some other (still present) word.

Our approach allows to utilize information from very large corpora. While the computationally demanding sampling procedure can be applied only on limited data, the unrepeated precomputation of statistics for reducibility estimates can easily exploit much larger data.

2 Precomputing PoS tag reducibility scores

We call a word (or a sequence of words) in a sentence *reducible*, if the sentence after removing the word remains grammatically correct. Although we cannot automatically recognize grammaticality of such newly created sentence, we can search for it in a large corpus. If we find it, we assume the word was reducible in the original sentence. It is obvious that the number of such reducible sequences of words found in a corpus is relatively low. However, it is sufficient for determining reducibility scores at least for individual types of words (part-of-speech tags).[2]

Assume a PoS n-gram $g = [t_1, \ldots, t_n]$. We go through the corpus and search for all its occurrences. For each such occurrence, we remove the respective words from the current sentence and check in the corpus whether the rest of the sentence occurs at least once elsewhere in the corpus.[3] If so, then such occurrence of PoS n-gram is reducible, otherwise it is not. We denote the number of such reducible occurrences of PoS n-gram g by $r(g)$. The number of all its occurrences is $c(g)$. The relative reducibility

* This research was supported by the grants GA201/09/H057 (Res Informatica), MSM0021620838, GAUK 116310, and by the European Commission's 7th Framework Program (FP7) under grant agreement n° 247762 (FAUST).

[1] Of course, all the above works had to respond to the notorious fact that there are many language phenomena precluding the ideal (word by word) sentence reducibility (e.g. in the case of prepositional groups, or in the case of subjects in English finite clauses). However, we borrow only the very core of the reducibility idea.

[2] Although we search for reducible sequences of word forms in the corpus, we compute reducibility scores for sequences of part-of-speech tags. This requires to have the corpus morphologically disambiguated.

[3] We do not take into account sentences with less then 10 words, because they could be nominal (without any verb) and might influence the reducibility scores of verbs.

unigrams	R	bigrams	R	trigrams	R
VB	0.04	VBN IN	0.00	IN DT JJ	0.00
TO	0.07	IN DT	0.02	JJ NN IN	0.00
IN	0.11	NN IN	0.04	NN IN NNP	0.00
VBD	0.12	NNS IN	0.05	VBN IN DT	0.00
CC	0.13	JJ NNS	0.07	JJ NN .	0.00
VBZ	0.16	NN .	0.08	DT JJ NN	0.04
NN	0.22	DT NNP	0.09	DT NNP NNP	0.05
VBN	0.24	DT NN	0.09	NNS IN DT	0.14
.	0.32	NN ,	0.11	NNP NNP .	0.15
NNS	0.38	DT JJ	0.13	NN IN DT	0.23
DT	0.43	JJ NN	0.14	NNP NNP ,	0.46
NNP	0.78	NNP .	0.15	IN DT NNP	0.55
JJ	0.84	NN NN	0.22	DT NN IN	0.59
RB	2.07	IN NN	0.67	NNP NNP NNP	0.64
,	3.77	NNP NNP	0.76	IN DT NN	0.80
CD	55.6	IN NNP	1.81	IN NNP NNP	4.27

Table 1: Reducibility scores of the most frequent PoS tag English n-grams.

$R(g)$ of a PoS n-gram g is then computed as

$$R(g) = \frac{1}{N} \frac{r(g) + \sigma_1}{c(g) + \sigma_2}, \quad (1)$$

where the normalization constant N, which expresses relative reducibility over all the PoS n-grams (denoted by G), causes the scores are concentrated around the value 1.

$$N = \frac{\sum_{g \in G}(r(g) + \sigma_1)}{\sum_{g \in G}(c(g) + \sigma_2)} \quad (2)$$

Smoothing constants σ_1 and σ_2, which prevent reducibility scores from being equal to zero, are set as follows: [4]

$$\sigma_1 = \frac{\sum_{g \in G} r(g)}{\sum_{g \in G} c(g)}, \qquad \sigma_2 = 1 \quad (3)$$

Table 1 shows reducibility scores of the most frequent English PoS n-grams. If we consider only unigrams, we can see that the scores for verbs are often among the lowest. Verbs are followed by prepositions and nouns, and the scores for adjectives and adverbs are very high for all three examined languages. That is desired, because the reducible unigrams will more likely become leaves in dependency trees.

3 Dependency Models

We introduce a new generative model that is different from the widely used Dependency Model with Valence (DMV).[5] Our generative model introduces *fertility* of a node. For a given head, we first generate the number of its left and right children (*fertility model*) and then we fill these positions by generating its individual dependents (*edge model*). If a zero fertility is generated, the head becomes a leaf.

Besides the fertility model and the edge model, we use two more models (*subtree model* and *distance model*), which force the generated trees to have more desired shape.

3.1 Fertility model

We express a fertility of a node by a pair of numbers: the number of its left dependents and the number of its right dependents.[6] Fertility is conditioned by part-of-speech tag of the node and it is computed following the Chinese restaurant process.[7] The formula for computing probability of fertility f_i of a word on the position i in the corpus is as follows:

$$P_f(f_i|t_i) = \frac{c^{-i}(\text{“}t_i, f_i\text{”}) + \alpha P_0(f_i)}{c^{-i}(\text{“}t_i\text{”}) + \alpha}, \quad (4)$$

where t_i is part-of-speech tag of the word on the position i, $c^{-i}(\text{“}t_i, f_i\text{”})$ stands for the count of words with PoS tag t_i and fertility f_i in the history, and P_0 is a prior probability for the given fertility which depends on the total number of node dependents denoted by $|f_i|$ (the sum of numbers of left and right dependents):

$$P_0(f_i) = \frac{1}{2^{|f_i|+1}} \quad (5)$$

This prior probability has a nice property: for a given number of nodes, the product of fertility probabilities over all the nodes is equal for all possible dependency trees. This ensures balance of this model during inference.

[4]This setting causes that even if a given PoS n-gram is not reducible anywhere in the corpus, its reducibility score is $1/(c(g) + 1)$.

[5]In DMV (Klein and Manning, 2004) and in the extended model EVG (Headden III et al., 2009), there is a *STOP* sign indicating that no more dependents in a given direction will be generated. Given a certain head, all its dependents in left direction are generated first, then the *STOP* sign in that direction, then all its right dependents and then *STOP* in the other direction. This process continues recursively for all generated dependents.

[6]For example, fertility “1-3” means that the node has one left and three right dependents, fertility “0-0” indicates that it is a leaf.

[7]If a specific fertility has been frequent for a given PoS tag in the past, it is more likely to be generated again.

Besides the basic fertility model, we introduce also an extended fertility model, which uses frequency of a given word form for generating number of children. We assume that the most frequent words are mostly function words (e.g. determiners, prepositions, auxiliary verbs, conjunctions). Such words tend to have a stable number of children, for example (i) some function words are exclusively leaves, (ii) prepositions have just one child, and (iii) attachment of auxiliary verbs depends on the annotation style, but number of their children is also not very variable. The higher the frequency of a word form, the higher probability mass is concentrated on one specific number of children and the lower Dirichlet hyperparameter α in Equation 4 is needed. The extended fertility is described by equation

$$P'_f(f_i|t_i, w_i) = \frac{c^{-i}(\text{“}t_i, f_i\text{”}) + \frac{\alpha_e}{F(w_i)} P_0(f_i)}{c^{-i}(\text{“}t_i\text{”}) + \frac{\alpha_e}{F(w_i)}}, \quad (6)$$

where $F(w_i)$ is a frequency of the word w_i, which is computed as a number of words w_i in our corpus divided by number of all words.

3.2 Edge model

After the fertility (number of left and right dependents) is generated, the individual slots are filled using the *edge model*. A part-of-speech tag of each dependent is conditioned by part-of-speech tag of the head and the edge direction (position of the dependent related to the head).[8]

Similarly as for the fertility model, we employ Chinese restaurant process to assign probabilities of individual dependent.

$$P_e(t_j|t_i, d_j) = \frac{c^{-i}(\text{“}t_i, t_j, d_j\text{”}) + \beta}{c^{-i}(\text{“}t_i, d_j\text{”}) + \beta|T|}, \quad (7)$$

where t_i and t_j are the part-of-speech tags of the head and the generated dependent respectively; d_j is a direction of edge between the words i and j, which can have two values: *left* and *right*. $c^{-i}(\text{“}t_i, t_j, d_j\text{”})$ stands for the count of edges $t_i \leftarrow t_j$ with the direction d_j in the history, $|T|$ is a number of unique tags in the corpus and β is a Dirichlet hyperparameter.

[8]For the edge model purposes, the PoS tag of the technical root is set to '<root>' and it is in the zero-th position in the sentence, so the head word of the sentence is always its right dependent.

3.3 Distance model

Distance model is an auxiliary model that prevents the resulting trees from being too flat.[9] This simple model says that shorter edges are more probable than longer ones. We define probability of a distance between a word and its parent as its inverse value,[10] which is then normalized by the normalization constant ϵ_d.

$$P_d(i, j) = \frac{1}{\epsilon_d}\left(\frac{1}{|i-j|}\right)^{\gamma} \quad (8)$$

The hyperparameter γ determines the weight of this model.

3.4 Subtree model

The subtree model uses the reducibility measure. It plays an important role since it forces the reducible words to be leaves and reducible n-grams to be subtrees. Words with low reducibility are forced towards the root of the tree. We define $desc(i)$ as a sequence of tags $[t_l, \ldots, t_r]$ that corresponds to all the descendants of the word w_i including w_i, i.e. the whole subtree of w_i. The probability of such subtree is proportional to its reducibility $R(desc(i))$. The hyperparameter δ determines the weight of the model; ϵ_s is a normalization constant.

$$P_s(i) = \frac{1}{\epsilon_s} R(desc(i))^{\delta} \quad (9)$$

3.5 Probability of the whole treebank

We want to maximize the probability of the whole generated treebank, which is computed as follows:

$$P_{treebank} = \prod_{i=1}^{n} (P'_f(f_i|t_i, w_i) \quad (10)$$

$$P_e(t_i|t_{\pi(i)}, d_i) \quad (11)$$

$$P_d(i, \pi(i)) \quad (12)$$

$$P_s(i)), \quad (13)$$

where $\pi(i)$ denotes the parent of the word on the position i. We multiply the probabilities of fertility, edge, distance from parent, and subtree over all

[9]Ideally, the distance model would not be needed, but experiments showed that it helps to infer better trees.

[10]Distance between any word and the technical root of the dependency tree was set to 10. Since each technical root has only one dependent, this value does not affect the model.

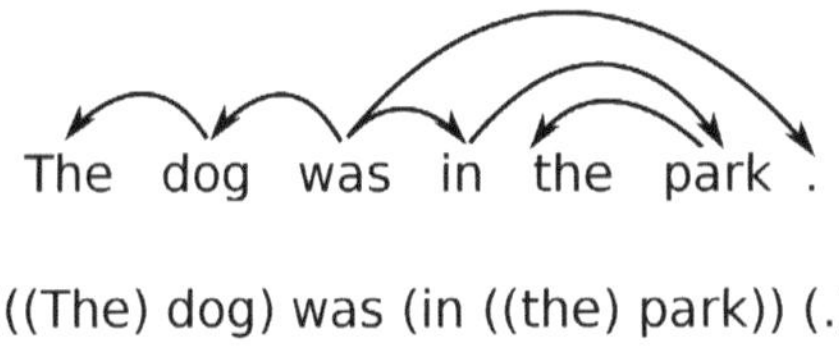

Figure 1: Arrow and bracketing notation of a projective dependency tree.

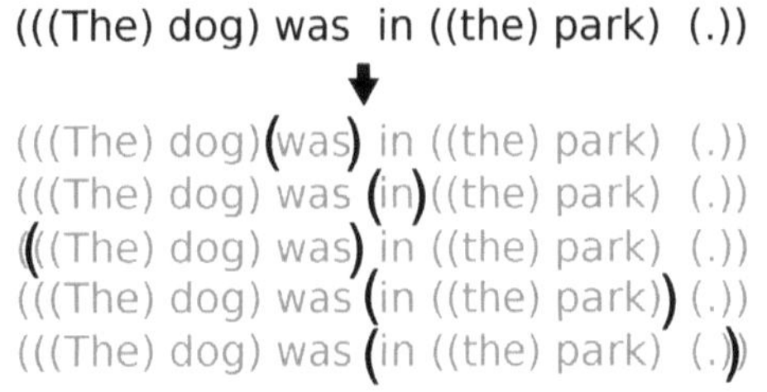

Figure 2: An example of small change in a projective tree. The bracket (in the park) is removed and there are five possibilities how to replace it.

words (nodes) in the corpus. The extended fertility model P'_f can be substituted by its basic variant P_f.

4 Sampling algorithm

For stochastic searching for the most probable dependency trees, we employ Gibbs sampling, a standard Markov Chain Monte Carlo technique (Gilks et al., 1996). In each iteration, we loop over all words in the corpus in a random order and change the dependencies in their neighborhood (a small change described in Section 4.2). In the end, "average" trees based on the whole sampling are built.

4.1 Initialization

Before the sampling starts, we initialize the projective trees randomly in a way that for each sentence, we choose randomly one word as the head and attach all other words to it.[11]

4.2 Small Change Operator

We use the bracketing notation for illustrating the small change operator. Each projective dependency tree consisting of n words can be expressed by n pairs of brackets. Each bracket pair belongs to one node and delimits its descendants from the rest of the sentence. Furthermore, each bracketed segment contains just one word that is not embedded deeper; this node is the segment head. An example of this notation is in Figure 1.

The small change is then very simple. We remove one pair of brackets and add another, so that the conditions defined above are not violated. An example of such change is in Figure 2.

From the perspective of dependency structures, the small change can be described as follows:

1. Pick a random non-root word w (the word *in* in our example) and find its parent p (the word *was*).
2. Find all other children of w and p (the words *dog*, *park*, and .) and denote this set by C.
3. Choose the new head out of w and p. Mark the new head as g and the second candidate as d. Attach d to g.
4. Select a neighborhood D adjacent to the word d as a continuous subset of C and attach all words from D to d. D may be also empty.
5. Attach the remaining words from C that were not in D to the new head g.

4.3 Building "average" trees

The "burn-in" period is set to 10 iterations. After this period, we begin to count how many times an edge occurs at a particular location in the corpus. This counts are collected over the whole corpus with the collection-rate 0.01.[12]

When the sampling is finished, the final dependency trees are built using such edges that belonged to the most frequent ones during the sampling. We employ the maximum spanning tree (MST) algorithm (Chu and Liu, 1965) to find them.[13] Tree projectivity is not guaranteed by the MST algorithm.

5 Experiments

We evaluated our parser on 10 treebanks included in the WILS shared-task data. Similarly to some previous papers on unsupervised parsing (Gillenwater et al., 2011; Spitkovsky et al., 2011), the tuning experiments were performed on English only. We used

[11] More elaborated methods for generating random trees converges to similar results. Therefore we conclude that the choice of the initialization mechanism is not so important here.

[12] After each small change is made, the edges from the whole corpus are collected with a probability 0.01.

[13] The weights of edges needed in MST algorithm correspond to the number of times they were present during the sampling.

language	tokens (mil.)	language	tokens (mil.)
Arabic	19.7	English	85.0
Basque	14.1	Portuguese	31.7
Czech	20.3	Slovenian	13.7
Danish	15.9	Swedish	19.2
Dutch	27.1		

Table 2: Wikipedia texts statistics

English development data for checking functionality of the individual models and for optimizing hyperparameter values. The best configuration of the parser achieved on English was then used for parsing all other languages. This simulates the situation in which we have only one treebank (English) on which we can tune our parser and we want to parse other languages for which we have no manually annotated treebanks.

5.1 Data

For each experiment, we need two kinds of data: a smaller treebank, which is used for sampling and for evaluation, and a large corpus, from which we compute n-gram reducibility scores. The induction of dependency trees and evaluation is done only on WILS testing data.

For obtaining reducibility scores, we used Wikipedia articles downloaded by Majliš and Žabokrtský (2012). Their statistics across languages are showed in Table 2. To make them useful, the necessary preprocessing steps must have been done. The texts were first automatically segmented and tokenized[14] and then they were part-of-speech tagged by TnT tagger (Brants, 2000), which was trained on the respective WILS training data. The quality of such tagging is not very high, since we do not use any lexicons[15] or pretrained models. However, it is sufficient for obtaining good reducibility scores.

5.2 Setting the hyperparameters

The applicability of individual models and their parameters were tested on English development data and full part-of-speech tags. The four hyperparameters α (fertility model), β (edge model), γ (distance model), and δ (subtree model), were set by a grid search algorithm, which found the following optimal values:

$$\alpha_e = 0.01, \quad \beta = 1, \quad \gamma = 1.5, \quad \delta = 1$$

5.3 Results

The best setting from the experiments on English is now used for evaluating our parser across all WILS treebanks. Besides using the standard part-of-speech tags (POS), the experiments were done also on coarse tags (CPOS) and universal tags (UPOS). From results presented in Table 3, it is obvious that our systems outperforms all the given baselines considering the average scores across all the testing languages. However, it is important to note that we used an additional source of information, namely large unannotated corpora for computing reducibility scores, while the baseline system (Gillenwater et al., 2011) use only the WILS datasets.

6 Conclusions and Future Work

We have described a novel unsupervised dependency parsing system employing new features, such as reducibility or fertility. The reducibility scores are extracted from a large corpus, and the computationally demanding inference is then done on smaller data.

In future work, we would like to estimate the hyperparameters automatically, for example by the Metropolis-Hastings technique (Gilks et al., 1996). Furthermore, we would like to add lexicalized models and automatically induced word classes instead of the PoS tags designed by humans. Finally, we would like to move towards deeper syntactic structures, where the tree would be formed only by content words and the function words would be treated in a different way.

References

Thorsten Brants. 2000. TnT - A Statistical Part-of-Speech Tagger. *Proceedings of the sixth conference on Applied natural language processing*, page 8.

Y. J. Chu and T. H. Liu. 1965. On the Shortest Arborescence of a Directed Graph. *Science Sinica*, 14:1396–1400.

[14]The segmentation to sentences and tokenization was performed using the TectoMT framework (Popel and Žabokrtský, 2010).

[15]Using lexicons or another pretrained models for tagging means using other sources of human annotated data, which is not allowed if we want to compare our results with others.

	baselines			Gillenwater et al. (2011)			our approach		
Treebank	random	left br.	right br.	CPOS	POS	UPOS	CPOS	POS	UPOS
Arabic PADT	37.0	5.2	**58.7**	14.9	14.5	23.4	12.7	57.2	52.0
Basque 3LB	9.8	32.4	22.5	**48.9**	41.8	30.0	21.0	25.5	22.3
Czech PDT	10.8	23.9	29.1	25.6	31.6	27.5	**49.1**	42.9	44.1
Danish CDT	24.7	13.3	47.4	31.8	27.2	26.3	48.4	41.4	**49.7**
Dutch Alpino	17.1	27.9	24.6	23.3	21.2	23.5	28.3	**44.2**	29.9
English Childes	12.8	34.8	22.2	48.8	**50.4**	36.2	54.2	44.2	49.3
English PTB	13.2	31.4	20.4	30.9	34.4	25.9	41.0	**50.3**	37.5
Portuguese Floresta	33.1	25.9	31.1	26.0	31.1	25.5	**50.2**	49.5	29.3
Slovene JOS	9.5	31.1	10.8	36.6	**53.3**	36.6	30.4	40.8	26.7
Swedish Talbanken	23.9	25.8	28.0	27.2	27.2	27.1	48.4	50.6	**52.6**
Average:	19.2	25.2	29.5	31.4	33.3	28.2	38.4	**44.7**	39.3

Table 3: Directed attachment scores on the WILS testing data (all sentences). Punctuation was excluded. Comparison with simple baselines and the given baseline system (Gillenwater et al., 2011).

Kim Gerdes and Sylvain Kahane. 2011. Defining dependencies (and constituents). In *Proceedings of Dependency Linguistics 2011*, Barcelona.

W. R. Gilks, S. Richardson, and D. J. Spiegelhalter. 1996. *Markov chain Monte Carlo in practice*. Interdisciplinary statistics. Chapman & Hall.

Jennifer Gillenwater, Kuzman Ganchev, João Graça, Fernando Pereira, and Ben Taskar. 2011. Posterior Sparsity in Unsupervised Dependency Parsing. *The Journal of Machine Learning Research*, 12:455–490, February.

William P. Headden III, Mark Johnson, and David McClosky. 2009. Improving unsupervised dependency parsing with richer contexts and smoothing. In *Proceedings of Human Language Technologies: The 2009 Annual Conference of the North American Chapter of the Association for Computational Linguistics*, NAACL '09, pages 101–109, Stroudsburg, PA, USA. Association for Computational Linguistics.

Dan Klein and Christopher D. Manning. 2004. Corpus-based induction of syntactic structure: models of dependency and constituency. In *Proceedings of the 42nd Annual Meeting on Association for Computational Linguistics*, ACL '04, Stroudsburg, PA, USA. Association for Computational Linguistics.

Sandra Kübler, Ryan T. McDonald, and Joakim Nivre. 2009. *Dependency Parsing*. Synthesis Lectures on Human Language Technologies. Morgan & Claypool Publishers.

Markéta Lopatková, Martin Plátek, and Vladislav Kuboň. 2005. Modeling syntax of free word-order languages: Dependency analysis by reduction. In Václav Matoušek, Pavel Mautner, and Tomáš Pavelka, editors, *Lecture Notes in Artificial Intelligence, Proceedings of the 8th International Conference, TSD 2005*, volume 3658 of *Lecture Notes in Computer Science*, pages 140–147, Berlin / Heidelberg. Springer.

Martin Majliš and Zdeněk Žabokrtský. 2012. Language richness of the web. In *Proceedings of LREC2012*, Istanbul, Turkey, May. ELRA, European Language Resources Association. In print.

Martin Popel and Zdeněk Žabokrtský. 2010. TectoMT: modular NLP framework. In *Proceedings of the 7th international conference on Advances in natural language processing*, IceTAL'10, pages 293–304, Berlin, Heidelberg. Springer-Verlag.

Valentin I. Spitkovsky, Hiyan Alshawi, and Daniel Jurafsky. 2011. Lateen EM: Unsupervised training with multiple objectives, applied to dependency grammar induction. In *Proceedings of the 2011 Conference on Empirical Methods in Natural Language Processing (EMNLP 2011)*.

Induction of Linguistic Structure with Combinatory Categorial Grammars

Yonatan Bisk and Julia Hockenmaier
Department of Computer Science
University of Illinois at Urbana-Champaign
201 N Goodwin Ave. Urbana IL, 61801
{bisk1,juliahmr}@illinois.edu

Abstract

Our system consists of a simple, EM-based induction algorithm (Bisk and Hockenmaier, 2012), which induces a language-specific Combinatory Categorial grammar (CCG) and lexicon based on a small number of linguistic principles, e.g. that verbs may be the roots of sentences and can take nouns as arguments.

1 Introduction

Much of the recent work on grammar induction has focused on the development of sophisticated statistical models that incorporate expressive priors (Cohen and Smith, 2010) or linguistic universals (Naseem et al., 2010; Boonkwan and Steedman, 2011) that have all been shown to be very helpful. But, with some notable exceptions, such as (Cohn et al., 2011), the question of what underlying linguistic representation to use has received considerably less attention. Our induction algorithm is based on Combinatory Categorial Grammar (Steedman, 2000), a linguistically expressive, lexicalized grammar formalism which associates words with rich syntactic categories that capture language-specific facts about basic word order and subcategorization. While Boonkwan and Steedman (2011) have shown that linguists can easily devise a language-specific inventory of such categories that allows a parser to achieve high performance in the absence of annotated training data, our algorithm automatically discovers the set of categories it requires to parse the sentences in the training data.

2 Combinatory Categorial Grammar (CCG)

The set of CCG categories is built recursively from two atomic types, $\mathtt{S}$ (sentence) and $\mathtt{N}$ (noun). Complex types are of the form $\mathtt{X/Y}$ or $\mathtt{X\backslash Y}$, and represent functions which combine with an argument of type $\mathtt{Y}$ to yield a constituent of type $\mathtt{X}$ as result. The slash indicates whether the $\mathtt{Y}$ precedes ($\backslash$) or follows (/) the functor. An English lexicon should contain categories such as $\mathtt{S\backslash N}$ and $\mathtt{(S\backslash N)/N}$ for verbs: both transitive and intransitive verbs subcategorize for a preceding subject, and the transitive verb additionally takes an object to its right. In this manner, the argument slots of lexical categories also define word-word dependencies between heads and their arguments (Clark and Hockenmaier, 2002; Hockenmaier and Steedman, 2007). Modifiers are generally of the form $\mathtt{X|X}$: in English, pre-nominal adjectives are $\mathtt{N/N}$, whereas adverbs may be $\mathtt{(N/N)/(N/N)}$, $\mathtt{S/S}$, or $\mathtt{S\backslash S}$, and prepositions can have categories such as $\mathtt{(N\backslash N)/N}$ or $\mathtt{(S\backslash S)/N}$. That is, CCG assumes that the direction of the corresponding dependency goes from the modifier to the head. This discrepancy between CCG and most other analyses can easily be removed under the assumption that all categories of the form $\mathtt{X|X}$ are modifiers whose dependencies should be reversed when comparing against other frameworks.

Adjacent constituents can be combined according to a small, universal set of combinatory rules. For the purposes of this work we restrict ourselves to function application and B^1 composition:

$$\mathtt{X/Y} \quad \mathtt{Y} \quad \Rightarrow \mathtt{X} \qquad (>)$$

Y	X\Y	$\Rightarrow$ X	(<)
X/Y	Y$\vert_i$Z	$\Rightarrow$ X$\vert_i$Z	($B^1_>$)
Y$\vert_i$Z	X\Y	$\Rightarrow$ X$\vert_i$Z	($B^1_<$)

Here the slash variable $|_i$ can be instantiated with either the forward or backward slash.

These rules allow derivations (parses) such as:

The	*man*	*ate*	*quickly*
DT	NNS	VBD	RB
N/N	N	S\N	S\S
N (>)		S\N (<B)	
S (<)			

CCG also has unary type-raising rules of the form

X	$\Rightarrow$ T/(T\X)	(>T)
X	$\Rightarrow$ T\(T/X)	(<T)

We only allow nouns to be type-raised, and impose the restriction that the argument T\N (or T/N) of the type-raised category has to already be present in the lexicon of the language.

This restricted set of combinatory rules provides sufficient power for reasonable parse accuracy but does not allow us to capture non-projective (crossing) dependencies.

Coordination is handled by a ternary rule

X	conj	X	$\Rightarrow$ X	(>)

which we binarize as:

X	X[conj]	$\Rightarrow$ X	(< &)
conj	X	$\Rightarrow$ X[conj]	(> &)

Punctuation, when present, can be absorbed by rules of the form

X	Pct	$\Rightarrow$ X	(< p)
Pct	X	$\Rightarrow$ X	(> p)

The iterative combination of these categories resulting in S or N is considered a successful parse. In order to avoid spurious ambiguities, we restrict our derivations to be normal-form (Hockenmaier and Bisk, 2010).

3 An algorithm for unsupervised CCG induction

We now describe our induction algorithm, which consists of two stages: category induction (creation of the grammar), followed by parameter estimation for the probability model.

3.1 Category induction

We assume there are two atomic categories, N (nouns or noun phrases) and S (sentences), a special conjunction category conj, and a special start symbol TOP. We assume that all strings we encounter are either nouns or sentences:

$$\text{N} \Rightarrow \text{TOP} \qquad\qquad \text{S} \Rightarrow \text{TOP}$$

We also assume that we can group POS-tags into four groups: nominal tags, verbal tags, conjunctions, and others. This allows us to create an initial lexicon $\mathcal{L}^{(0)}$, which only contains entries for atomic categories, e.g. for the English Penn Treebank tag set (Marcus et al., 1993):

$$\text{N} : \{\text{NN}, \text{NNS}, \text{NNP}, \text{PRP}, \text{DT}\}$$
$$\text{S} : \{\text{MD}, \text{VB}, \text{VBZ}, \text{VBG}, \text{VBN}, \text{VBD}\}$$
$$\text{conj} : \{\text{CC}\}$$

We force any string that contains one or more verbs (besides VBG in English), to be parsed with the S $\Rightarrow$ TOP rule.

Since the initial lexicon would only allow us to parse single word utterances (or coordinations thereof), we need to induce complex functor categories. The lexicon entries for atomic categories remain, but all POS-tags, including nouns and conjunctions, will be able to acquire complex categories during induction. We impose the following constraints on the lexical categories we induce:

1. Nouns (N) do not take any arguments.
2. The heads of sentences (S|...) and modifiers (X|X, (X|X)|(X|X)) may take N or S as arguments.
3. Sentences (S) may only take nouns (N) as arguments.
(We assume S\S and S/S are modifiers).
4. Modifiers (X/X or X\X) can be modified by categories of the form (X/X)|(X/X) or (X\X)|(X\X).
5. The maximal arity of any lexical category is 3.
6. Since (S\N)/N is completely equivalent to (S/N)\N, we only allow the former category.

Induction is an iterative process. At each stage, we aim to parse all sentences S_i in our training corpus $\mathcal{D} = \{S_1, ..., S_D\}$ with the current lexicon

$\mathcal{L}^{(t)}$. In order to parse a sentence $S = w_0...w_n$, all words $w_i \in S$ need to have lexical categories that allow a complete parse (resulting in a constituent TOP that spans the entire sentence). Initially, only some words will have lexical categories:

The	*man*	*ate*	*quickly*
DT	NNS	VBD	RB
-	N	S	-

We assume that any word may modify adjacent constituents:

The	*man*	*ate*	*quickly*
DT	NNS	VBD	RB
N/N	N, S/S	S, N\N	S\S

We also assume that any word that previously had a category other than N (which we postulate does not take any arguments) can take any adjacent non-modifier category as argument, leading us here to introduce S\N for the verb:

The	*man*	*ate*	*quickly*
DT	NNS	VBD	RB
N/N	N, S/S	S, N\N, S\N	S\S

With these categories, we obtain the correct parse:

```
The     man     ate     quickly
DT      NNS     VBD     RB
-----   -----   -----   -------
N/N     N       S\N     S\S
--------------> ---------------<B
      N               S\N
-------------------------------<
               S
```

We then update the lexicon with all new tag-category pairs that have been found, excluding those that did not lead to a successful parse:

N/N : {DT}   S\N : {VBD, VBZ}   S\S : {RB, NNS, IN}

The first stage of induction can only introduce functors of arity 1, but many words, such as prepositions or transitive verbs, require more complex categories, leading us to complete, but incorrect parses such as

```
The     man     eats    with    friends
DT      NNS     VBZ     IN      NNS
-----   -----   -----   -----   -------
N/N     N       S\N     S\S     S\S
-------------->  --------------<B
      N               S\N
                 ----------------------<B
                          S\N
---------------------------------------<
                   S
```

During the second iteration, we can discover additional simple, as well as more complex, categories. We now discover transitive verb categories:

```
The     man     ate      chips
DT      NNS     VBD      NNS
-----   -----   -------  -----
N/N     N       (S\N)/N  N
-------------->  ---------------->
      N               S\N
---------------------------------<
               S
```

The second stage also introduces a large number of complex modifiers of the form (X/X)|(X/X) or (X\X)|(X\X), e.g.:

The	*man*	*ate*	*very*	*quickly*
DT	NNS	VBD	RB	RB
N/N, (S/S)/(S/S)	N, S/S (N\N)/(N\N) (N/N)\(N/N)	S, N\N, S\N (S/S)\(S/S) (S\S)/(S\S)	S\S, (S\S)/(S\S) (N\N)\(N\N)	S\S, (S\S)\(S\S)

The final induction step takes adjacent constituents that can be derived from the existing lexicon into account. This allows us to induce (S\S)/N for IN, since we can combine *a* and *friend* to N.

3.2 Parameter estimation

After constructing the lexicon, we parse the training corpus, and use the Inside-Outside algorithm (Lari and Young, 1991), a variant of the Expectation-Maximization algorithm for probabilistic context-free grammars, to estimate model parameters. We use the baseline model of Hockenmaier and Steedman (2002), which is a simple generative model that is equivalent to an unlexicalized PCFG. In a CFG, the set of terminals and non-terminals is disjoint, but in CCG, not every category can be lexical. Since this model is also the basis of a lexicalized model that captures dependencies, it distinguishes between lexical expansions (which produce words), unary expansions (which are the result of type-raising or the TOP rules), binary expansions where the head is the left child, and binary expansions whose head is the right child. Each tree is generated top-down from the start category TOP. For each (parent) node, first its expansion type $exp \in \{\text{Lex}, \text{Unary}, \text{Left}, \text{Right}\}$ is generated. Based on the expansion type, the model then produces either the word w, or the category of the head child (H), and, possibly the category of the non-head sister category (S):

Lexical	$p_e(\text{exp}=\text{Lex} \mid \text{P}) \times p_w(w \mid \text{P}, \text{exp}=\text{Lex})$
Unary	$p_e(\text{exp}=\text{Unary} \mid \text{P}) \times p_{\text{H}}(\text{H} \mid \text{P}, \text{exp}=\text{Unary})$
Left	$p_e(\text{exp}=\text{Left} \mid \text{P}) \times p_{\text{H}}(\text{H} \mid \text{P}, \text{exp}=\text{Left})$ $\times\, p_S(\text{S} \mid \text{P}, \text{H}, \text{exp}=\text{Left})$
Right	$p_e(\text{exp}=\text{Right} \mid \text{P}) \times p_{\text{H}}(\text{H} \mid \text{P}, \text{exp}=\text{Right})$ $\times\, p_S(\text{S} \mid \text{P}, \text{H}, \text{exp}=\text{Right})$

3.3 Dependency generation

We use the following regime for generating dependencies from the resulting CCG derivations:

1. Arguments Y are dependents of their heads X|Y
2. Modifiers X|X are dependents of their heads X or X|Y.
3. The head of the entire string is a dependent of the root node (0)
4. Following the CoNLL-07 shared task representation (Johansson and Nugues, 2007), we analyze coordinations (X_1 conj X_2) as creating a dependency from the first conjunct, X_1, to the conjunction conj, and from conj to the second conjunct X_2.

In the case of parse failures we return a right-branching dependency tree.

3.4 Training details

The data provided includes fine, coarse and universal part-of-speech tags. Additionally, the data was split into train, test and development sets though the organizers encouraged merging the data for training. Finally, while punctuation was present, it was not evaluated but potentially provided an additional source of signal during training and test. We chose from among these options and maximum sentence length based on performance on the development set. We primarily focused on training with shorter sentences but grew the dataset if necessary or if, as is the case in Arabic, there was very little short sentence data. Our final training settings were:

Language	Tags	Max Len	Punc
Arabic	Fine	40	✓
Basque	Coarse	20	
Childes	Fine	20	✓
Czech	Fine	10	
Danish	Fine	20	✓
Dutch	Fine	10	✓
Slovene	Fine	10	✓
Swedish	Fine	15	
PTB	Fine	10	
Portuguese	Fine	10	

In the case of Czech, we only trained on the test-set because the data set was so large and the results from randomly downsampling the merged dataset were equivalent to simply using the previously defined test-set.

3.5 Future directions

Since our current system is so simple, there is ample space for future work. We plan to investigate the effect of more complex statistical models and priors that have been shown to be helpful in dependency grammar-based systems. We also wish to relax the assumption that we know in advance which part-of-speech tags are nouns, verbs, or conjunctions.

4 Final observations regarding evaluation

Although the analysis of constructions involving basic head-argument and head-modifier dependencies is generally uncontroversial, many common constructions allow a number of plausible analyses. This makes it very difficult to evaluate and compare different unsupervised approaches for grammar induction. The corpora used in this workshop also assume different conventions for a number of constructions. Figure 1 shows the three different types of analysis for coordination adopted by the corpora used in this shared task (as well as the standard CCG analysis). The numbers to the side indicate for each corpus what percentage of our system's error rate is due to missed dependencies within coordinated structures (i.e between a conjunction and a conjunct, or between two conjuncts). It is important to note that the way in which we extract dependencies from coordinations is somewhat arbitrary (and completely independent of the underlying probability model, which currently captures no explicit de-

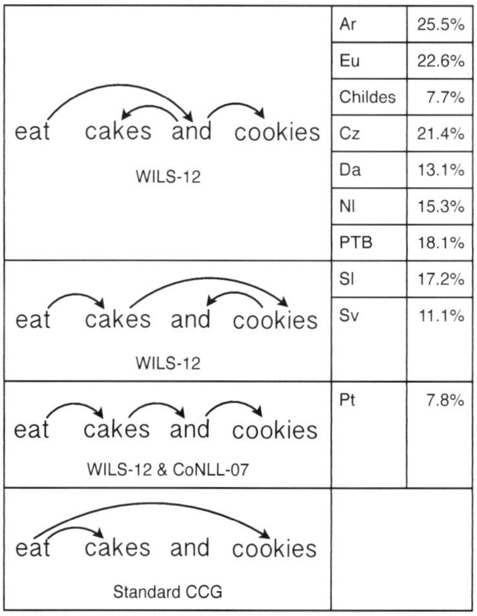

Figure 1: Different analyses of coordination in the various corpora used in this shared task. Our system adopts the CoNLL-07 convention, instead of the standard CCG analysis. For the development set of each corpus, we also indicate what percentage of the errors our system makes is due to missed coordination dependencies.

pendencies). These systematic differences of analysis are also reflected in our final results. The only exception is the Childes corpus, where coordination is significantly rarer.

However, this is a general problem. There are many other constructions for which no agreed-upon standard exists. For example, the Wall Street Journal data used in this shared task assumes a dependency between the verb of the main clause and the verb of a subordinate clause, whereas the CoNLL-07 analysis stipulates a dependency between the main verb and the subordinating conjunction:

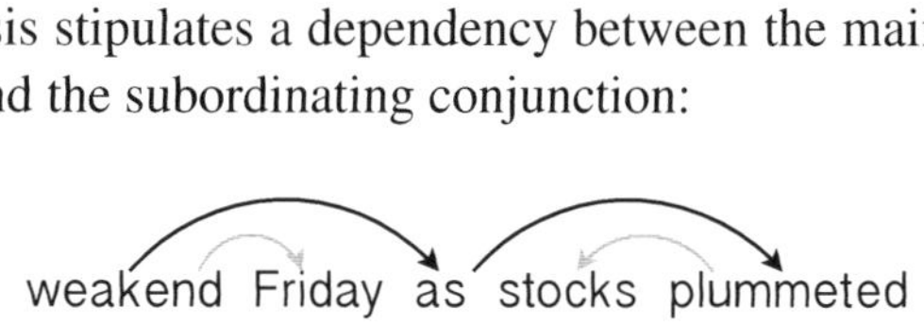

(a) CoNLL-07

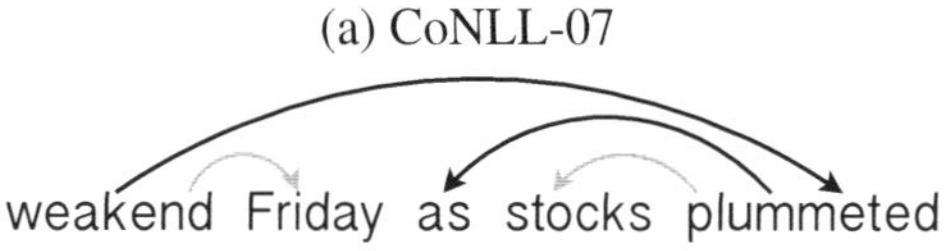

(b) WILS-12

We therefore believe that much further work is required to address the problems surrounding evaluation and comparison of unsupervised induction systems adequately. Even if the community cannot agree on a single gold standard, systems should not be penalized for producing one kind of linguistically plausible analysis over another. The systematic divergences that arise with coordination for our approach are relatively easy to fix, since we only need to change the way in which we read off dependencies. But this points to a deeper underlying problem that affects the entire field.

Acknowledgements

This research is supported by the National Science Foundation through CAREER award 1053856 and award 0803603.

References

Yonatan Bisk and Julia Hockenmaier. 2012. Simple Robust Grammar Induction with Combinatory Categorial Grammars. In *Association for the Advancement of Artificial Intelligence*.

Prachya Boonkwan and Mark Steedman. 2011. Grammar Induction from Text Using Small Syntactic Prototypes. In *International Joint Conference on Natural Language Processing*, pages 438–446, November.

Stephen Clark and Julia Hockenmaier. 2002. Evaluating a wide-coverage CCG parser. In *Proceedings of the LREC Beyond PARSEVAL workshop*, page 2002, Las Palmas, Spain.

S. B. Cohen and N. A. Smith. 2010. Covariance in unsupervised learning of probabilistic grammars. *Journal of Machine Learning Research*, 11:3017–3051.

Trevor Cohn, Phil Blunsom, and Sharon Goldwater. 2011. Inducing tree-substitution grammars. *Journal of Machine Learning Research*, pages 3053–3096, November.

Julia Hockenmaier and Yonatan Bisk. 2010. Normal-form parsing for Combinatory Categorial Grammars with generalized composition and type-raising. In *COLING*.

Julia Hockenmaier and Mark Steedman. 2002. Generative models for statistical parsing with Combinatory Categorial Grammar. In *Association for Computational Linguistics*, pages 335–342.

Julia Hockenmaier and Mark Steedman. 2007. CCGbank: a corpus of CCG derivations and dependency structures extracted from the Penn Treebank. *Computational Linguistics*, pages 355–396, January.

Richard Johansson and Pierre Nugues. 2007. Extended constituent-to-dependency conversion for english. In *Proceedings of NODALIDA 2007*, Tartu, Estonia.

K Lari and S Young. 1991. Applications of stochastic context-free grammars using the inside-outside algorithm. *Computer speech & language*, 5(3):237–257, January.

Mitchell P. Marcus, Beatrice Santorini, and Mary Ann Marcinkiewicz. 1993. Building a large annotated corpus of English: the Penn Treebank. *Computational Linguistics*, 19(2):313–330.

Tahira Naseem, Harr Chen, Regina Barzilay, and Mark Johnson. 2010. Using universal linguistic knowledge to guide grammar induction. In *Empirical Methods in Natural Language Processing*, pages 1234–1244, October.

Mark Steedman. 2000. The syntactic process. *MIT Press*, January.

Turning the pipeline into a loop: Iterated unsupervised dependency parsing and PoS induction

Christos Christodoulopoulos[†], **Sharon Goldwater**[‡], **Mark Steedman**[‡]
School of Informatics
University of Edinburgh
[†]christos.c@ed.ac.uk [‡]{steedman,sgwater}@inf.ed.ac.uk

1 Motivation

Most unsupervised dependency systems rely on gold-standard Part-of-Speech (PoS) tags, either directly, using the PoS tags instead of words, or indirectly in the back-off mechanism of fully lexicalized models (Headden et al., 2009).

It has been shown in supervised systems that using a hierarchical syntactic structure model can produce competitive sequence models; in other words that a parser can be a good tagger (Li et al., 2011; Auli and Lopez, 2011; Cohen et al., 2011). This is unsurprising, as the parser uses a rich set of hierarchical features that enable it to look at a less localized environment than a PoS tagger which in most cases relies solely on local contextual features. However this interaction has not been shown for the unsupervised setting. To our knowledge, this work is the first to show that using dependencies for unsupervised PoS induction is indeed useful.

2 Iterated learning

Although most unsupervised systems depend on gold-standard PoS information, they can also be used in a fully unsupervised pipeline. One reason for doing so is to use dependency parsing as an extrinsic evaluation for unsupervised PoS induction (Headden et al., 2008). As discussed in that paper (and also by Klein and Manning (2004)) the quality of the dependencies drops with the use of induced tags. One way of producing better PoS tags is to use the dependency parser's output to influence the PoS inducer, thus turning the pipeline into a loop.

The main difficulty of this approach is to find a way of incorporating dependency information into a PoS induction system. In previous work

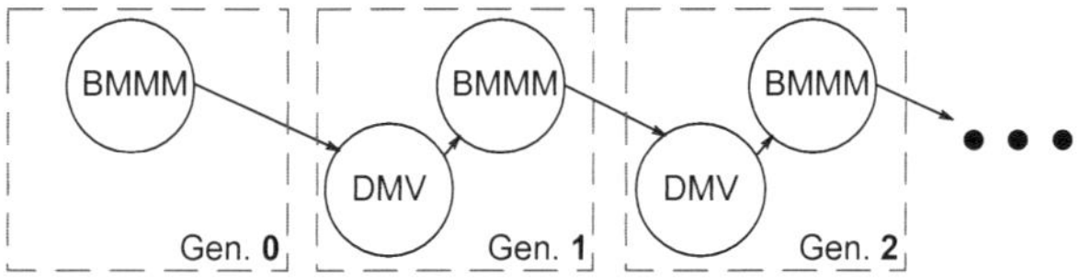

Figure 1: The iterated learning paradigm for inducing both PoS tags and dependencies.

(Christodoulopoulos et al., 2011) we have described BMMM: a PoS induction system that makes it is easy to incorporate multiple features either at the type or token level. For the dependency induction system we chose the DMV model of Klein and Manning (2004) because of its simplicity and its popularity. Both systems are described briefly in section 3.

Using these two systems we performed an *iterated learning* experiment. The term is borrowed from the language evolution literature meaning "the process by which the output of one individual's learning becomes the input to other individuals' learning" (Smith et al., 2003). Here we treat the two systems as the individuals[1] that influence each other in successive generations starting from a run of the original BMMM system without dependency information (fig. 1). We start with a run of the basic BMMM system using just context and morphology features (generation 0) and use the output to train the DMV. To complete the first generation, we then use the induced dependencies as features (as described in section 4) for a new run of the BMMM system.

As there is no single objective function, this setup

[1]This is not directly analogous to the language evolution notion of iterated learning; here instead of a single type of individual we have two separate systems that learn/model different representations.

does not guarantee that either the quality of PoS tags or the dependencies will improve after each generation. However, in practice this iterated learning approach works well (as we discuss in section 4).

3 Component models

3.1 DMV model

The basic DMV model (Klein and Manning, 2004) generates dependency trees based on three decisions (represented by three probability distributions) for a given head node: whether to attach children in the left or right direction; whether or not to stop attaching more children in the specific direction given the adjacency of the child in that direction; and finally whether to attach a specific child node. The probability of an entire sentence is the sum of the probabilities of all the possible derivations headed by ROOT.

The DMV model can be seen as (and is equivalent to) a Context Free Grammar (CFG) with only a few rules from head nodes to generated children and therefore the model parameters can be estimated using the Inside-Outside algorithm (Baker, 1979).

3.2 BMMM model

The Bayesian Multinomial Mixture Model (Christodoulopoulos et al., 2011), illustrated in figure 2, assumes that all tokens of a given word type belong to a single syntactic class, and each type is associated with a number of features (e.g., morphological or contextual features), which form the observed variables. The generative process first chooses a hidden class z for each word type and then chooses values for each of the observed features of that word type, conditioned on the class. Both the distribution over classes θ and the distributions over each kind of feature $\phi^{(t)}$ are multinomials drawn from Dirichlet priors α and $\beta^{(t)}$ respectively. A main advantage of this model is its ability to easily incorporate features either at the type or token level; as in Christodoulopoulos et al. (2011) we assume a single type-level feature m (morphology, drawn from $\phi^{(m)}$) and several token-level features $f^{(1)} \dots f^{(T)}$ (e.g., left and right context words and, in our extension, dependency features).

Inference in the model is performed using a collapsed Gibbs sampler, integrating out the model parameters and sampling the class label z_j for each

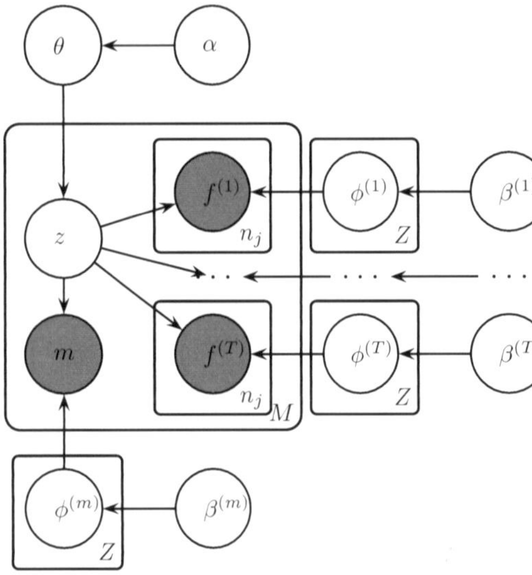

Figure 2: The BMMM with T kinds of token-level features ($f^{(t)}$ variables) and a single kind of type-level feature (morphology, m). M is the total number of word types, Z the number of classes, and n_j the number of tokens of type j.

word type j from the following posterior distribution:

$$P(z_j \mid \mathbf{z}_{-j}, \mathbf{f}, \alpha, \beta) \propto P(z_j \mid \mathbf{z}_{-j}, \alpha, \beta) P(\mathbf{f}_j \mid \mathbf{f}_{-j}, \mathbf{z}, \alpha, \beta) \quad (1)$$

where the first factor $P(z_j)$ is the prior distribution over classes (the mixing weights) and the second (likelihood) factor $P(\mathbf{f}_j)$ is the probability given class z_j of all the features associated with word type j. Since the different kinds of features are assumed to be independent, the likelihood can be rewritten as:

$$P(\mathbf{f}_j \mid \mathbf{f}_{-j}, \mathbf{z}, \alpha, \beta) = P(f_j^{(m)} \mid \mathbf{f}_{-j}^{(m)}, \mathbf{z}, \alpha, \beta) \cdot \prod_{t=1}^{T} P(\mathbf{f}_j^{(t)} \mid \mathbf{f}_{-j}^{(t)}, \mathbf{z}, \beta) \quad (2)$$

and, as explained in Christodoulopoulos et al. (2011), the joint probability of all the token level features of kind t for word type j is computed as:

$$P(\mathbf{f}_j^{(t)} \mid \mathbf{f}_{-j}^{(t)}, z_j = z, \mathbf{z}_{-j}, \beta) = \frac{\prod_{k=1}^{K^{(t)}} \prod_{i=0}^{n_{jk}-1} (n_{jk,z} + i + \beta)}{\prod_{i=0}^{n_j-1} (n_{\cdot,z} + i + F\beta)} \quad (3)$$

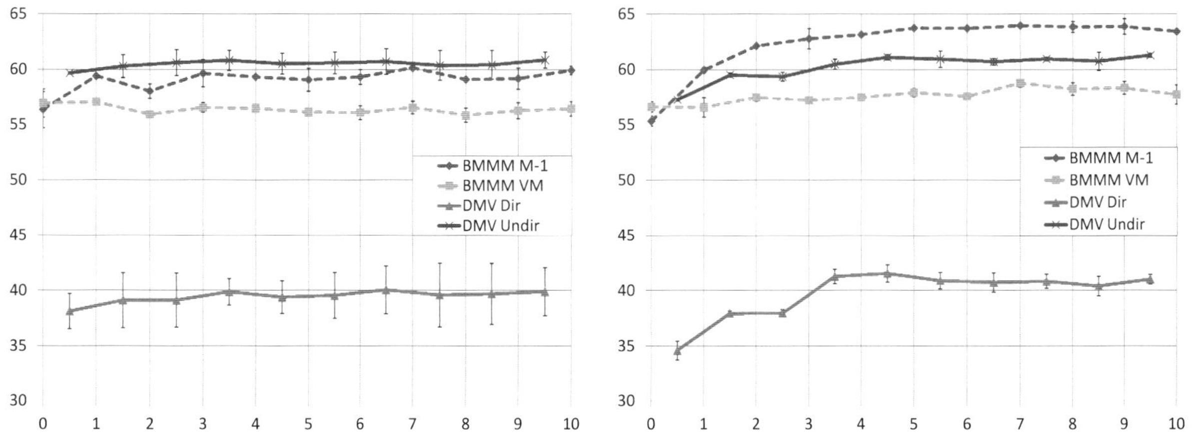

(a) Using only directed dependencies as features

(b) Using directed and undirected dependencies as features

Figure 3: Developmental results on WSJ10. The performance of the PoS inducer is shown in terms of many-to-1 accuracy (BMMM M1) and V-Measure accuracy (BMMM VM) and the performance of the dependency inducer is shown using directed and undirected dependency accuracy (DMV Dir and DMV Undir respectively).

where $K^{(t)}$ is the dimensionality of $\phi^{(t)}$ and n_{jk} is the number of instances of feature k in word type j.

4 Experimental design

Because the different kinds of features are assumed to be independent in the BMMM, it is easy to add more features into the model; this simply increases the number of factors in equation 2. To incorporate dependency information, we added a feature for word-word dependencies. In the model, this means that for a word type j with n_j tokens, we observe n_j dependency features (each being the head of one token of j). Like all other features, these are assumed to be drawn from a class-specific multinomial $\phi_z^{(d)}$ with a Dirichlet prior $\beta^{(d)}$.

Using lexicalized head dependencies introduces sparsity issues in much the same way contextual information does. In the case of context words, the BMMM and most vector-based clustering systems use a fixed number of most frequent words as features; however in the case of dependencies we use the induced PoS tags of the previous generation as grouping labels: we aggregate the head dependency counts of words that have the same PoS tag, so the dimension of $\phi_z^{(d)}$ is just the number of PoS tags.

The dependency features are used in tandem with the features used in the original BMMM system, namely the 100 most frequent context words (± 1 context window), the suffixes extracted from the Morfessor system (Creutz and Lagus, 2005) and the extended morphology features of Haghighi and Klein (2006).

For designing the iterated learning experiments, we used the 10-word version of the WSJ corpus (WSJ10) as development data and ran the iterative learning process for 10 generations. To evaluate the quality of the induced PoS tags we used the many-to-1 (M1) and V-Measure (VM) metrics and for the induced dependencies we used directed and undirected accuracy.

Figure 3a presents the developmental result of the iterated learning experiments on WSJ10 where only directed dependencies where used as features. We can see that although there was some improvement in the PoS induction score after the first generation, the rest of the metrics show no significant improvement throughout the experiment.

When we used undirected dependencies as features (figure 3b) the improvement over iterations was substantial: nearly 8.5% increase in M1 and 1.3% in VM after only 5 iterations. We can also see that the results of the DMV parser are improving as well: 7% increase in directed and 3.8% in undirected accuracy. This is to be expected, since as Headden et al. (2008) show, there is a (weak) correlation between the intrinsic scores of a PoS inducer and the performance of an unsupervised dependency parser trained on the inducer's output.

Using the same development set we selected the remaining system parameters; for the BMMM we fixed the number of induced classes to the number of gold-standard PoS tags for each language and used 500 sampling iterations with annealing. For the DMV model we used 20 EM iterations. Finally we used observed that after 5 generations the rate of improvement seems to level, so for the rest of the languages we use only 5 learning iterations.

References

Michael Auli and Adam Lopez. 2011. A comparison of loopy belief propagation and dual decomposition for integrated CCG supertagging and parsing. In *Proceedings of ACL-HLT*, pages 470–480.

James K. Baker. 1979. Trainable grammars for speech recognition. *The Journal of the Acoustical Society of America*, 65(S1):S132, June.

Christos Christodoulopoulos, Sharon Goldwater, and Mark Steedman. 2011. A Bayesian mixture model for pos induction using multiple features. In *Proceedings of EMNLP*, pages 638–647, Edinburgh, Scotland, UK., July.

Shay B. Cohen, Dipanjan Das, and Noah A. Smith. 2011. Unsupervised structure prediction with non-parallel multilingual guidance. In *Proceedings of EMNLP*, pages 50–61.

Mathias Creutz and Krista Lagus. 2005. Inducing the morphological lexicon of a natural language from unannotated text. In *In Proceedings of AKRR*, volume 5, pages 106–113.

Aria Haghighi and Dan Klein. 2006. Prototype-driven learning for sequence models. In *Proceedings of NAACL*, pages 320–327.

William P. Headden, David McClosky, and Eugene Charniak. 2008. Evaluating unsupervised part-of-speech tagging for grammar induction. In *Proceedings of COLING*, pages 329–336.

William P. Headden, Mark Johnson, and David McClosky. 2009. Improving unsupervised dependency parsing with richer contexts and smoothing. In *Proceedings of NAACL*, pages 101–109.

Dan Klein and Christopher D. Manning. 2004. Corpus-based induction of syntactic structure: models of dependency and constituency. In *Proceedings of ACL*.

Zhenghua Li, Min Zhang, Wanxiang Che, Ting Liu, Wenliang Chen, and Haizhou Li. 2011. Joint models for chinese POS tagging and dependency parsing. In *Proceedings of EMNLP*, pages 1180–1191.

Kenny Smith, Simon Kirby, and Henry Brighton. 2003. Iterated learning: a framework for the emergence of language. *Artif. Life*, 9(4):371–386.

Hierarchical clustering of word class distributions

Grzegorz Chrupała
gchrupala@lsv.uni-saarland.de
Spoken Language Systems
Saarland University

Abstract

We propose an unsupervised approach to POS tagging where first we associate each word type with a probability distribution over word classes using Latent Dirichlet Allocation. Then we create a hierarchical clustering of the word types: we use an agglomerative clustering algorithm where the distance between clusters is defined as the Jensen-Shannon divergence between the probability distributions over classes associated with each word-type. When assigning POS tags, we find the tree leaf most similar to the current word and use the prefix of the path leading to this leaf as the tag. This simple labeler outperforms a baseline based on Brown clusters on 9 out of 10 datasets.

1 Introduction

Unsupervised induction of word categories has been approached from three broad perspectives. First, it is of interest to cognitive scientists who model syntactic category acquisition by children (Redington et al. 1998, Mintz 2003, Parisien et al. 2008, Chrupała and Alishahi 2010), where the primary concern is matching human performance patterns and satisfying cognitively motivated constraints such as incremental learning.

Second, learning categories has been cast as unsupervised part-of-speech tagging task (recent work includes Ravi and Knight (2009), Lee et al. (2010), Lamar et al. (2010), Christodoulopoulos et al. (2011)), and primarily motivated as useful for tagging under-resourced languages.

Finally, learning categories has also been researched from the point of view of feature learning, where the induced categories provide an intermediate level of representation, abstracting away and generalizing over word form features in an NLP application (Brown et al. 1992, Miller et al. 2004, Lin and Wu 2009, Turian et al. 2010, Chrupala 2011, Täckström et al. 2012). The main difference from the part-of-speech setting is that the focus is on evaluating the performance of the learned categories in real tasks rather than on measuring how closely they match gold part-of-speech tags. Some researchers have used both approaches to evaluation.

This difference in evaluation methodology also naturally leads to differing constraints on the nature of the induced representations. For part-of-speech tagging what is needed is a mapping from word tokens to a small set of discrete, atomic labels. For feature learning, there are is no such limitation, and other types of representations have been used, such as low-dimensional continuous vectors learned by neural network language models as in Bengio et al. (2006), Mnih and Hinton (2009), or distributions over word classes learned using Latent Dirichlet Allocation as in Chrupala (2011).

In this paper we propose a simple method of mapping distributions over word classes to a set of discrete labels by hierarchically clustering word class distributions using Jensen-Shannon divergence as a distance metric. This allows us to effectively use the algorithm of Chrupala (2011) and similar ones in settings where using distributions directly is not possible or desirable. Equivalently, our approach can be seen as a generic method to convert a soft clustering to hard clustering while conserving much of the information encoded in the original soft cluster assignments. We evaluate this method on the unsupervised part-of-speech tagging task on ten datasets in nine languages as part of the shared task at the NAACL-HLT 2012 Workshop on Inducing Linguistic Structure.

2 Architecture

Our system consists of the following components (i) a soft word-class induction model (ii) a hierarchical clustering algorithm which builds a tree of word class distributions (iii) a labeler which for each word type finds the leaf in the tree with the most similar word-class distribution and outputs a prefix of the path leading to that leaf.

2.1 Soft word-class model

We use the probabilistic soft word-class model proposed by Chrupala (2011), which is based on Latent Dirichlet Allocation (LDA). LDA was introduced by Blei et al. (2003) and applied to modeling the topic structure in document collections. It is a generative, probabilistic hierarchical Bayesian model which induces a set of latent variables, which correspond to the topics. The topics themselves are multinomial distributions over words.

The generative structure of the LDA model is the following:

$$\begin{aligned} \phi_k &\sim \text{Dirichlet}(\beta), & k &\in [1, K] \\ \theta_d &\sim \text{Dirichlet}(\alpha), & d &\in [1, D] \\ z_{n_d} &\sim \text{Categorical}(\theta_d), & n_d &\in [1, N_d] \\ w_{n_d} &\sim \text{Categorical}(\phi_{z_{n_d}}), & n_d &\in [1, N_d] \end{aligned} \tag{1}$$

Chrupala (2011) interprets the LDA model in terms of word classes as follows: K is the number of classes, D is the number of unique word types, N_d is the number of context features (such as right or left neighbor) associated with word type d, z_{n_d} is the class of word type d in the n_d^{th} context, and w_{n_d} is the n_d^{th} context feature of word type d. Hyperparameters α and β control the sparseness of the vectors θ_d and ϕ_k.

Inference in LDA in general can be performed using either variational EM or Gibbs sampling. Here we use a collapsed Gibbs sampler to estimate two sets of parameters: the θ_d parameters correspond to word class probability distributions given a word type while the ϕ_k correspond to feature distributions given a word class. In the current paper we focus on θ_d which we use to represent a word type d as a distribution over word classes.

Soft word classes are more expressive than hard categories. They make it easy and efficient to express shared ambiguities: Chrupala (2011) gives an example of words used as either first names or surnames, where this shared ambiguity is reflected in the similarity of their word class distributions.

Another important property of soft word classes is that they make it easy to express graded similarity between words types. With hard classes, a pair of words either belong to the same class or to different classes, i.e. similarity is a binary indicator. With soft word classes, we can use standard measures of similarity between probability distributions to judge how similar words are to each other. We take advantage of this feature to build a hierarchical clustering of word types.

2.2 Hierarchical clustering of word types

In some settings, e.g. in the unsupervised part-of-speech tagging scenario, words should be labeled with a small set of discrete labels. The question then arises how to map a probability distribution over word classes corresponding to each word type in the soft word class setting to a discrete label. The most obvious method would be to simply output the highest scoring word class, but this has the disadvantage of discarding much of the information present in the soft labeling.

What we do instead is to create a hierarchical clustering of word types using the Jensen-Shannon (JS) divergence between the word-class distributions as a distance function. JS divergence is an information-theoretic measure of dissimilarity between two probability distributions (Lin 1991). It is defined as follows:

$$JS(P, Q) = \frac{1}{2}\left(D_{\text{KL}}(P, M) + D_{\text{KL}}(Q, M)\right) \tag{2}$$

where M is the mean distribution $\frac{P+Q}{2}$ and D_{KL} is the Kullback-Leibler (KL) divergence:

$$D_{\text{KL}}(P, Q) = \sum_i P(i) \log_2 \frac{P(i)}{Q(i)} \tag{3}$$

Unlike KL divergence, JS divergence is symmetric and is defined for any pair of discrete probability distributions over the same domain.

We use a simple agglomerative clustering algorithm to build a tree hierarchy over the word class distributions corresponding to word types (see Algorithm 1). We start with a set of leaf nodes, one for each of D word types, containing the unnormalized word-class probabilities for the corresponding word type: i.e. the co-occurrence counts of word-type and word-class, $n(z, d)$, output by the Gibbs sampler.

We then merge that pair of nodes (P, Q) whose JS divergence is the smallest, remove these two nodes from the set, and add the new merged node with two branches. We proceed in this fashion until we obtain a single root node.

When merging two nodes we sum their co-occurrence count tables: thus the nodes always contain unnormalized probabilities which are normalized only when computing JS scores.

Algorithm 1 Bottom-up clustering of word types

$S = \{n(\cdot, d) \mid d \in [1, D]\}$
while $|S| > 1$ **do**
    $(P, Q) = \mathrm{argmin}_{(P,Q) \in S \times S}\, JS(P, Q)$
    $S \leftarrow S \setminus \{P, Q\} \cup \{\mathrm{merge}(P, Q)\}$

The algorithm is simple but not very efficient: if implemented carefully it can be at best quadratic in the number of word types. However, in practice it is unnecessary to run it on more than a few hundred word types which can be done very quickly. In the experiments reported on below we build the tree based only on the 1000 most frequent words.

Figure 1 shows two small fragments of a hierarchy built from 200 most frequent words of the English CHILDES dataset using 10 LDA word classes.

2.3 Tree paths as labels

Once the tree is built, it can be used to assign a label to any word which has an associated word class distribution. In principle, it could be used to perform either type-level or token-level tagging: token-level distributions could be composed from the distributions associated with current word type (θ) and the distributions associated with the current context features (ϕ). Since preliminary experiments with token-level tagging were not successful, here we focus exclusively on type-level tagging.

Given the tree and a word-type paired with a class distribution, we generate a path to a leaf in the tree

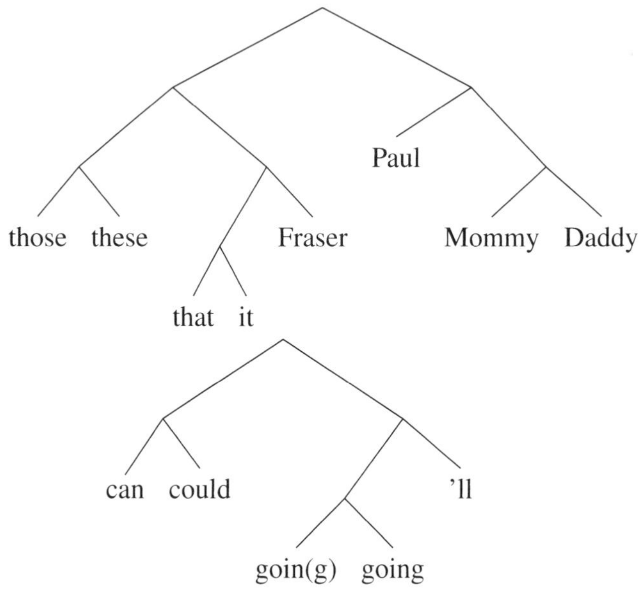

Figure 1: Two fragments of a hierarchy over word class distributions

as follows. If the word is one of the ones used to construct the tree, we simply record the path from the root to the leaf containing this word. If the word is not at any of the leaves (i.e. it is not one of the 1000 most frequent words), we traverse the tree, at each node comparing the JS divergence between the word and the left and right branches, and then descend along the branch for which JS is smaller. We record the path until we reach a leaf node.

We can control the granularity of the labeling by varying the length of the prefix of the path from the root to the leaf.

3 Experiments

We evaluate our method on the unsupervised part-of-speech tagging task on ten dataset in nine languages as part of the shared task.

For each dataset we run LDA word class induction[1] on the union of the unlabeled sentences in the train, development and test sets, setting the number of classes $K \in \{10, 20, 40, 80\}$, and build a hierarchy on top of the learned word-class probability distributions as explained above. We then label the development set using path prefixes of length $L \in \{8, 9, \ldots, 20\}$ for each of the trees, and record

[1] We ran 200 Gibbs sampling passes, and set the LDA hyper-parameters to $\alpha = \frac{10}{K}$ and $\beta = 0.1$.

Dataset	K	L	Brown	HCD
Arabic	40	13	39.6	**51.4**
Basque	40	16	39.5	**48.3**
Czech	80	8	42.1	**42.4**
Danish	40	19	50.2	**56.8**
Dutch	40	10	43.3	**54.8**
English CH	10	12	64.1	**67.8**
English PTB	40	8	**61.6**	60.2
Portuguese	80	10	51.7	**52.4**
Slovene	80	19	44.5	**46.6**
Swedish	20	17	51.8	**56.1**

Table 1: Evaluation of coarse-grained POS tagging on test data

Dataset	K	L	Brown	HCD
Arabic	40	13	42.2	**52.9**
Basque	40	16	38.5	**54.4**
Czech	40	19	45.3	**46.8**
Danish	40	20	49.2	**63.6**
Dutch	20	12	49.4	**53.4**
English CH	10	12	66.0	**78.2**
English PTB	80	14	**62.0**	61.3
Portuguese	80	11	52.9	**54.7**
Slovene	80	20	45.8	**51.9**
Swedish	20	17	51.8	**56.1**

Table 2: Evaluation of coarse-grained POS tagging on test data

the V-measure (Rosenberg and Hirschberg 2007) against gold part-of-speech tags. We choose the best-performing pair of K and L and use this setting to label the test set. We tune separately for coarse-grained and fine-grained POS tags. Other than using the development set labels to tune these two parameters our system is unsupervised and uses no data other than the sentences in the provided data files.

Table 1 and Table 2 show the best settings for the coarse- and fine-grained POS tagging for all the datasets, and the V-measure scores on the test set achieved by our labeler (HCD for Hierarchy over Class Distributions). Also included are the scores of the official baseline, i.e. labeling with Brown clusters (Brown et al. 1992), with the number of clusters set to match the number of POS tags in each dataset.

The best K stays the same when increasing the granularity in the majority of cases (7 out of 10). On the CHILDES dataset of child-directed speech,

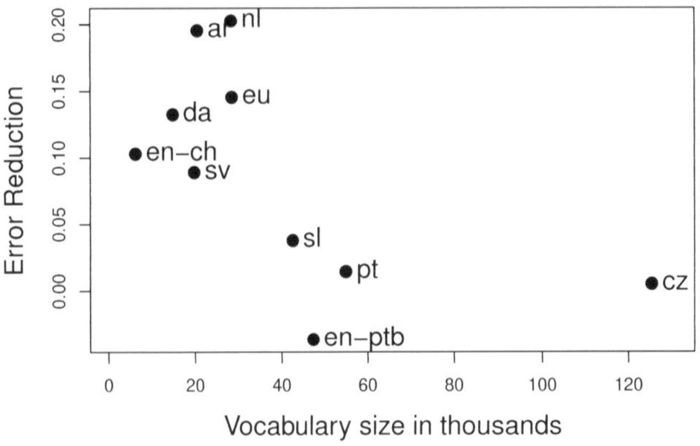

Figure 2: Error reduction as a function of vocabulary size

which has the smallest vocabulary of all, the optimal number of LDA classes is also the smallest (10). As expected, the best path prefix length L is typically larger for the fine-grained labeling.

Our labels outperform the baseline on 9 out of 10 datasets, for both levels of granularity. The only exception is the English Penn Treebank dataset, where the HCD V-measure scores are slightly lower than Brown cluster scores. This may be taken as an illustration of the danger arising if NLP systems are exclusively evaluated on a single dataset: such a dataset may well prove to not be very representative.

Part of the story seems to be that our method tends to outperform the baseline by larger margins on datasets with smaller vocabularies[2]. The scatter-plot in Figure 2 illustrates this tendency for coarse-grained POS tagging: Pearson's correlation is -0.6.

4 Conclusion

We have proposed a simple method of converting a set of soft class assignments to a set of discrete labels by building a hierarchical clustering over word-class distributions associated with word types. This allows to use the efficient and effective LDA-based word-class induction method in cases where a hard clustering is required. We have evaluated this

[2]We suspect performance on datasets with large vocabularies could be improved by increasing the number of frequent words used to build the word-type hierarchy; due to time constraints we had to postpone verifying it.

method on the POS tagging task on which our approach outperforms a baseline based on Brown clusters in 9 out of 10 cases, often by a substantial margin.

In future it would be interesting to investigate whether the hierarchy over word-class distributions would also be useful as a source of features in a semi-supervised learning scenario, instead, or in addition to using word-class probabilities as features directly. We would also like to revisit and further investigate the challenging problem of token-level labeling.

References

Bengio, Y., Schwenk, H., Senécal, J., Morin, F., and Gauvain, J. (2006). Neural Probabilistic Language Models. *Innovations in Machine Learning*, pages 137–186.

Blei, D., Ng, A., and Jordan, M. (2003). Latent dirichlet allocation. *The Journal of Machine Learning Research*, 3:993–1022.

Brown, P. F., Mercer, R. L., Della Pietra, V. J., and Lai, J. C. (1992). Class-based n-gram models of natural language. *Computational Linguistics*, 18(4):467–479.

Christodoulopoulos, C., Goldwater, S., and Steedman, M. (2011). A bayesian mixture model for part-of-speech induction using multiple features. In *EMNLP*.

Chrupala, G. (2011). Efficient induction of probabilistic word classes with LDA. In *IJCNLP*.

Chrupała, G. and Alishahi, A. (2010). Online Entropy-based Model of Lexical Category Acquisition. In *CoNLL*.

Lamar, M., Maron, Y., Johnson, M., and Bienenstock, E. (2010). Svd and clustering for unsupervised pos tagging. In *ACL*.

Lee, Y., Haghighi, A., and Barzilay, R. (2010). Simple type-level unsupervised pos tagging. In *EMNLP*.

Lin, D. and Wu, X. (2009). Phrase clustering for discriminative learning. In *ACL/IJCNLP*.

Lin, J. (1991). Divergence measures based on the shannon entropy. *Information Theory, IEEE Transactions on*, 37(1):145–151.

Miller, S., Guinness, J., and Zamanian, A. (2004). Name tagging with word clusters and discriminative training. In *HLT/NAACL*.

Mintz, T. (2003). Frequent frames as a cue for grammatical categories in child directed speech. *Cognition*, 90(1):91–117.

Mnih, A. and Hinton, G. (2009). A scalable hierarchical distributed language model. In *NIPS*.

Parisien, C., Fazly, A., and Stevenson, S. (2008). An incremental bayesian model for learning syntactic categories. In *CoNLL*.

Ravi, S. and Knight, K. (2009). Minimized models for unsupervised part-of-speech tagging. In *ACL/IJCNLP*.

Redington, M., Crater, N., and Finch, S. (1998). Distributional information: A powerful cue for acquiring syntactic categories. *Cognitive Science: A Multidisciplinary Journal*, 22(4):425–469.

Rosenberg, A. and Hirschberg, J. (2007). V-measure: A conditional entropy-based external cluster evaluation measure. In *EMNLP/CoNLL*.

Turian, J., Ratinov, L., and Bengio, Y. (2010). Word representations: A simple and general method for semi-supervised learning. In *ACL*.

Täckström, O., McDonald, R., and Uszkoreit, J. (2012). Cross-lingual word clusters for direct transfer of linguistic structure. In *NAACL*.

Combining the Sparsity and Unambiguity Biases for Grammar Induction

Kewei Tu
Departments of Statistics and Computer Science
University of California, Los Angeles
Los Angeles, CA 90095, USA
tukw@ucla.edu

Abstract

In this paper we describe our participating system for the dependency induction track of the PASCAL Challenge on Grammar Induction. Our system incorporates two types of inductive biases: the sparsity bias and the unambiguity bias. The sparsity bias favors a grammar with fewer grammar rules. The unambiguity bias favors a grammar that leads to unambiguous parses, which is motivated by the observation that natural language is remarkably unambiguous in the sense that the number of plausible parses of a natural language sentence is very small. We introduce our approach to combining these two types of biases and discuss the system implementation. Our experiments show that both types of inductive biases are beneficial to grammar induction.

1 Introduction

Grammar induction refers to the induction of a formal grammar from a corpus of unannotated sentences. There has been significant progress over the past decade in the research of natural language grammar induction. A variety of approaches and techniques have been proposed, most of which are designed to induce probabilistic dependency grammars. The PASCAL Challenge on Grammar Induction aims to provide a thorough evaluation of approaches to natural language grammar induction. The challenge includes three tracks: inducing dependency structures using the gold standard part-of-speech tags, inducing both dependency structures and part-of-speech tags directly from text, and an open-resource track which allows other external resources to be used. Ten corpora of nine different languages are used in the challenge: Arabic (Hajič et al., 2004), Basque (Aduriz et al., 2003), Czech (Hajič et al., 2000), Danish (Buch-Kromann et al., 2007), Dutch (Beek et al., 2002), English WSJ (Marcus et al., 1993), English CHILDES (Sagae et al., 2007), Portuguese (Afonso et al., 2002), Slovene (Erjavec et al., 2010), and Swedish (Nivre et al., 2006). For each corpus, a large set of unannotated sentences are provided as the training data, along with a small set of annotated sentences as the development data; the predictions on the unannotated test data submitted by challenge participants are evaluated against the gold standard annotations.

We participate in the track of inducing dependency structures from gold standard part-of-speech tags. Our system incorporates two types of inductive biases in learning dependency grammars: the sparsity bias and the unambiguity bias. The sparsity bias favors a grammar with fewer grammar rules. We employ two different approaches to inducing sparsity: Dirichlet priors over grammar rule probabilities and an approach based on posterior regularization (Gillenwater et al., 2010). The unambiguity bias favors a grammar that leads to unambiguous parses, which is motivated by the observation that natural language is remarkably unambiguous in the sense that the number of plausible parses of a natural language sentence is very small. To induce unambiguity in the learned grammar we propose an approach named unambiguity regularization based on the posterior regularization framework (Ganchev et al., 2010). To combine Dirichlet priors with unambiguity regularization, we derive a mean-field variational inference algorithm. To combine the sparsity-inducing posterior regularization approach with unambiguity regularization, we employ a simplistic approach that optimizes the two regularization terms separately.

The rest of the paper is organized as follows. Section 2 introduces the two approaches that we employ to induce sparsity. Section 3 introduces the unambiguity bias and the unambiguity regularization approach. Section 4 discusses how we combine the sparsity bias with the unambiguity bias. Section 5 provides details of our implementation and training procedure. Section 6 concludes the paper.

2 Sparsity Bias

A sparsity bias in grammar induction favors a grammar that has fewer grammar rules. We employ two different approaches to inducing sparsity: Dirichlet priors over grammar rule probabilities and an approach based on posterior regularization (Gillenwater et al., 2010).

A probabilistic grammar consists of a set of probabilistic grammar rules. A discrete distribution is defined over each set of grammar rules with the same left-hand side, and a Dirichlet distribution can be used as the prior of the discrete distribution. Denote vector θ of dimension K as the parameter of a discrete distribution. Then a Dirichlet prior over θ is defined as:

$$P(\theta; \alpha_1, \ldots, \alpha_K) = \frac{1}{B(\alpha)} \prod_{i=1}^{K} \theta_i^{\alpha_i - 1}$$

where $\alpha = (\alpha_1, \ldots, \alpha_K)$ are the hyperparameters, and $B(\alpha)$ is the normalization constant. Typically, all the hyperparameters are set to the same value. It can be shown that if the hyperparameters are less than 1, then the Dirichlet prior assigns larger probabilities to vectors that have more elements close to zero. Therefore, Dirichlet priors can be used to encourage parameter sparsity. It has been found that when applied to dependency grammar induction, Dirichlet priors with hyperparamters set to values less than 1 can slightly improve the accuracy of the learned grammar over the maximum-likelihood estimation (Cohen et al., 2008; Gillenwater et al., 2010).

Gillenwater et al. (2010) proposed a differnt approach to inducing sparsity in dependency grammar induction based on the posterior regularization framework (Ganchev et al., 2010). They added a regularization term to the posterior of the grammar that penalizes the number of unique dependency types in the parses of the training data. More specifically, their objective function is:

$$J(\theta) = \log p(\theta|\mathbf{X}) - \min_q \Bigg(\mathbf{KL}(q(\mathbf{Z})||p_\theta(\mathbf{Z}|\mathbf{X})) + \sigma_s \sum_{cp} \max_i \mathbf{E}_q[\phi_{cpi}(\mathbf{X}, \mathbf{Z})] \Bigg)$$

where θ is the parameter of the grammar, $\mathbf{X}$ is the training data, $\mathbf{Z}$ is the dependency parses of the training data $\mathbf{X}$, σ_s is a constant that controls the strength of the regularization term, c and p range over all the tags of the dependency grammar, i ranges over all the occurrences of tag c in the training data $\mathbf{X}$, and $\phi_{cpi}(\mathbf{X}, \mathbf{Z})$ is an indicator function of whether tag p is the dependency head of the i-th occurrence of tag c in the dependency parses $\mathbf{Z}$. This objective function is optimized using a variant of the expectation-maximization algorithm (EM), which contains an E-step that optimizes the auxiliary distribution q using the projected subgradient method. It has been shown that this approach achieves higher degree of sparsity than Dirichlet priors and leads to significant improvement in accuracy of the learned grammars.

3 Unambiguity Bias

The unambiguity bias favors a grammar that leads to unambiguous parses on natural language sentences (Tu and Honavar, 2012). This bias is motivated by the observation that natural language is remarkably unambiguous in the sense that the number of plausible parses of a natural language sentence is very small in comparison with the total number of possible parses. To illustrate this, we randomly sample an English sentence from the Wall Street Journal and parse the sentence using the Berkeley parser (Petrov et al., 2006), one of the state-of-the-art English language parsers. The estimated total number of possible parses of this sentence is 2×10^{20} (by assuming a complete Chomsky normal form grammar with

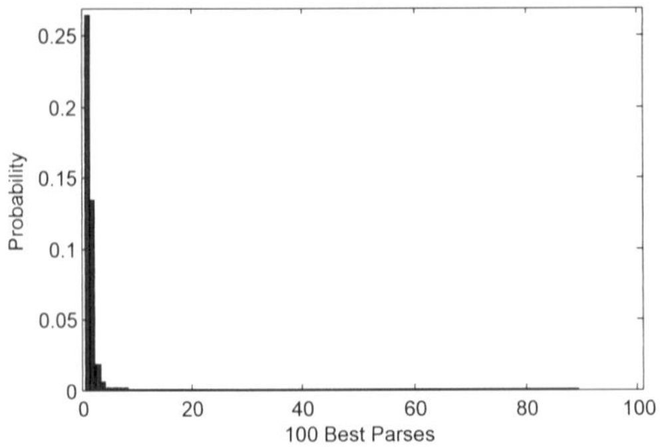

Figure 1: The probabilities of the 100 best parses of the sample sentence.

the same number of nonterminals as in the Berkeley parser). However, as shown in Figure 1, most of the parses have probabilities that are negligible compared with the probability of the best parse.

To induce unambiguity in the learned grammar, we derive an approach named *unambiguity regularization* (Tu and Honavar, 2012) based on the posterior regularization framework (Ganchev et al., 2010). Specifically, we add into the objective function a regularization term that penalizes the entropy of the parses given the training sentences. Let $\mathbf{X}$ denote the set of training sentences, $\mathbf{Z}$ denote the set of parses of the training sentences, and θ denote the rule probabilities of the grammar. Our objective function is

$$J(\theta) = \log p(\theta|\mathbf{X}) - \min_{q} \left(\mathbf{KL}(q(\mathbf{Z})||p_\theta(\mathbf{Z}|\mathbf{X})) + \sigma_u H(q)\right)$$

where σ_u is a nonnegative constant that controls the strength of the regularization term; q is an auxiliary distribution. The first term in the objective function is the log posterior probability of the grammar parameters given the training corpus, and the second term minimizes the KL-divergence between the auxiliary distribution q and the posterior distribution of $\mathbf{Z}$ while also minimizes the entropy of q. This objective function is optimized using coordinate ascent in our approach. It can be shown that the behavior of our approach is controlled by the value of the parameter σ_u. When $\sigma_u = 0$, our approach reduces to the standard EM algorithm. When $\sigma_u \geq 1$, our approach reduces to the Viterbi EM algorithm, which considers only the best parses of the training sentences in the E-step. When $0 < \sigma_u < 1$, our approach falls between standard EM and Viterbi EM: it applies a softmax function to the distribution of the parse z_i of each training sentence x_i in the E-step:

$$q(z_i) = \alpha_i p_\theta(z_i|x_i)^{\frac{1}{1-\sigma_u}}$$

where α_i is the normalization factor. To compute q, note that $p_\theta(z_i|x_i)$ is the product of a set of grammar rule probabilities, so we can raise all the rule probabilities of the grammar to the power of $\frac{1}{1-\sigma_u}$ and then run the normal E-step of the EM algorithm. The normalization of q is included in the normal E-step. We refer to the algorithm in the case of $0 < \sigma_u < 1$ as the *softmax-EM* algorithm.

The choice of the value of σ_u is important in unambiguity regularization. Considering that in grammar induction the initial grammar is typically very ambiguous, the value of σ_u should be set large enough to induce unambiguity. On the other hand, natural language grammars do contain some degree of ambiguity, so the value of σ_u should not be set too large. One way to avoid choosing a fixed value of σ_u is to anneal its value. We start learning with a large value of σ_u (e.g., $\sigma_u = 1$) to strongly push the learner away from the highly ambiguous initial grammar; then we gradually reduce the value of σ_u, possibly ending with $\sigma_u = 0$, to avoid inducing excessive unambiguity in the learned grammar.

4 Combining Sparsity and Unambiguity Biases

To incorporate Dirichlet priors over grammar rule probabilities into our unambiguity regularization approach, we derive a mean-field variational inference algorithm (Tu and Honavar, 2012). The algorithm alternately optimizes $q(\theta)$ and $q(\mathbf{Z})$. The optimization of $q(\theta)$ is exactly the same as in the standard mean-field variational inference with Dirichlet priors, in which we obtain a set of weights that are summarized from $q(\theta)$ (Kurihara and Sato, 2004). The optimization of $q(\mathbf{Z})$ is similar to the E-step of our approach discussed in section 3: when $0 < \sigma_u < 1$, we raise all the weights to the power of $\frac{1}{1-\sigma_u}$ before running the normal step of computing $q(\mathbf{Z})$ in the standard mean-field variational inference; and when $\sigma_u \geq 1$, we use the weights to find the best parse of each training sentence and assign probability 1 to it.

The sparsity-inducing posterior regularization approach and our unambiguity regularization approach are based on the same posterior regularization framework. To combine these two approaches, the standard method is to optimize a linear combination of the sparsity and unambiguity regularization terms in the E-step of the posterior regularization algorithm. Here we employ a simplistic approach instead which optimizes the two regularization terms separately in the E-step. Specifically, we first ignore the sparsity regularization term and optimize $q(\mathbf{Z})$ with respect to the unambiguity regularization term using the approach discussed in section 3. The optimization result is an intermediate distribution $q'(\mathbf{Z})$. Then we ignore the unambiguity regularization term and optimize $q(\mathbf{Z})$ to minimize the sparsity regularization term as well as the KL-divergence between $q(\mathbf{Z})$ and $q'(\mathbf{Z})$.

5 Implementation and Experiments

Our system was built on top of the PR-Dep-Parsing package[1]. We implemented both approaches introduced in section 4, i.e., unambiguity regularization with Dirichlet priors and combined posterior regularization of sparsity and unambiguity. For the latter, we did not implement the $\sigma_u \geq 1$ case and the annealing of σ_u because of time constraint.

We preprocessed the corpora to remove all the punctuations as denoted by the universal POS tags. One exception is that for the English WSJ corpus we did not remove the $ symbol because we found that removing it significantly decreased the accuracy of the learned grammar. We combined the provided training, development and test set as our training set. We trained our system on the fine POS tags except for the Dutch corpus. In the Dutch corpus, the fine POS tags are the same as the coarse POS tags except that each multi-word unit is annotated with the concatenation of the POS tags of all the component words, making the training data for such tags extremely sparse. So we chose to use the coarse POS tags for the Dutch corpus.

We employed the informed initialization proposed in (Klein and Manning, 2004) and ran our two approaches on the training set. We tuned the parameters by coordinate ascent on the development set. The parameters that we tuned include the maximal length of sentences used in training, the valence and back-off strength of the E-DMV model, the hyperparameter α of Dirichlet priors, the type (PR-S or PR-AS) and strength σ_s of sparsity-inducing posterior regularization, and the strength σ_u of unambiguity regularization. Sparsity-inducing posterior regularization has a high computational cost. Consequently, we were not able to run our second approach on the English CHILDES corpus and the Czech corpus, and performed relatively limited parameter tuning of the second approach on the other eight corpora.

Table 1 shows, for each corpus, the approach and the parameters that we found to perform the best on the development set and were hence used to learn the final grammar that produced the submitted predictions on the test set. Each of our two approaches was found to be the better approach for five of the ten corpora. The sparsity bias was found to be beneficial (i.e., $\alpha < 1$ if Dirichlet priors were used, or $\sigma_s > 0$ if sparsity-inducing posterior regularization was used) for six of the ten corpora. The unambiguity bias was found to be beneficial (i.e., $\sigma_u > 0$) for seven of the ten corpora. This implies the usefulness of both types of inductive biases in grammar induction. For only one corpus, the English CHILDES corpus, neither the sparsity bias nor the unambiguity bias was found to be beneficial, probably because this corpus is a collection of child language and the corresponding grammar might be less sparse and more ambiguous than adult grammars.

6 Conclusion

In this paper we have described our participating system for the dependency induction track of the PASCAL Challenge on Grammar Induction. Our system incorporates two types of inductive biases: the sparsity bias and the unambiguity bias. The sparsity bias favors a grammar with fewer grammar rules. We employ two types of sparsity biases: Dirichlet priors over grammar rule probabilities and the sparsity-inducing posterior regularization. The unambiguity bias favors a grammar that leads to unambiguous parses, which is motivated by the observation that natural language is remarkably unambiguous in the sense that the number of plausible

[1]Available at `http://code.google.com/p/pr-toolkit/`

Corpus	Approach	Parameters
Arabic	Dir+UR	maxlen = 20, valence = 4/4, back-off = 0.1, $\alpha = 10^{-5}$, $\sigma_u = 0.75$
Basque	PR+UR	maxlen = 10, valence = 3/3, back-off = 0.1, PR-AS, $\sigma_s = 100$, $\sigma_u = 0$
Czech	Dir+UR	maxlen = 10, valence = 3/3, back-off = 0.1, $\alpha = 1$, $\sigma_u = 1 - 0.1 \times iter$
Danish	PR+UR	maxlen = 20, valence = 2/1, back-off = 0.33, PR-AS, $\sigma_s = 100$, $\sigma_u = 0.5$
Dutch	PR+UR	maxlen = 10, valence = 3/3, back-off = 0, PR-S, $\sigma_s = 140$, $\sigma_u = 0$
English WSJ	Dir+UR	maxlen = 10, valence = 2/2, back-off = 0.33, $\alpha = 1$, $\sigma_u = 1 - 0.01 \times iter$
English CHILDES	Dir+UR	maxlen = 15, valence = 4/4, back-off = 0.1, $\alpha = 10$, $\sigma_u = 0$
Portuguese	PR+UR	maxlen = 15, valence = 2/1, back-off = 0, PR-AS, $\sigma_s = 140$, $\sigma_u = 0.5$
Slovene	PR+UR	maxlen = 10, valence = 4/4, back-off = 0.1, PR-AS, $\sigma_s = 140$, $\sigma_u = 0$
Swedish	Dir+UR	maxlen = 10, valence = 4/4, back-off = 0.1, $\alpha = 1$, $\sigma_u = 1 - 0.5 \times iter$

Table 1: For each corpus, the approach and the parameters that we found to perform the best on the development set and were hence used to learn the final grammar that produced the submitted predictions on the test set. In the second column, "Dir+UR" denotes our approach of unambiguity regularization with Dirichlet priors, and "PR+UR" denotes our approach of combined posterior regularization of sparsity and unambiguity. The parameters in the third column are explained in the main text.

parses of a natural language sentence is very small. We propose an approach named unambiguity regularization to induce unambiguity based on the posterior regularization framework. To combine Dirichlet priors with unambiguity regularization, we derive a mean-field variational inference algorithm. To combine the sparsity-inducing posterior regularization approach with unambiguity regularization, we employ a simplistic approach that optimizes the two regularization terms separately. We have also introduced our implementation and training procedure for the challenge. Our experimental results show that both types of inductive biases are beneficial to grammar induction.

References

I. Aduriz, M. J. Aranzabe, J. M. Arriola, A. Atutxa, A. Diaz de Ilarraza, A. Garmendia, , and M. Oronoz. 2003. Construction of a basque dependency treebank. In *Proc. of the 2nd Workshop on Treebanks and Linguistic Theories (TLT)*.

Susana Afonso, Eckhard Bick, Renato Haber, and Diana Santos. 2002. "floresta sintá(c)tica": a treebank for Portuguese. In *Proceedings of the 3rd Intern. Conf. on Language Resources and Evaluation (LREC)*, pages 1968–1703.

Van Der Beek, G. Bouma, R. Malouf, G. Van Noord, and Rijksuniversiteit Groningen. 2002. The alpino dependency treebank. In *In Computational Linguistics in the Netherlands (CLIN*, pages 1686–1691.

Matthias Buch-Kromann, Jürgen Wedekind, , and Jakob Elming. 2007. The copenhagen danish-english dependency treebank v. 2.0. http://www.buch-kromann.dk/matthias/cdt2.0/.

Shay B. Cohen, Kevin Gimpel, and Noah A. Smith. 2008. Logistic normal priors for unsupervised probabilistic grammar induction. In *NIPS*, pages 321–328.

Tomaz Erjavec, Darja Fiser, Simon Krek, and Nina Ledinek. 2010. The jos linguistically tagged corpus of slovene. In *LREC*.

Kuzman Ganchev, João Graça, Jennifer Gillenwater, and Ben Taskar. 2010. Posterior regularization for structured latent variable models. *Journal of Machine Learning Research*, 11:2001–2049.

Jennifer Gillenwater, Kuzman Ganchev, João Graça, Fernando Pereira, and Ben Taskar. 2010. Sparsity in dependency grammar induction. In *ACL '10: Proceedings of the ACL 2010 Conference Short Papers*, pages 194–199, Morristown, NJ, USA. Association for Computational Linguistics.

Jan Hajič, Alena Böhmová, Eva Hajičová, and Barbora Vidová-Hladká. 2000. The Prague Dependency Treebank: A Three-Level Annotation Scenario. In A. Abeillé, editor, *Treebanks: Building and Using Parsed Corpora*, pages 103–127. Amsterdam:Kluwer.

Jan Hajič, Otakar Smrž, Petr Zemánek, Jan Šnaidauf, and Emanuel Beška. 2004. Prague arabic dependency treebank: Development in data and tools. In *In Proc. of the NEMLAR Intern. Conf. on Arabic Language Resources and Tools*, pages 110–117.

Mark Johnson, Thomas L. Griffiths, and Sharon Goldwater. 2007. Bayesian inference for pcfgs via markov chain monte carlo. In *HLT-NAACL*, pages 139–146.

Dan Klein and Christopher D. Manning. 2004. Corpus-based induction of syntactic structure: Models of dependency and constituency. In *Proceedings of ACL*.

Kenichi Kurihara and Taisuke Sato. 2004. An application of the variational Bayesian approach to probabilistic contextfree grammars. In *IJCNLP-04 Workshop beyond shallow analyses*.

Mitchell P. Marcus, Beatrice Santorini, and Mary Ann Marcinkiewicz. 1993. Building a large annotated corpus of english: The penn treebank. *COMPUTATIONAL LINGUISTICS*, 19(2):313–330.

Joakim Nivre, Jens Nilsson, and Johan Hall. 2006. Talbanken05: A Swedish Treebank with Phrase Structure and Dependency Annotation. In *Proceedings of the fifth international conference on Language Resources and Evaluation (LREC2006), May 24-26, 2006, Genoa, Italy*, pages 1392–1395. European Language Resource Association, Paris.

Slav Petrov, Leon Barrett, Romain Thibaux, and Dan Klein. 2006. Learning accurate, compact, and interpretable tree annotation. In *ACL-44: Proceedings of the 21st International Conference on Computational Linguistics and the 44th annual meeting of the Association for Computational Linguistics*, pages 433–440, Morristown, NJ, USA. Association for Computational Linguistics.

Kenji Sagae, Eric Davis, Alon Lavie, Brian MacWhinney, and Shuly Wintner. 2007. High-accuracy annotation and parsing of childes transcripts. In *Proceedings of the Workshop on Cognitive Aspects of Computational Language Acquisition*, CACLA '07, pages 25–32, Stroudsburg, PA, USA. Association for Computational Linguistics.

Kewei Tu and Vasant Honavar. 2012. Unambiguity regularization for unsupervised learning of probabilistic grammars. Technical report, Computer Science, Iowa State University.

Author Index

Association for Computational Linguistics
209 N. Eighth Street
Stroudsburg, Pennsylvania 18360

proceedings.com

2nd Workshop on Natural Language Processing Techniques for Educational Applications 2015

Co-located with ACL-IJCNLP 2015

Beijing, China
31 July 2015